THE JPS BIBLE COMMENTARY

ECCLESIASTES קהלת

The JPS Torah Commentary

GENERAL EDITOR *Nahum M. Sarna*
LITERARY EDITOR *Chaim Potok*

GENESIS *Nahum M. Sarna*
EXODUS *Nahum M. Sarna*
LEVITICUS *Baruch A. Levine*
NUMBERS *Jacob Milgrom*
DEUTERONOMY *Jeffrey H. Tigay*

The JPS Bible Commentary

THE HAFTAROT *Michael Fishbane*

The Five Megillot and Jonah
GENERAL EDITOR *Michael Fishbane*

JONAH *Uriel Simon*
ESTHER *Adele Berlin*
ECCLESIASTES *Michael V. Fox*

THE JPS BIBLE COMMENTARY

ECCLESIASTES קהלת

The Traditional Hebrew Text with the New JPS Translation

Commentary by MICHAEL V. FOX

THE JEWISH PUBLICATION SOCIETY

PHILADELPHIA 2004 / 5764

First edition.
The Jewish Publication Society
2100 Arch Street, 2nd floor
Philadelphia, PA 19103

Composition by El Ot Ltd. (English text) and Varda Graphics (Hebrew text)
Design by Adrianne Onderdonk Dudden
Manufactured in the United States of America

04 05 06 07 08 09 10 11 12 10 9 8 7 6 5 4 3 2 1

Library of Congress Cataloging-in-Publication Data

Bible. O.T. Ecclesiastes. Hebrew. 2004
Ecclesiastes: the traditional Hebrew text with the new JPS translation / commentary by Michael V. Fox. — 1st ed.
p. cm. — (The JPS Bible commentary)
Text of Ecclesiastes in Hebrew and English; commentary in English.
"Masoretic Hebrew text, Codex Leningrad B19A, taken from Biblia Hebraica Stuttgartensia (BHS) 1967/77, 1983, by the Deutsche Bibelgesellschaft, Stuttgart."
Includes bibliographical references and index.
ISBN 0-8276-0742-3
1. Bible. O.T. Ecclesiastes—Commentaries. I. Fox, Michael V., 1940–
II. Bible. O.T. Ecclesiastes. English. Jewish Publication Society. 2004.
III. Title. IV. Series.
BS1473.F69 2004
223'.8077—dc22 *2003025151*

GENESIS *ISBN 0-8276-0326-6*
EXODUS *ISBN 0-8276-0327-4*
LEVITICUS *ISBN 0-8276-0328-2*
NUMBERS *ISBN 0-8276-0329-0*
DEUTERONOMY *ISBN 0-8276-0330-4*
Five-volume set ISBN 0-8276-0331-2
JONAH *ISBN 0-8276-0672-9*
ESTHER *ISBN 0-8276-0699-0*
ECCLESIASTES *ISBN 0-8276-0742-3*
HAFTAROT *ISBN 0-8276-0691-5*

The publication of this book was made possible by
a gift in memory of Bernard Frank
by his wife, children, and grandchildren.

For my grandchildren
and their parents

CONTENTS

ACKNOWLEDGMENTS

I have benefited greatly from the contributions of two learned and rigorous editors. Professor Michael Fishbane's erudition and exegetical powers helped me shape and enrich my interpretation. Rabbi David Sulomm Stein's interpretive sensitivity and keen sense of English style helped me clarify and present my ideas.

Also, my wife Jane discussed certain issues of interpretation with me and heightened my awareness of readers' perceptions.

INTRODUCTION

Ecclesiastes is a strange and disquieting book. It gives voice to an experience not usually thought of as religious: the pain and frustration engendered by an unblinking gaze at life's absurdities and injustices. The man speaking in Ecclesiastes, "Koheleth," sees things that are distressing to observe: the distortions and inequities that pervade the world; the ineffectuality of human deeds; the frailty and limitations of human wisdom and righteousness. This awareness coexists with a firm belief in God—whose power, justice, and unpredictability are sovereign.

Koheleth is not a methodical thinker who has worked out a systematic world view and now presents it in organized fashion. There is much irregularity and repetition in the way he develops his thought, and much tension among his observations and beliefs. Some of his ideas pull in opposite directions, and many run counter to familiar religious principles. But Koheleth is not alone in his frustration and disillusionment at life's injustices and human failures. This is a facet of human experience, and especially Jewish experience—one that weighs heavy after the atrocities of the mid-twentieth century, which was surely a time when "man's calamity overwhelms him" (8:6b).

Koheleth faces life's inequities and absurdities—and refuses to impose pat and reassuring "meanings" on them. Yet he maintains a faith in God's rule and fundamental justness, and he looks for ways to create a meaningful life in a world where so much is senseless. The presence of the Book of Ecclesiastes in the canon of sacred scripture brings this type of thought into the compass of authentic Jewish religious reflection.

Koheleth has some unusual things to say, and his views should not be forced to fit presuppositions of what a biblical book *must* say. One need not grant the truth of all his opinions; the other biblical authors would not have. Koheleth's hard and lonely theology is only one man's view of the world and his glimpse of the Infinite. All truths are partial, all thinkers inadequate. Koheleth's teachings are one motif—a poignant and significant discord in the larger symphony of the biblical canon.

Title and Author

The title of the book in Hebrew is *Koheleth* (or *Qohelet*) after the name of the character who speaks in it. The English title—taken from the ancient Greek rendering of "Koheleth"—is "Ecclesiastes," meaning "member of the assembly." The book is sometimes called "the Preacher," based on an interpretation of "Koheleth" as one who preaches to the assembly *(kahal)*. The name "Koheleth" probably means one who teaches the public; see Comment to 1:1. Recently scholars have been making a useful distinction between "Ecclesiastes" (the book) and "Koheleth" (the speaker), which will be elaborated below.

Koheleth was traditionally identified with Solomon on the basis of 1:1 and 1:12, though in the book he is not given that name. Solomon was the epitome of the wise and wealthy king (1 Kings 3:12, 5:9–14; 1 Chron. 29:25; 2 Chron. 1:12; etc.). Further, Solomon was the only "son of David" to have ruled over all Israel (1:12), because when he died, the kingdom split in two, after which the Davidic dynasty reigned only in Judah, the southern kingdom. Koheleth's activities and self-description also fit Solomon, who possessed wealth and wisdom in abundance and was best qualified to speak credibly about their inadequacies. ("If any other person had said 'Utterly futile [*Havel havalim;* 1:1],' people would have said, 'This one has never had a penny for food!'" [Deut. R. 1:5].) One opinion held that Solomon wrote Ecclesiastes in his old age (Song R. 1:1 § 10), and indeed Koheleth gives the impression of speaking from the vantage point of an old man looking back on life.[1]

Since the nineteenth century, critical scholarship has not regarded Solomon as the actual author, on several grounds. First of all, the book's language and background assumptions indicate a postexilic dating, as is discussed below. Second, the epilogue (12:9) does not speak of Koheleth as king. Koheleth takes on the role of king only in 1:12–2:26. After that, he reveals the perspective of a nonroyal sage, a member of the class who may have contact with rulers and would have reason to fear their erratic anger (8:2–4, 9). And third, Koheleth blames the royal administrative apparatus for social injustices (5:7). This is something that Solomon, who founded the Judean royal administration, would not have been likely to do.

Though modern scholars do not think that Koheleth was Solomon, almost all of them believe that the author wants us to make that identification. The author's intention, however, appears to be more subtle. After all, if he had wanted the reader to think that the speaker really was Solomon, he could have called him by that name, as do several other Jewish writings (the biblical Proverbs and Song of Songs and the post-biblical Odes of Solomon, Testament of Solomon, and Psalms of Solomon).

This commentary assumes that Koheleth is a persona—a fictional figure through whom the author speaks. This persona, at least in the first two chapters, is portrayed as a king whose lineaments are taken from the biblical image of Solomon. For purposes of the intellectual exercise that Koheleth undertakes, the author wants us to conceive of the persona's wisdom, power, and prosperity as Solomonic in quantity and quality—at least in 1:2–2:26—without necessarily trying to make us believe that Koheleth truly was Solomon or to give the book full Solomonic authority.

Ecclesiastes and Wisdom Literature

The broad literary category to which Ecclesiastes belongs is Wisdom Literature. This is the body of writings that offer advice on how to succeed in life as well as reflections on its meanings and problems. In the Bible, these books include Proverbs, Job, and certain Psalms of similar character (Pss. 1, 19 [vv. 8–15], 34, 37, 111–112, 119). Somewhat later are the noncanonical book of Ben Sira (also known as Ecclesiasticus), the Wisdom of Solomon, some texts among the Dead Sea Scrolls, and *Pirke Avot.* Ecclesiastes combines both practical counsels (such as are predominant in Proverbs and Ben Sira) and reflections on the problems of life and religion (like the book of Job).

Wisdom Literature was ancient and widespread in the ancient Near East, where it was cultivated in literate and sophisticated scribal circles (see Prov. 25:1) and often directed to young men who would join the high officialdom and even serve in the royal court (as is implied in Prov. 16:14, 22:29, 25:6–7; Eccl. 8:2b–4). Most teachings, however, are of general relevance and some are folk proverbs from varied walks of life.[2]

Numerous Wisdom writings are extant from ancient Egypt and Mesopotamia, ranging from the third millennium B.C.E. to Hellenistic times. There is strong evidence that some of these books, or at least some of their sayings and teachings, were translated and transmitted in ancient Israel and that they influenced the book of Proverbs.[3] The author of Ecclesiastes would not have known Egyptian Wisdom directly, but literary forms and ideas current in international wisdom could have been accessible to him through the medium of the Israelite Wisdom tradition.

One foreign work that the author of Ecclesiastes might have known directly is the Book of Ahiqar.[4] This very popular Wisdom book, early translated into several languages, was known (in Aramaic) to the Jews of Elephantine, Egypt, in the Persian period and later, and the story of Aḥiqar is mentioned in the pseudepigraphal book of Tobit. See Comment to 8:4.

As in all ancient Wisdom Literature (with the exception of Prov. 31:1–9[5]), the speaker in Ecclesiastes is a man addressing a male audience and treating their concerns.[6] (Rather than obscuring Koheleth's orientation, the present commentary largely uses gender-marked words when paraphrasing Koheleth's statements about mankind. While most of what he says is true of all humans, he simply does not seem to have women in mind.)

Ecclesiastes and Philosophy

Ecclesiastes is the closest the Bible comes to philosophy, which is the intellectual, rational contemplation of fundamental human issues, with no recourse to revelation or tradition.

Koheleth says that he set out "to study and to probe with wisdom all that happens under the sun" (1:13). The boldest, most radical notion in the book is not Koheleth's contradictions, his pessimism, or his observations of injustices. It is the belief that the individual can and should proceed toward truth by means of his own powers of perception and reasoning; and that he can in this way discover truths previously unknown. There are no external rules, no doctrines or traditions to which his conclusions must conform. This is the approach of philosophy, and its appearance in

Ecclesiastes probably reflects a Jewish awareness of this type of thinking among foreign intellectuals.

Koheleth's philosophical endeavor is unique in Hebrew writings before the Middle Ages. (Jewish philosophy in Hellenistic times was otherwise recorded in Greek, not Hebrew.) To the degree that Ecclesiastes approaches philosophy, it requires a special kind of analysis: an attention to the precise meaning of its key terms, a description of its reasoning and argumentation, and a synthesis of conclusions.

Koheleth stands apart from other ancient Near Eastern sages in his determination to discover truth based on individual reason and experience alone. He does not look to revelation or tradition for guidance. He believes that he can discover what is good to do in life by acquiring wisdom and using it to examine and contemplate the world. This is the stance of Greek philosophy. Also, as Hengel observes, in Koheleth we find "the personally engaged, critical individuality of an acute observer and independent thinker" that goes beyond the matter-of-fact anonymity of earlier Israelite wisdom.[7] Koheleth can legitimately be called a philosopher, even though he does not approach his task with the organized rationality characteristic of the Greek philosophers.

Koheleth's focus on individual experience, in particular the perception of pleasure, bears a significant resemblance to Hellenistic popular philosophy, whose central purpose was to find the way to individual happiness by the use of the powers of reason. The Epicureans sought happiness through pleasure and freedom from fear. The Stoics thought to find it in the shedding of desires and passions. Both schools agreed that the inner realm of human experience is the locus of freedom and happiness. The goal Koheleth sets himself in 2:3—to discover "what is good for men to do under the heavens during the few days of their life"—was central to Greek philosophy.

Various of Koheleth's ideas have special affinities with Stoicism, with its belief in the preordination of events by God; strong restrictions on free will; the repetition of history in periodic cycles; and the doctrine of the four elements—fire, air, water, and earth.[8] The latter was a common Greek notion especially important to the Stoics. (Koheleth apparently considers the four elements as comprising the totality of the physical world, because he mentions them in 1:4–7 to demonstrate that *everything* is *hevel* ["absurd"; 1:2].)

These general similarities, though significant, do not demonstrate a direct knowledge of Greek philosophy. They do support the hypothesis that the author was aware of some concerns and attitudes of philosophical thinking current in the Hellenistic age.[9]

Literary Forms

Ecclesiastes combines a number of literary forms and genres found in earlier literature.

Maxims and Proverbs Much of the book is a collection of (short) proverbs and (longer) maxims giving advice and encapsulating observations on the ways of the world. Most Wisdom Literature is cast in this form. In both form and substance, Eccl. 4:17–5:6, 7:1–12, 16–21, 8:1b–8, 9:17–10:20, and 11:1–6 are series of proverbs, most of which would be at home in more conventional Wisdom books. Though Koheleth's unorthodox, pessimistic, and aggrieved reflections give the book a peculiar character, he was a wisdom teacher and proverb-maker (12:9), and he has practical advice to offer as well.

Autobiography Koheleth tells his own story. His discourse is in the tradition of the fictional autobiography, known from Mesopotamia. In these texts, a character, historical or otherwise, who is often a king, relates his experiences and draws lessons from them, some of which are self-critical.[10] In like manner, Koheleth identifies himself as king, speaks about his search for wisdom, reports his conclusions, and recognizes his own limitations. Fictional autobiographies draw upon formulas known from actual royal inscriptions, in which a king boasts of his accomplishments. In Ecclesiastes, similar formulas appear in 1:12–2:9; see Comment to 1:12.

Royal Testament This is an Egyptian Wisdom genre in which the speaker, a king, relates his experiences to his son and gives advice applicable to him in particular. This genre includes the Instruction to Merikare and the Instruction of Amenemhet.

Narrative Koheleth's autobiography is framed by a narrator's voice, that of the speaker of the epilogue (12:9–14). This voice refers to Koheleth in the third person also in 1:1–2, 7:27, and 12:8. The epilogist looks back at Koheleth and praises his wisdom, but also reminds us that wisdom has its limits and is not a man's primary concern. The epilogue is usually thought to have been appended by a pious scribe who sought to tone down the book's unorthodoxy, but it may well belong to the author himself, who has previously quoted the words of a persona, Koheleth.

It is important to read Ecclesiastes as a narrative, not simply as a collection of proverbs and epigrams each one of which can be understood in itself and is intended to be independently valid.[11] We cannot assume that any one statement of Koheleth's expresses the *book's* teaching.

Koheleth's discourse is reflexive. He looks at himself and reports what he planned, did, experienced, and thought. Some of his feelings and thoughts may be temporary and transitional, left behind at a more mature stage in Koheleth's development, as when he says that he had earlier come to loathe life (2:17; cf. 4:3). He bares his soul in all its twistings and turnings, ups and downs, taking his readers with him on a sometimes arduous journey to knowledge—a knowledge that turns out to be very incomplete. Thus his readers are not only to absorb Koheleth's teachings, they are also to observe him as he walks a rocky and winding path toward understanding and acceptance of life's frustrations and uncertainties. The journey itself is important.

Dating

Though traditionally dated to the time of Solomon in the late tenth century B.C.E., Ecclesiastes is clearly postexilic. Numerous words and linguistic usages are more characteristic of rabbinic Hebrew than of the classical (preexilic) biblical language.[12] The high frequency of Aramaisms also points to a postexilic date, when Jews in Palestine increasingly used Aramaic, while still using Hebrew as the predominant literary language and even speaking it in some areas. (Indeed, one theory holds that Ecclesiastes was translated from an Aramaic original.[13]) Mention of the "province" *(medinah)* as the place where the reader lives (5:7) indicates that Jews were living in an empire, either Persian or Hellenistic. This same verse describes a layered and burdensome bureaucratic apparatus, such as prevailed in the Hellenistic empires (333–63 B.C.E.). Also, the mention of a race in 9:11 ("The race is not won by the swift") points to a Hellenistic setting, when footraces, a practice originating in Greek competitions, were a prominent event in public athletics.[14] There is also evidence for the influence of Greek thought, with which Jews came into contact in the Hellenistic age, in the third or early second centuries B.C.E. (see below, p. xxix).[15]

The latest date to which the book can be assigned is about 180 B.C.E. Ben Sira, writing in Jerusalem at that time, was almost certainly acquainted with Ecclesiastes, quoting and rephrasing it in the way he does other scripture. Moreover, some fragments of Ecclesiastes found among the Dead Sea Scrolls are dated in the second century B.C.E.. Thus a third-century B.C.E. dating is the most likely.

Place in Jewish Literature

In the Biblical Canon. Ecclesiastes appears in the third division of the Hebrew Bible, the Writings *(Ketuvim)*. The Talmud (*Bava Batra* 14b) places the Solomonic books after Job and in the order Proverbs, Ecclesiastes, Song of Songs. Of the scrolls *(megillot)* used for synagogal reading on the festivals and in printed Bibles, Ecclesiastes is the third.

Ancient rabbinic literature discusses the status of Ecclesiastes in Scripture. In the Mishnah, the question is raised as to whether earlier sages, in the days of Hillel and Shammai, had disputed whether the book "makes the hands [ritually] unclean," which is the rabbinic locution for inspired scripture. (The discussion comes to the conclusion that the sages had indeed debated the issue and determined that the book is sacred; Yadayim 3:5.) Another early discussion asked whether, in light of the book's self-contradictions, it had once been withdrawn from public use *(nignaz)* (B. Shabbat 30b). Others posed the further challenge that the book was merely "Solomon's wisdom" and thus not divinely inspired (B. Megillah 7a). Still others expressed concern that the book's commendation of pleasure might "encourage hedonism" (Pes. de-R. Kah. 8a) or "induce an inclination to heresy" (ibid.; Koh. R. 1:3). They raised eyebrows at the call to follow one's heart and eyes in 11:9a (see Comment).

In none of their discussions were the Rabbis actually deliberating whether to grant or deny Ecclesiastes canonical status. This was already a fact for them. These discussions were an intellectual exercise whose purpose was to raise the difficulties the book presents in order to resolve them.

And how did the Rabbis resolve those difficulties? The most important evidence cited was the book's framework, 1:3 and 12:13–14. They understood 1:3 to praise exertions in the study of Torah (see Comment), while 12:13–14 unambiguously requires fear of God and obedience to divine commandments. With these religious principles securely bracketing the book, considerable scope could be allowed for deliberation on daring ideas.

Contemporary readers, too, often express puzzlement that Ecclesiastes could have gotten into the Bible. The assumption behind this puzzlement is that the canon of Scripture arose from theological deliberation, with the Rabbis evaluating books for their doctrinal suitability. In actuality, the formation of the biblical canon appears to have been a historical development, not a deliberative one. Books that were in circulation in the Second Temple community and were believed to come from the classical period of literature, prior to Ezra and Nehemiah, gradually came to be regarded as Scripture. The belief that Solomon was the author of Ecclesiastes made its acceptance as Scripture possible.[16] Once it was included among the sacred scriptures, exegesis found ways to make it theologically palatable.

In the Liturgy Reading Ecclesiastes as part of synagogue liturgy is not mentioned in early or even gaonic rabbinic literature. However, by the eleventh century, some Jewish communities were reading Ecclesiastes as a holiday lection during Sukkot. Today the book is read on Sukkot among most Ashkenazim on the intermediate Sabbath of Sukkot—or on the eighth day of the holiday (Shemini Atzeret), if that falls on the Sabbath. The practice has been embraced by many Sephardic and Mizraḥi synagogues.

The reason for the association with Sukkot may be simply that the other holidays already were assigned scrolls on the basis of their content (Song of Songs on Passover; Ruth on Shavuot; Lamentations on the Ninth of Av; Esther on Purim). Subsequently, thematic motives were suggested for reading Ecclesiastes in Sukkot. These are that Koheleth recommends rejoicing, which is the mood of Sukkot; that he declares the transience of human life, which is well symbolized by a temporary booth; and that autumn is the season evocative of mortality.

Structure and Unity

Structure. The question of an overarching structure and cohesiveness is one of the most vexing issues in the study of Ecclesiastes. On the one hand, the book is not a collection of miscellaneous proverbs like most of the Book of Proverbs. On the other hand, it is hard to find some design that would organize the book's components and guide the reader in comprehending the parts and the whole.

The test of any inferred structure or design is whether it matches the reader's experience—that is, whether it emerges from your own reading, and whether awareness of it helps you organize the book's thoughts and deepens your understanding of its message. Numerous scholars have tried to uncover structures or designs in the book;[17] few of their proposals have received widespread acceptance. The most influential is that of A. Wright, who sees a complex hierarchical design based on keywords and repeated phrases.[18] The main rubrics of his proposed structure are as follows:

Initial poem (1:2–11)

- I. Koheleth's investigation of life (1:12–6:9)
- II. Koheleth's conclusions (6:10–11:6)
  - Introduction (6:10–12)
  - A. Man cannot find out what is good for him to do (7:1–8:17)
  - B. Man does not know what will come after him (9:1–11:6)

Concluding poem (11:7–12:8)

Epilogue (12:9–14)

These units are also subdivided. In support of his division, Wright adduces certain key phrases that delimit units by marking their beginning and ending. For example, his four subdivisions of II.A (7:1–14, 15–24, 25–29; 8:1–17) end with phrases signifying "not finding out" or "who can find out?"

Wright's hypothesis faces a number of objections: the criteria for unit division are not well-defined phrases; the key phrases are not always at the *end* of the unit, where they "should" be; the units are of very different size and character; and the plan does not match the content. Similar criticisms apply to other attempts to uncover hidden structures in Ecclesiastes.

Some of the material in Ecclesiastes is well placed. The book begins with a general principle (1:3), continues with a thematic prelude, introduces the persona and his background, describes his task, previews his results, and then proceeds with his investigation. The last unit, 12:1–7, is climactic and could stand nowhere else. These things are evident to all, but the arrangement in other parts of the book seems rather haphazard. However, units of several verses exist that deal with a single theme. These often have a significant internal organization and will be outlined in the commentary. Often, too, the beginnings of units are indicated by introductory phrases such as "I said to myself" (2:1), "I further observed" (4:1); and "There is an evil I have observed under the sun" (6:1). Such locutions mark phases in Koheleth's investigation.

In spite of the lack of an organized literary structure, the book displays a deep cohesiveness. This shows above all in the constant presence of a single consciousness mediating all the book's observations, counsels, and evaluations. In most Wisdom books, the author—real or fictional—stays well in the background; the speaker gives advice, but, with rare exceptions, one gets little sense of an individual personality or his thought processes. In Ecclesiastes, however, we see a distinctive and memorable character who both comments on the world and describes how he reached his conclusions (see especially 1:12–18 and 2:1–26). Everything we read is filtered through the speaker's consciousness. In 1:12–14 we read:

> I, Koheleth, was king in Jerusalem over Israel. I set my mind to study and to probe with wisdom all that happens under the sun.—An unhappy business, that, which God gave men to be concerned with! I observed all the happenings beneath the sun, and I found that all is futile and pursuit of wind.

The credibility and interest of these claims would be diminished if the author had written in an impersonal fashion, saying, for example:

> Studying and probing with wisdom all that happens under the sun is an unhappy business, which God gave men to be concerned with! All the happenings beneath the sun are futile and pursuit of wind.

The second version gives us a series of dogmatic pronouncements, whereas in Ecclesiastes we follow the struggles of a deeply committed thinker as he works his way to his conclusions, some unhappy and frustrated, some affirmative and productive. This is close to the heart of the book's message: life's absurdities frustrate the rational mind. The author lets us see this happening to Koheleth.

Unity Some commentators believe that several passages were added to the book by later scribes. Most modern commentators regard the epilogue (12:9–14) as an appendix added by a later scribe or "editor." Some commentators, especially those writing around the turn of the twentieth century (for example, Barton; see below), identified certain statements as additions intended to make the book more religiously conventional or theologically acceptable. Examples are affirmations of God's justice and the need for human piety (e.g., 2:26 [up to "That too is futile . . ."], 3:17, 7:26b, 8:11–14, 12:11–14) and proverbs typical of Wisdom Literature (e.g., 4:5; 5:3, 7; 7:1a, 3, 5, 6–9).

The problem with this approach is that it assumes that Koheleth was a consistently radical, pessimistic, and skeptical thinker. However, the statements considered traditional and conservative use vocabulary and style typical of Ecclesiastes, and they are often intertwined with observations of life's inequities and absurdities, as in 8:11–14. Moreover, the putative additions do not fulfill the purposes ascribed to their authors. They create contradictions, not religiously traditional statements. Nor are they always located *after* the unorthodox opinions they are supposed to neutralize. Thus, in 8:14, the observation of injustice is allowed the last word, whereas if the pious sentences (vv. 12b–13) were meant to be a corrective, they should have concluded the unit.

Koheleth is not consistent. The contradictions noted by the earliest exegetes are an important part of his work and should be interpreted, not expunged or smoothed out by strained harmonizations. Koheleth sees a world that is full of inconsistencies and contradictions. These are what he calls *hevel*.

Keywords

Ecclesiastes uses certain words repeatedly as keywords that indicate the book's major themes and give coherence to its varied contents. These words are all found elsewhere in the language—in postbiblical if not in biblical Hebrew—and, with the exception of *hevel,* their uses in Ecclesiastes are all paralleled elsewhere. What is special is the choice and frequency of the words the author uses to convey Koheleth's thoughts and the connotations they bring to the fore. The following words have a higher frequency in Ecclesiastes than in any other book of the Bible. (They are listed in alphabetical order of their transliteration.) Some of the ways they are rendered in the New Jewish Publication Society [NJPS] translation are given first.

'Amal עמל, *"toil."* (NJPS renderings: *NOUN:* "gains, wealth, fortune, toiling, means, labor, earnings"; *VERB:* "earn, toil, make, try strenuously, acquire") The noun *'amal* basically means arduous, wearisome labor (e.g., 4:8, 5:15, and 6:7). It can also refer to the earnings that such toil produces (e.g., 2:19). Likewise, as a verb, *'amal* can mean "to toil" or "to earn." It is often difficult to determine exactly what Koheleth intends, whether the toil or the earnings—or the two together.

The scope of *'amal* includes more than remunerative labors. Even walking to the city is "toil" (10:15), as are intellectual exertions (2:22, 8:17). The word is so broad that life's experiences in general can be called "toil." See Comment to 4:9. Taking pleasure in one's *'amal* (3:12) is equivalent to taking pleasure in one's life (3:13). In 8:15 and 9:9, too, *'amal* seems to refer to life generally.

NJPS usually translates *'amal* with words meaning earnings and wealth. My view is that with few exceptions, *'amal* refers to the effort of toil; see Comment to 1:3. Koheleth is really concerned with the efficacy of work rather than the value of material wealth.

'Asah עשה, *"do, make happen"; ma'aseh* מעשה, *"work, event."* (NJPS renderings: *'asah:* "build up, practice, lay out, bring to pass, do"—and a variety of other verbs implying doing, earning, and causing to happen; *ma'aseh:* "happenings, possessions, fortune, what goes on, all the things [that God brings to pass], happening, miseries [for "bad *ma'aseh*"], enterprise"—and a variety of other nouns for events, possessions, and deeds) In Ecclesiastes, these two common words each have three different meanings. The verb *'asah* can mean (1) "to do"; (2) "to cause to happen" (3:11, 14a, 14b); 7:14, 8:17, 11:5); or (3) "to earn" (possibly 2:11). The passive, *na'asah,* means "be done," or "occur" (1:9, 13). The cognate noun *ma'aseh* has corresponding meanings: (1) "deed" or "work" (3:11b, 8:17, 9:10, 11:5, etc.); (2) "event" or "what happens" (1:9), especially in the phrases *ma'aseh ha-'elohim* ("the events that God makes happen"; 7:13, 8:17, 11:5; variant in 3:11) and *ha-ma'aseh 'asher na'asah taḥat ha-shemesh* ("the things that happen under the sun"; 1:14, 2:17, 4:1, etc., plus the parallel in 1:13); and (3) "property," that is to say, the results of work (2:4, 2:11, and 5:5, though the first two citations are ambiguous).[19]

In each instance, context must determine which meaning is most appropriate, but the identification of the meanings "occur" and "event" is important to understanding the book. Koheleth is examining what happens in life—that is to say, all of life—and not only deeds. *Ma'aseh ha-'elohim* is God's ongoing governance of the world (and not the original creation, as might be supposed if we translated it as "the work of God").

Underlying this usage is Koheleth's deterministic worldview. What happens in life is ultimately *ma'aseh ha-'elohim,* "that which God has made happen."

Ḥelek חלק, *"portion, possession."* (NJPS renderings: "all I got, portion, share, what you can get") The noun *ḥelek* means something one receives and possesses, irrespective of its adequacy or duration. In Ecclesiastes, a *ḥelek* is sometimes wealth itself (2:21; cf. 11:2). More often, a *ḥelek* is the pleasure derived from wealth (2:10, 3:22, 5:17, 5:18, 9:9). Other experiences, even unpleasant ones, can be our *ḥelek* (9:6). They belong to us, if just for the moment.

For Koheleth, a portion is not necessarily a "profit" *(yitron)*. We can have a portion in our work—namely, pleasure (2:10)—and it is good. Yet for Koheleth, this is not enough of a "plus" to constitute a "profit" (2:11). See below on *yitron*.

Hevel הבל, *"senseless[ness], absurd[ity]."* (NJPS renderings: "futility, futile, amounts to nothing, fleeting, illusory, brief span, frustration, nothingness") *Hevel* is the central motif of the book: *Everything* is *hevel* (1:2; 12:8). *Hevel* literally means "breath" or "vapor." Ecclesiastes uses it metaphorically. The different translations reflect the ways the metaphor has been understood.

(a) *Vanity*. This is the most ancient and widespread understanding of *hevel*. "All is vanity" means that the things of this world ("under the sun") are trite and worthless. ("Vanity" does not mean "pride" in this context.) Those who translate *hevel* as "vanity" tend to see Koheleth as a pious moralist who chides people for pursuing worldly frivolities rather than spiritual values.

(b) *Futile*. NJPS usually renders *hevel* as "futile, futility." This translation suggests a focus on *actions*. According to this understanding, the central concern of the book is the productivity of human work and the value of its products.

(c) *Ephemeral*. Translating *hevel* thus implies that Koheleth is primarily troubled by life's brevity.

(d) *Incomprehensible*. The implication of this rendering is that Koheleth is modestly asserting the limitations of human reason. Rashbam, who understands *hevel* to mean "futile" in most contexts, says in his comment on 8:10–13 that there, *hevel* is "a matter which is hidden from humans and which they are unable to perceive clearly and do not understand . . . [Koheleth] calls this '*hevel*,' for people wonder and are amazed at it." Some modern commentators understand *hevel* similarly.

(e) *Absurd* or *senseless*. In the view propounded in the present commentary, *hevel* means "senseless" or "absurd," not in the sense of ludicrous but in the sense of counter-rational, a violation of reason. Facts or scenarios (which would not naturally be called futile or brief) are judged to be absurd. Thus in 8:14, Koheleth comments on *the fact* that people often receive a fate the opposite of what they deserve. In 2:18–26, what is *hevel* is the fact that the wealth Koheleth laboriously accumulated will go to someone else after his death—someone who did not work for it, no less. This violates Koheleth's sense of fairness and reason. Koheleth sees numerous such contradictions in the world, which violate rational expectations and lead him to call everything *hevel*.

Ḥokhmah חכמה, *"wisdom"; ḥakham* חכם, *"wise, wise man."* (NJPS renderings: *ḥokhmah:* "wisdom, wise, skill"; *ḥakham:* "wise man, wise, sage") The term *ḥokhmah* is very broad. It may be translated "wisdom," but it includes more than the English word does. Knowledge, reasoning powers, crafts, and expertise of all sorts are called *ḥokhmah*. It is both the knowledge gained by learning and the intellectual powers that can analyze and evaluate that learning.

Ḥokhmah does not necessarily connote moral virtue (as "wisdom" usually does in English). True, in Proverbs, wisdom is always a moral virtue, and this is part of the special message of that book. But in most of the Bible, it can refer to any kind of cleverness, skill, or savvy.

In Ecclesiastes, *ḥokhmah* is a practical and intellectual faculty, not inherently ethical. It sometimes is ingenuity—the faculty that would be expected to bring a man wealth (2:9, 19, 21), or save a city from attack (9:13–15), or enable an obscure man to rise to power (4:13–16). *Ḥokhmah* can also be manifest as good sense, which is the faculty that promotes success in personal behavior and human relations; examples are 2:3, 7:10, and 8:1. Finally, it is sometimes used of the rational intellect, the faculty employed in investigation and discovery of truths (1:13, 18; 7:23; 8:16). This usage seems to be an innovation of the book's author.

Re'ut ruaḥ רעות רוח; *ra'yon ruaḥ* רעיון רוח, *"pursuit of wind."* (NJPS rendering: "pursuit of wind") *Re'ut ruaḥ* is an ambiguous expression, since *re'ut* can mean "pursuit," "shepherd," "desire," or "thought"; and *ruaḥ* can mean "wind," "spirit," or "desire." *Re'ut ruaḥ* is usually understood to signify a futile pursuit or desire (cf. Hos. 12:2). Possibly it means "windy [i.e., useless] thoughts." In 2:22, *ra'yon* refers to thoughts, in particular troublesome notions and anxieties that buzz around in one's head at night; thus too in Daniel (4:16; 5:6, 10; 7:28; etc.). In Eccl. 4:6, *re'ut ruaḥ* is the opposite of calm labor. Some associate the word with the root *r-'-'* ("to break"). Moreover, though not etymologically related, the words *re'ut* and especially *ra'yon* are reminiscent of the word *ra'* ("bad"). Thus the phrase *re'ut ruaḥ* (with its variants) is rich in the potential for wordplays and secondary connotations. *Re'ut ruaḥ* is almost always paired with *hevel* and also implies senselessness, whether in deeds or in thoughts.

Simḥah שמחה, *"enjoyment, pleasure"; samaḥ* שמח, *"get pleasure, enjoy oneself."* (NJPS renderings: *simḥah:* "merriment, enjoyment, merrymaking, gladness"; *samaḥ:* "enjoy, acclaim, get pleasure, make merry") Koheleth often praises *simḥah,* "pleasure" or "enjoyment," sometimes using the verb *samaḥ*. Elsewhere in the Bible, *simḥah* refers to feelings ranging from deep joy and happiness (e.g., Isa. 30:29; Ps. 126:3) to mere amusements (e.g., Prov. 21:17), even joyless ones (Isa. 22:13a).

Simḥah in Ecclesiastes is often translated "happiness" or "joy." This gives the impression that Koheleth is urging the reader to embrace joy or happiness. Such advice would be self-evident if not trite. Also, it is pointless to advise people to be happy, for it is not something that can be chosen at will.

At best, one can choose to indulge in agreeable and pleasant activities, and this is what Koheleth recommends: the embrace of pleasure or enjoyment—eating and drinking and such activities as listed in 9:7–9. He hopes that pleasure will bring some happiness, or at least diversion (5:19). (Nevertheless, one can indulge in pleasures without achieving happiness; Koheleth himself had much *simḥah* [2:10] but little happiness and no joy [2:11, 17–18].) Happiness is, by its very nature, meaningful and gratifying. Thus Koheleth is more a "preacher of pleasure" than a "preacher of joy," as some commentators consider him.[20]

Tov טוב; *tovah* טובה, *"good."* (NJPS renderings: "mirth, better, worthwhile, enjoyment, pleases, good, better, best, wealth, fortunate, happy"—and a variety of other terms for goodness and pleasure) *Tov* means "goodness" of any sort. Ecclesiastes uses it in a number of ways, including as a synonym for *simḥah,* "pleasure." This usage is found elsewhere but is most common in Ecclesiastes. "To do good" (3:12) and "to see good" (2:1, 3:13, 5:17, 6:6; cf. 2:24) mean to enjoy something. (In 7:20, however, "good" is used in an ethical sense.) As an adjective, *tov* can mean "pleasing" (2:26) or "merry" (9:7). As a noun, *tovah* means "goods" or "valuables" (5:10; 6:3). By using this word to designate the experience he values most, Koheleth is suggesting that "pleasure" *(tov)* is inherently "good" *(tov)*.

Yitron יתרון; *yoter* יותר; *motar* מותר, *"profit."* (NJPS renderings: "advantage [*usually*], real value, superior, value, the good") *Yitron,* used in rabbinic Hebrew but not elsewhere in the Bible, is a commercial term meaning "profit." Koheleth employs it in a strict sense, to mean surplus returns from one's investment of work. This may be an adequate remuneration or a nonmonetary benefit, such as pleasure equal to the toil invested in it. Whatever we gain from a business (and life) is a "portion" (e.g., 2:10), and this is good. But unless we go beyond breaking even and achieve a surplus gain, we have not, in Koheleth's stringent reckoning, realized a "profit" (2:11). This alone Koheleth would consider adequate compensation for life's miseries.

The Challenges of Scriptural Citation, Translation, and Commentary

This commentary series takes as its basis the New Jewish Publication Society translation (NJPS), which followed the Masoretic text. The present commentary departs from NJPS in many ways, both in details and in fundamental concepts. It will often take issue with NJPS and present an alternative rendering for the reader's consideration. (All translations in the present commentary, besides NJPS, are the author's.)

A central principle of NJPS is to render a Hebrew term by whichever English term fits the context most precisely, as this is interpreted by the translator. Consequently, a variety of words are used to translate Ecclesiastes' characteristic terms (see Keywords, above). To help the reader follow the recurring motifs designated by the keywords, the Hebrew will be supplied in brackets in the lemma before each Comment as necessary.

Also, in quoting the interpreters, it is often necessary to adjust the translation to *their* idea of its meaning. Thus quotations in the body of the commentary often depart considerably from NJPS.

These disagreements should alert the reader to an important fact of Ecclesiastes-study: the book is in places extremely difficult. The reasons for this are manifold: The language is unlike the Hebrew of the rest of the Bible, with syntax that is often strange and vocabulary that is frequently idiosyncratic. The sentences are often ambiguous for a variety of reasons, such as unclear antecedents for pronouns (in 4:13–16, for example). Moreover, the text in some places was corrupted in the course of centuries of copying. (The foregoing difficulties are often disguised in translation, which substitutes a meaningful English sentence for an obscure Hebrew one.) Another source of difficulty is the fact that the book often expresses contradictory ideas. Such problems do not preclude an intelligent engagement with a translated text, but the reader should realize that often in the Bible, and especially in Ecclesiastes, much remains uncertain and much work remains.

Because Ecclesiastes is such a problematic book, the translation and interpretations proposed in this commentary are not intended to be the sole way of reading Ecclesiastes, but rather the way this commentator finds most satisfactory. The proposals are offered as explorations of the book's meaning and message.

Ecclesiastes does not simply call for assent. (Indeed, Koheleth does not claim certainty even about his own findings.) By carefully studying the book, rereading it, and testing one's own perceptions against others', the reader gradually makes progress toward a fuller and more subtle understanding of the book's message and underlying presuppositions. Understanding Ecclesiastes requires engagement, exploration, dissent, and rethinking—the very activities that characterize Koheleth himself.

Major Sources Cited and Overview of Interpretations

Ancient Versions and Related Works

Ben Sira. Joshua b. Sira: a Jewish sage, author of the eponymous Wisdom book known also as Ecclesiasticus; ca. 180 B.C.E. Ben Sira almost certainly knew Ecclesiastes, reusing and reshaping some of its phraseology and proverbs.

Peshitta. An ancient translation into Syriac, a dialect of Aramaic, undertaken in Mesopotamia in the third to eighth centuries C.E.

Septuagint. An ancient Greek translation, probably from the first century C.E. In the case of Ecclesiastes, it stays close to the Hebrew, translating word-for-word whenever possible. This technique allows us to reconstruct some ancient Hebrew variants in the text the translator used.

Targum. An ancient Aramaic translation. The Targum of Ecclesiastes is highly paraphrastic and is a repository of older midrashim. Text: Mikra'ot Gedolot. English translation by Peter Knobel, in *The Targum of Qohelet*. The Aramaic Bible, XV. Collegeville, MN: Michael Glazier, 1991.

Wisdom, Egyptian and Mesopotamian. Egyptian texts are quoted from M. Lichtheim, *Ancient Egyptian Literature*; 3 vols., Berkeley: Univ. of California, 1973–80 (= *AEL*). Mesopotamian texts are quoted mostly from B. Foster, *Before the Muses*, Bethesda, MD: CDL Press, 1993.

Commentaries Mentioned

The present commentary draws extensively upon its predecessors, though they could not be fully cited at every step. For fuller argumentation, technical discussions, and references to scholarship, see my book, *A Time to Tear Down and A Time to Build Up: A Rereading of Ecclesiastes* (Grand Rapids, MI: Eerdmans, 1999).

MIDRASH We should distinguish between *midrash* (or *derash*) as a hermeneutic, or interpretive methodology, and *midrash* as the interpretation itself. In the latter sense, a "midrash" can be a unit of interpretation—one interpretation of a verse—or one of the compilations of midrashic interpretations. These compilations were composed mainly from the third to eleventh centuries C.E., but the material is older.

As a hermeneutic, midrash focuses on each verse or its components, not on an entire book. It seeks, first, to harmonize the verse with the entirety of the Bible, in the belief that the Bible speaks with a single voice, which is ultimately God's. As such, it must in all ways accord with the beliefs of the expositors, which is to say, the theology and law of rabbinic Judaism. Second, midrash seeks to draw out the fullness of meaning potential in the verse. It makes use of a variety of homiletical techniques, including historical comparisons, personal anecdotes, wordplays, different readings of Hebrew words, and, above all, reapplication of associated biblical verses. Midrashic compilations also incorporate interpretations that are fairly straightforward, usually without drawing a distinction among the different types.

The midrashic hermeneutic attempts to bring forth the limitless range of meanings of the biblical text. It thus embraces a multiplicity of interpretations. (In contrast, a different approach to interpretation, *peshat* exegesis, arose and flourished in the Middle Ages. Commonly but misleadingly called "literalist," the *peshat* approach attends to the plain sense of the passage and tries to understand the verse within the rules of grammar and to locate its meaning in its literary and historical context. It aims at the author's specific intention and will exclude other readings as inaccurate, even when these produce a reading in harmony with the assumptions of the faith. Modern critical exegesis follows the basic principles of *peshat* exegesis, while sometimes recognizing that biblical texts may be multivocal.)

Midrashic interpretations of Ecclesiastes are found in many midrashim, in the Talmuds, and the Targum (discussed above). Most of the midrashim relevant to Ecclesiastes are collected and organized by chapter and verse in Midrash Koheleth Rabbah.[21] For the purposes of the present commentary, it is usually sufficient to refer to Koheleth Rabbah as the source of the midrashic interpretations mentioned, though these usually appeared first in other texts, often in different form or ascribed to different sages. Also, the medieval commentators cite and incorporate midrashic interpretations. Rashi's exegesis in particular continues the midrashic tradition, even though he generally aims at the *peshat*.

Midrash Koheleth Rabbah (Koh. R.). Jerusalem: Makhon Hamidrash HaMevoar, 1993. English translation by A. Cohen, *Midrash Rabbah,* vol. VIII (New York: Soncino Press, 3rd edn., 1983). Compiled in the ninth or tenth century C.E.

Pesikta de-Rav Kahana (Pes. de-R. Kah.); edited by B. Mandelbaum (New York: JTS, 1962). A series of homilies on holidays and special Sabbaths. English translation: Jacob Neusner, *Pesiqta deRab Kahana: An Analytical Translation*. Atlanta: Scholars Press, 1987.

TRADITIONAL COMMENTARIES Of the rich exegetical literature by Jewish scholars of ancient and medieval times, the following are mentioned in the present commentary.

Alsheikh (Moshe b. Ḥayyim Alsheikh), 1508–1601, Safed. Published Czernowitz, 1855.

Ibn Ezra (Abraham ibn Ezra), 1089–1164, mainly Spain. Rabbinic Bible.

Ibn Tibbon (Samuel ibn Tibbon), 1160–1238, France; see note 28.

Ibn Yaḥyah (Yosef b. David ibn Yaḥyah), 1494–1534, Italy. Bologna, 1539.

Rashi (R. Solomon b. Isaac), 1040–1105, France. Rabbinic Bible.

Rashbam (R. Samuel b. Meir), 12th century, France. Text and English translation by Sara Japhet and Robert Salters, *The Commentary of R. Samuel ben Meir: Rashbam on Qoheleth*. Jerusalem, 1985.

Sa'adia Gaon, 882–942, Egypt, Palestine, Babylonia. Translated from Judeo-Arabic by David Fränkel, Romania, 1903.

Sforno (Obadiah b. Jacob Sforno), c. 1470–c. 1550. *Kitvey Rabbi Ovadiah Seforno*. Ed. Zeev Gotlieb, Jerusalem, 1987.

MODERN COMMENTARIES

Moses Mendelssohn, *Bei'ur Li-mgillat Koheleth,* 1729–86, Germany (commentary: 1770).[22]

Shadal (Samuel David Luzzatto), 1800–65, Italy. Commentary on Ecclesiastes (1860–63).[23]

And of the large number of twentieth-century commentaries (Hebrew or English) on Ecclesiastes, the following recent works are worthy of special note:

G. A. Barton, *Ecclesiastes* (ICC). Edinburgh: T. & T. Clark (1908; repr. 1959).

Elias Bickermann, *Four Strange Books of the Bible*. New York: Schocken, 1967, 141–67.

James L. Crenshaw, *Ecclesiastes* (OT Library). Philadelphia: Westminster, 1987.

Michael V. Fox, *A Time to Tear Down and A Time to Build Up: A Rereading of Ecclesiastes*. Grand Rapids, MI: Eerdmans, 1999.[24]

H. L. Ginsberg, *Koheleth* קהלת. Jerusalem: M. Newman, 1961.

Robert Gordis, *Koheleth, the Man and his World*. New York: Bloch, 1955.

Tremper Longman III, *The Book of Ecclesiastes* (NICOT). Grand Rapids, MI: Eerdmans, 1998.

Roland E. Murphy, *Ecclesiastes* (WBC). Waco, TX: Word, 1992.

Choon-Leong Seow, *Ecclesiastes* (Anchor Bible). Garden City, NY: Doubleday-Anchor, 1997.

Major Interpretations

Every interpretation of Ecclesiastes must answer three questions: What is Koheleth negating and complaining about? What is he affirming and recommending? What are his underlying reasons for each?

Rather than recounting the full history of exegesis here,[25] the following survey summarizes a representative sampling of interpretative approaches.

MIDRASH Despite the diversity in origins and character of Koheleth Rabbah, certain themes and ideas run through the collection; together these convey a basically unified understanding of the book. Variants of this view are incorporated in all Jewish commentaries until modern times.[26] The following précis would, for example, summarize Rashi's view as well.

> King Solomon, having experienced both the world's glories and its disappointments, wrote the Book of Ecclesiastes in old age to teach the futility of mundane strivings and the insignificance of earthly goods. These he judges trivial and transient (as *hevel* was understood to mean). By contrast, of enduring value are matters that are *not* "beneath the sun," but belong instead to the transcendent, spiritual realm, including eternal life. These are study of Torah and good deeds. The advice to "eat and drink" signifies study of Torah. One must resign oneself to God's will, for all his works are good. Injustices will be rectified and righteousness rewarded, if not in this life then in eternal life.

The Midrash profoundly reorients the theology of Ecclesiastes, particularly in regard to the problem of reward and punishment. Whereas for Koheleth the existence of wrongs and inequities are hard facts that stubbornly defy resolution, for the Midrash these troubles—which the Rabbis were fully cognizant of—dissolve in the larger pattern of the divine order. Since God *must* be just, absolutely and in all ways, wisdom reveals apparent injustices to be illusory when seen from the right perspective. God's justice will triumph, perhaps in this life, in unexpected and sometimes mysterious ways, and surely in eternity. Solomon, it is assumed, must have known this in his wisdom, and if read correctly, his work must reveal its truth.

ABRAHAM IBN EZRA Ibn Ezra, perhaps the greatest of medieval interpreters, developed an exegetical method based on philological discipline and adherence to rational judgment. In applying this to Ecclesiastes, he sought to discover underlying continuity in Koheleth's thought. For example, he connected 10:12–15 and 10:16–19 (seemingly on unrelated topics) by reasoning that Koheleth, after mentioning the vapid words of the fool in 10:14, goes on to say (in v. 16) that if a fool like this were king, the situation would be very grave. How much the more so if he were also a youth!

Ibn Ezra puts much effort into resolving the contradictions in Ecclesiastes, believing that no wise man would contradict his own words. To resolve contradictory assertions regarding divine justice in 8:12–14, for example, he asserts that "It will be well with those who revere God" (8:12b) pronounces the general rule, whereas "sometimes an upright man is requited according to the conduct of the scoundrel [etc.]" (8:14) observes an anomaly, something that happens "at rare intervals."

According to Ibn Ezra, Solomon teaches that all human works are ephemeral and insignificant. God's work is perfect, but humans are flawed. Only the fear of God, reached through the acquisition of wisdom (identified with Torah) can bring happiness.

RASHBAM (RABBI SAMUEL B. MEIR)[27] Rashbam was a *peshat* exegete who gave attention to the subtleties of style and language. He tried to sort out the logical incongruities in Ecclesiastes by drawing semantic distinctions. With regard to pleasure, for example, Koheleth is said to repudiate frivolous and extravagant pleasures *(seḥoq, simḥah)* but to affirm happiness (also called *simḥah*), which means contentment in one's lot. As for wisdom, Rashbam distinguishes two types: ordinary, practical wisdom, which teaches how to get along in life, versus "profound wisdom," which probes God's motives, justice, and the mysteries of creation. Accordingly, Koheleth is seen to conclude that ordinary wisdom is accessible and useful, whereas but profound wisdom is unattainable and its pursuit brings frustration and sorrow. Humans should accept their ignorance and transience, enjoy life in moderation, study Torah, trust in—and fear—God, and keep His commandments.

SAMUEL B. JUDAH IBN TIBBON[28] The commentary of Samuel ibn Tibbon, famed as the Hebrew translator of Maimonides' *Guide of the Perplexed,* exemplifies the medieval philosophical approach. He analyzes Ecclesiastes' thought in neo-Aristotelian terms. Samuel considers the book to be Solomon's argument against those sages of his time who believed that everything in the material world—including the human soul—is subject to corruption and hence cannot be immortal. Fearing that students of wisdom might be influenced by these contentions, Solomon posits the other sages' presuppositions for the purposes of argumentation and proceeds by dialectic to refute them. Those sages, he says, succeeded in demonstrating only that the part of the soul that comes from "under the sun" is mortal. They cannot prove that the part of the soul that comes from above the sun, the acquired intellect, is subject to corruption. Since this is not impossible, one can argue for its possibility. Being an initial defense of the possibility of immortality, Ecclesiastes must be the first of Solomon's works.

MOSHE ALSHEIKH Alsheikh, a leading halakhic scholar and preacher, developed his sermons into Bible commentaries infused with ethical and philosophical meditations. His homiletical commentary on Ecclesiastes expounds Koheleth's message as a call to asceticism and piety. According to this view, Koheleth repudiates the pleasures of this life in favor of the "world to come," the life after death. He declares the present world to be a vapor. At birth, we humans leave our eternal home and enter the evanescent and corruptible material world. This we must regard as a temporary abode and not set our hearts on enjoying its fruits, such as food, drink, and fine clothes. We must instead regard these things as naught. Otherwise, "better ... the stillbirth" (6:3) because everyone's spirit will return to God" (12:7) devoid of all good and filthy with sins. We must prepare for return to the eternal world by storing up Torah and good deeds to bring back to the King's palace. As for apparent violations of divine providence, we must consider the totality of what a person has done and undergone, for a righteous person may currently be suffering for prior sins and a wicked person temporarily benefiting from prior merits.

MOSES MENDELSSOHN[29] Mendelssohn, the leading philosopher of Jewish modernism at the turn of the eighteenth to nineteenth centuries, sought to help European Jews, who were in the first stages of emancipation, make the transition to modern European culture and thought while remaining faithful to traditional Jewish faith and practice. His Hebrew commentary on the Bible was intended to revive the art of biblical exegesis and introduce Jews to modern, philosophical approaches to biblical interpretation. According to Mendelssohn, Ecclesiastes was written to defend two doctrines of natural philosophy: providence and the immortality of the soul. Koheleth shows the inadequacy of worldly wisdom, when this is not supplemented by the superior truths of revealed religion, as imparted in the Torah. Koheleth is in dialogue with skeptics and unbelievers, some of whose statements he cites in order to refute or to expose their unfortunate consequences. The book's conclusions: We should choose the middle path and develop all our faculties; the Torah calls for a balance between fear of God on the one hand and love and joy on the other; and pursuit of wealth is acceptable if combined with study of Torah and good deeds (see Comment to 11:9).

The watershed in the interpretation of Ecclesiastes was the mid–nineteenth century. Earlier, commentators were largely constrained by a set of assumptions about what Solomon *must* have believed, such as the immortality of the soul, the supreme importance of Torah and good deeds, and the ultimate inviolability of God's justice. Exegesis that did not discover these principles in the book was unthinkable. But in the nineteenth century, critical Bible study began to flourish, and it was no longer necessary to conform Ecclesiastes to other books of the Bible. Ecclesiastes could take on a darker, less pious countenance.

SHADAL (SAMUEL DAVID LUZZATTO) Shadal, an Italian rabbinic scholar who was also learned in classical and modern languages and philosophy, employed modern philology and critical practices in the study of Jewish literature and philosophy. In a remarkable rhymed essay written in 1823 or 1824 but published only in 1860, this Italian rabbi and Hebraist became one of the very first scholars to describe Koheleth as a radical, even heretical, thinker. Shadal makes no attempt to harmonize Ecclesiastes with traditional religious doctrines.

Shadal boldly insists that Koheleth plainly denies the immortality of the soul, asserts determinism, and recommends carnal pleasures. Koheleth is not Solomon. Solomon would not have said such things, nor would he have written in a style that Shadal considers defective, obscure, and repetitive. The language of the book, moreover, is highly Aramaized and postexilic in character. Shadal concludes that Ecclesiastes was written shortly after the Babylonian captivity and falsely ascribed to Solomon. When later sages saw that they could not banish the book, they tried to temper its heresy by adding 11:9b; 12:1a, and 7b.

At several points in his commentary, Shadal interprets Koheleth in this fashion, then chides him for the selfishness and superficiality of his values, which are what lead him to despair. In contrast, someone who takes pleasure in others' happiness and knows the joy of righteousness and kindness finds the rewards that Koheleth deems impossible.

Critical scholars of the late nineteenth century and most of the twentieth favored the view that Koheleth is skeptical, pessimistic, and hedonistic, and that the pious sentiments in the book are later interpolations. Commentators started to appreciate Koheleth as a skeptical or "realistic" religious thinker who challenged traditional doctrines.

GEORGE A. BARTON (1908) Koheleth probed life relentlessly and found "the older religious conceptions of his people inadequate and the newer ones unproven" (p. 49). There is no permanent satisfaction in earthly activity. All labor is vain. There is nothing better than to eat and drink and gain "animal satisfaction" (p. 47). God holds human beings in an iron vice of fate and imposes ignorance upon them to inspire fear of God. Oppression and injustice prove that humans are like beasts. Immortality is questionable.

Koheleth nevertheless counsels an obedient and reverent religious stance. "His conception of God is dark, but such religion as he has is sincere" (p. 48). Koheleth's outlook has forced him to pessimism, but his advice is "manly and healthy, if not inspiring" (p. 49). He preaches "a gospel of healthy work and the full enjoyment of life's rounds of duties and opportunities" (p. 50).

According to Barton, the original Book of Ecclesiastes was extensively supplemented by glosses by a "Chasid" (a pious glossator of the Pharisaic persuasion) and a "Chakam" (a Wisdom glossator who added proverbs from conventional wisdom) (43–46).[30]

H. L. GINSBERG (1961)[31] Ginsberg's exegesis, which was influential in the NJPS translation of Ecclesiastes, portrays Koheleth as profoundly pessimistic and fatalistic. According to Ginsberg, the book concludes that all is futile and nugatory. This is true even of wisdom. The same emotions, experiences, and activities recur endlessly in human life. God determines the time for every event, which humans may try to discover but to no avail. The nature of phenomena is determined for eternity, and they never cease. This is true even of fear of heaven, oppression, righteous judgment, and wickedness. Death wipes away the advantages of wisdom and other talents. The only thing of real value is the enjoyment of material goods.

In the late twentieth century, commentators began addressing the literary forms, features, and rhetoric of the book. The number of alleged additions dwindled drastically. Some scholars came to view Koheleth as a persona rather than as the book's actual author. Some commentators are more inclined to read the book—including the epilogue—as a unity rather than excavating its literary development.

MARTIN HENGEL (1974) In *Judaism and Hellenism* (1.115–30), Hengel situates Ecclesiastes in its Hellenistic context, dating the book about 270–220 B.C.E. Hellenistic religion underwent a crisis in the Ptolemaic period, undergoing widespread loss of faith in the traditional gods and their replacement by the impersonal concept of fate. It was an age of considerable skepticism and anxiety about justice, human freedom, and divine care for human beings. (Some other Hellenistic traits are mentioned above in Dating.)

The author probably encountered Greek ideas not in the writings of the philosophers but in the popular views of the Greek bourgeoisie—among the officials, merchants, and soldiers in Ptolemaic Judea.[32] He sought to deal with these within the tradition of Wisdom, with its roots in classical Hebrew literature.

The meeting with Hellenism, according to Hengel, had several results. The individuality of the author's personality broke through. His "unprejudiced, detached observation" led to a radical criticism of the doctrine of retribution. His concept of a God lost an immediate personal relationship to mankind and it threatened to become ossified. Terms for destiny insinuated themselves between God and human, and God became almost—but not fully—equivalent to fate. Now all that humans could do was to resign themselves to God's control and enjoy life to the extent possible.

Under the impact of the spiritual crisis of early Hellenism, Koheleth could no longer make sense of traditional wisdom and piety, but he would not abandon the religion of his ancestors. Thus he fused the external stimuli with traditional principles in a unique fashion.

ROLAND E. MURPHY (1992) A variety of attitudes are heard in Ecclesiastes. Some of the tensions between Koheleth's statements arise because Koheleth cites ideas of conventional wisdom in order to limit their applicability. As Murphy understands it, Koheleth recognizes the value of life, wealth, toil, and wisdom, but these prove inadequate when seen under the shadow of death. Koheleth is often in conflict with traditional Wisdom teaching, especially its claim to provide security, yet he affirms wisdom and remains within its traditions, employing its methods and literary genres. It is because Koheleth loves life and wisdom that he is grieved by death and by life's vanity.

CHOON-LEONG SEOW (1997) In Seow's reading, Ecclesiastes has a fairly affirmative worldview. Koheleth focuses on the human condition and sees that mortals are not in control of events or of their own destiny, nor can they understand it. *Hevel* refers to whatever cannot be grasped or controlled. "Everything is *hevel*" does not mean that everything is meaningless or insignificant, but that the meaning of life and the rationale of its inequities escape human comprehension. Furthermore, God is transcendent and wholly other, with absolute control. Humans must accept what happens, whether good or bad. We must respond spontaneously to life, even in the midst of uncertainties, and be receptive to both the possibilities life offers and aware of the limitations of our humanness.

MICHAEL V. FOX (1999) This book is effectively summarized in the next section. The book should also be consulted for a more extensive discussion of textual and linguistic problems as well as analytical essays on various topics in Ecclesiastes' thought.

The Teachings of Ecclesiastes

The Problem. The underlying issue that Ecclesiastes addresses is the possibility of *meaningfulness* in life. For events to be meaningful, they would have to cohere in a comprehensible picture. Deed and consequence must correspond securely and predictably. The righteous *should* be rewarded, the wicked punished; the one who toils *should* get to enjoy the full fruits of his work; the wise *should* have a life the polar opposite of the fool's, and something *should* distinguish them in death.

A life with a strict correspondence between deed and consequence, virtue and reward, vice and punishment, would make sense. But Koheleth sees that this does not happen, and he is weighed down by the collapse of meaning, as revealed by the contradictions that pervade life. These are antinomies, contradictory propositions that seem equally valid. These antinomies should not be eliminated by harmonization, for they are the essence of what Koheleth observes. He is not consistent because the world he sees is not consistent.

Koheleth is frustrated that life does not make sense in this way, that the mass of disjointed deeds and events cannot be drawn together into a coherent and significant picture. The irrationality of the world is his fundamental grievance, and his other complaints—such as the brevity of life, the futility of effort, the triviality of worldly goods, the vulnerability of wisdom, and the anomalies in divine justice—are secondary to this one and serve to confirm it. Frustrated by such incoherence and irrationality, Koheleth calls the world *hevel*—"senseless" or "absurd."

Affirmations Koheleth is not a nihilist. "Everything is absurd" is to be understood as expressing a general characterization of life, not as an absolute proposition negating all possible activities and values. As well as tearing down, Koheleth builds up, showing how we can recover and reconstruct meanings. He does not arrive at a grand logic (or theology) that makes sense of everything, but he does recommend modest and small-scale accommodations in our individual lives.

Koheleth does find some things worthwhile: moderate work; temperate enjoyment of the pleasures that come to hand; love and friendship; gaining and using whatever wisdom is within our capacity; being reasonably righteous; fearing God; and hoping for divine justice. These are our portion and should be embraced, even if they do not constitute a "profit" *(yitron)* by Koheleth's rigorous standards, and even if they are contaminated by the absurdity that pervades our world.

These valuable things are brief, limited, and uncertain, but they are enough to make life worth living. Thus Koheleth comes to realize that despite all its unfairness and absurdity, life itself is good, to be grasped all the more eagerly for its brevity, given death's finality (9:7–10; 11:7).

Koheleth's affirmations—the things he recommends as worthwhile—all look inward, to each individual's benefit. Koheleth does not tell us to pursue justice, though he sees injustice. He does not tell us to comfort the oppressed, though he sees their discomfort. His concerns are internal: what troubles people, what cheers them up, how they can get along in a world in which much is determined but also opaque. There are practical things we can do to reduce the risks, but the only real realm of freedom and control is the human heart—the realm of emotions, thoughts, and attitudes. We are to enjoy whatever pleasures that God makes possible and avoid whatever sorrow we can look away from. This, we may note, is Stoic doctrine.

God While Koheleth does not use the metaphor of a divine king, he does see God as the absolute and transcendent ruler, rather like the human potentate described in 8:2b–4: powerful, autocratic, unpredictable, and rather dangerous. The will of God—who controls all events and all fates (9:1), and whose deeds cannot be undone (7:13)—is absolute. The richly anthropomorphic and anthropopathic language used of God elsewhere in the Bible has faded to a few pale references to divine emotions (2:25; 5:6; 9:1). Ascribing human form and feelings to deity is a way of expressing divine accessibility, concern, and immediacy.[33] These qualities are represented only vestigially in Koheleth's transcendent God.

Koheleth speaks of God with no warmth and expects no fellowship from Him. God controls the details of human life but keeps a distance. The warning that "God is in heaven and you are on earth" (5:1) describes an unbridgeable gap, not only divine loftiness and majesty. Koheleth's God is a distant and all-powerful force who can be feared but not loved. He does not seem like a God who would be open to prayer. Indeed, this deity has no particular relationship to Israel and is exclusively called *'elohim* ("God"), a generic term—never *YHWH* (translated "the LORD"), the personal name of God in ancient Israel.

Though rather steely and remote, this deity is not hostile. After giving good things to people, God wants them to enjoy the pleasure potential in it (9:7). Yet Koheleth expects little divine help or reward. Being obedient and treading warily in all that concerns God at best reduces the danger of provoking His anger (5:5b) rather than yielding any positive benefit or fellowship. Those whom God favors do receive benefits

(2:25), but this favor is unpredictable and does not necessarily correspond to moral deserts, since the beneficiary may be a fool (2:19; and see Comment to 2:26).

Sometimes God seems arbitrary, if not downright perverse, as when He sets humans a hopeless task (3:10–11), or gives a man wealth but does not allow him to enjoy it (6:2), or hides knowledge from humans for no apparent reason (7:14). He keeps people deeply ignorant. One does not even know whether God loves or hates him; in other words, what kind of fate awaits him (9:1).

Koheleth insists that God is just. The world does seem to operate, for the most part, on comprehensible principles of reward and punishment. Fools harm themselves; the wise generally do better (10:12f., 15). Laziness spoils one's property. Deeds, as a rule, have appropriate effects. The very wicked and foolish die before their time (7:17).

Koheleth believes, or at least tries to believe, that God will eventually execute justice (3:17; 11:9b). The righteous, in principle at least, live long and the wicked die young (8:11–12a, 14). But Koheleth does not see this happening at present and fears that justice will come too late (8:10–11, 14). God allows injustices and oppressions and—by offering no comfort to the oppressed—seems indifferent to their suffering (4:1). This is very different from the God in most of the Bible, such as when He declares, for example, "I, I am He who comforts you" (Isa. 51:12).

This is not an encouraging theology, nor is it meant to be. For Koheleth seeks to open eyes to the world as he sees it, and this world is a grim one—rather like that of the Ptolemaic empire itself, autocratic and indifferent to its subjects. In most of the Bible, God has relations, whether loving or hostile, to nations and individuals; and God—though not fully predictable—almost always acts in accordance with transparent principles of justice. But the entirety of biblical thought does not reside in every book. Ecclesiastes must be read as one voice adding a unique perspective to the diverse collection of ideas that constitute the Bible.

Doubt and Belief Modern commentators have almost always depicted Koheleth as a skeptic, a precursor of the modern doubter or radical who seeks to undermine traditional and conventional beliefs. This is a mischaracterization. Koheleth never sets forth a conventional idea as an erroneous dogma that he proposes to defeat or modify. He never distances himself from the principles he finds contradicted. (For this reason, it is highly misleading to insert phrases, as NJPS sometimes does, that ascribe an opinion to someone else, in the absence of any indicator in the text; see Comment to 8:12–14.) Koheleth holds to conflicting ideas, and he is troubled.

Koheleth places himself among the wise and shows no awareness that his observations clash with the beliefs of *other* sages. He does not attack the principle of retributive justice—that good is rewarded, evil is punished, appropriately and proportionately. He believes in divine justice but sees it contradicted, and—rather than working out a smooth solution as a theologian might, or rejecting the principle as a skeptic might—Koheleth throws up his hands in frustration and calls what he sees *hevel*. Then he urges us to open ourselves to whatever good things the moment offers.

Another Voice: the Epilogue The epilogue (12:9–14) is commonly considered an addition by a later scribe, but it may well be the words of the anonymous *author,* who has heretofore presented Koheleth, a persona, and quoted his teachings. (Some distinguish two epilogues, 12:9–12 and 12:13–14.)

The epilogue looks back and evaluates Koheleth from a more conventional and conservative standpoint, assuring the reader that he was a wise and eloquent teacher, but also warning that the words of the wise hold certain dangers. What is most important? Fearing God, obeying His commandments, and living in awareness of God's ultimate judgment. For Koheleth too, these are bedrock truths that experience can collide with but not dislodge.

Notes to the Introduction

1. This was not the only opinion expressed before modern times. Maimonides ascribed the epilogue to "those who edited the book," indicating that he considered Ecclesiastes to be a later collection of Solomon's thoughts. Ibn Ezra mentions, and rejects, an opinion that the book is a collection of teachings from the "assembly" *(kahal)* of Solomon's disciples.

2. Helpful introductions to Israelite Wisdom Literature are Roland E. Murphy, *The Tree of Life* (Grand Rapids, MI: Eerdmans, 1996) and James L. Crenshaw, *Old Testament Wisdom* (Louisville, KY: Westminster John Knox, 1998).

3. The most important foreign resource for Israelite Wisdom was the Egyptian Instruction of Amenemope (*AEL* 1.146–63). There is good evidence that Prov. 22:17–23:11 was based on a Hebrew or Aramaic translation of Amenemope; see, among many works, Glendon Bryce, *A Legacy of Wisdom* (Lewisburg, PA: Bucknell, 1979), 39–134.

4. Translations: James B. Pritchard, *Ancient Near Eastern Texts Related to the Old Testament* (Princeton: Princeton University Press, 1955), 427–30. Text and translation: James M. Lindenberger, *The Aramaic Proverbs of Aḥiqar* (Baltimore: Johns Hopkins University, 1983).

5. It is vaguely possible that the audiences of a few other texts were thought to include daughters as well as sons, but this is not the norm; see M. V. Fox, *Proverbs 1–9* (Anchor Bible; Garden City, NY: Anchor-Doubleday, 1999), 80, n. 83.

6. In Ecclesiastes, the toiler is a man (called by the gender-specific term *'ish* in 6:2, 3), who may or may not have a wife. The reader is advised to enjoy life with a "woman you love" (9:8). Women come into consideration only insofar as they are a source of pleasure (9:9a; possibly 2:8b) or misery (7:26–8:1a) to men. In the light of 7:25–8:1a, it is improbable that Koheleth—unlike the book of Proverbs (12:4; 14:1; 31:10–31)—would have conceded the existence of a wise woman. In short, Koheleth has a male audience in mind.

7. Martin Hengel, *Judaism and Hellenism* (transl. J. Bowden). Philadelphia: Fortress, 1974, 1.116.

8. Koheleth's connection to Stoicism has been argued by a number of scholars, most thoroughly and cautiously by Dominic Rudman, *Determinism in the Book of Ecclesiastes* (Sheffield, England: Sheffield Academic Press, 2001), 173–99 and passim. See also John Gammie, "Stoicism and anti-Stoicism in Qoheleth," *Hebrew Annual Review* 9 (1985), 169–87.

9. Elias Bickermann, *Four Strange Books of the Bible* (New York: Schocken, 1967), 141–67, is especially helpful in situating Ecclesiastes in the social and intellectual environment of Hellenism.

10. Akkadian fictional autobiographies are described and compared to Koheleth by Tremper Longman III, *Fictional Akkadian Autobiographies* (Winona Lake, IN: Eisenbrauns, 1991).

11. For a literary study of Ecclesiastes as an autobiographical narrative see Eric S. Christianson, *A Time to Tell* (Sheffield, England: Sheffield Academic Press, 1998).

12. For example, the Book of Ecclesiastes employs two Persian words, *pardesim* ("groves, orchards"; 2:5) and *pitgam* ("sentence"; 8:11), and contact with Persia did not precede the sixth century B.C.E. (After the Persian period, these words continued in use in Hebrew and Aramaic.)

Many other words occur only in the later biblical books or subsequent later stages of Hebrew. Examples are: *ḥutz min* ("except for"; 2:25); *kevar* ("already"; 1:10; 2:12; etc.); *medinah* ("province"; 5:7); and *shalat* ("rule, control"; 2:19; 8:9). Several syntactic usages point to a later stage of biblical Hebrew. For example, the conjunction *she-* "that" (rather than *'asher*) is very rare in preexilic Hebrew but becomes standard in rabbinic Hebrew. In Ecclesiastes, the frequencies of *she-* and *'asher* are about equal. Also, the form *'ani* is used exclusively for "I," displacing *'anokhi,* which was used alongside *'ani* in preexilic times.

The evidence for dating the language of Ecclesiastes is carefully assembled and evaluated by Antoon Schoors, *The Preacher Sought to Find Pleasing Words* (Leuven: Peeters, 1992; vol. I, passim), who follows the great majority of commentators in identifying it as Late Biblical Hebrew. This would situate the book during the Persian period

(535–332 B.C.E.) or the early Hellenistic period (332 to the middle of the second century B.C.E.). Seow (16–20) argues that it belongs specifically to the Persian period, but the evidence for this limitation is inadequate.

13. Ginsberg (*Koheleth,* 30–42) argued that the difficult Hebrew text of Ecclesiastes is a translation of a lost Aramaic original and, moreover, that this translation is full of errors that must be corrected by reconstructing the Aramaic behind it, then translating *it.* The theory of an Aramaic original is plausible, given the discovery of certain books in Hebrew and Aramaic at Qumran (particularly Tobit), but the arguments Ginsberg brings are not adequate. This theory has been criticized (but not disproved) by Gordis (399–499); Whitley (*Koheleth,* 106–110); and A. Schoors, *The Preacher,* passim.

14. The word for "race," *merotz* (9:11), does not occur elsewhere in the Bible. The context refers not just to running or a chase (as Seow claims, p. 307), but competition. It is an event in which the swiftest runners normally win and receive a reward, like the rewards for other skills in 9:11.

15. A number of scholars have investigated the possibility of various sorts of Hellenistic-Greek influences on Ecclesiastes and made the case for situating the book in the Hellenistic thought-world. Treatments of this issue in English include Martin Hengel's *Judaism and Hellenism,* 1.115–28; Charles Whitley's *Koheleth, His Language and Thought* (Beihefte für die Zeitschrift für die alltestamentlicher Wissenschaft 148; Berlin: W. de Gruyter, 1979), 165–175; M. V. Fox, *A Time to Tear Down,* § 1.41 (with further references); and most modern commentaries.

16. Menahem Haran, האסופה המקראית (Jerusalem: Bialik, 1996) 301–2 and chap. 5. The Alexandrian Jewish community, and subsequently the Christian Church, included the Wisdom of Solomon and the Odes of Solomon in their canon. These works, composed in Greek, were not in use among the predecessors and founders of rabbinic Judaism.

17. Structures and designs proposed by modern scholars are conveniently summarized by A. G. Wright ("The Riddle of the Sphinx: The Structure of the Book of Qoheleth," *Catholic Bible Quarterly* 30 [1968], 313–34) and R. E. Murphy (*Ecclesiastes,* xxxv–xli). Earlier attempts to discern a structure are summarized by C. D. Ginsburg, *Coheleth,* 27–245.

18. "The Riddle of the Sphinx."

19. Ginsberg (*Koheleth,* 13, 15–16) identified "earn" and "property" as two of the meanings of *'asah* and its derivatives, and he made the important observation that derivatives of the root *'-s-h* often denote "occurrence and happening." He notes that *ma'aseh* often means "occurrence" in rabbinic Hebrew.

20. See especially R. N. Whybray, "Qoheleth, Preacher of Joy" (*Journal for the Study of the Old Testament* 23 [1982], 87–98) and his commentary, *Ecclesiastes,* New Century Bible Commentary (Grand Rapids, MI: Eerdmans, 1989).

21. Koheleth Rabbah and Rashbam are surveyed and quoted at length in Ruth Sandberg, *Rabbinic Views of Qohelet* (Lewiston, NY: Mellen, 1999). She classifies select interpretations by their "mode of interpretation" and emphasizes the wide diversity in rabbinic understandings.

22. In *Gesammelte Schriften,* ed. F. Bamberger et al. (Stuttgart–Bad Cannstatt: Frommann, 1972), 14.145–207.

23. Published in *Otzar Neḥmad* (ed. Ignaz Blumenfeld, Vienna), vol. 3 (1860), 15–25 (Introduction), and in vol. 5 (1863), 47–93 (Commentary). In the introduction, Luzzatto says that he wrote this interpretation when he was twenty-four (i.e., in 1823–4), but now has unspecified hesitations about his earlier theories.

24. This is a development of an earlier study, *Qohelet and His Contradictions* (Sheffield, England: JSOT Supplements, 1987).

25. On the history of Koheleth interpretation see M. V. Fox, "Qohelet," in John H. Hayes (editor), *Dictionary of Biblical Interpretation* (Nashville: Abingdon, 1999), 2.346–54. For summaries of Jewish and Christian interpretations up to 1860 see C. D. Ginsburg, *Coheleth,* 27–245.

26. Early Christian commentators took essentially the same approach. They tended to denigrate the value of mundane goods even more emphatically, and they saw salvation in Christ as the implied solution to the triviality of earthly life.

27. Rashbam's hermeneutics and his approach to contradictions are treated by Japhet and Salters, *Rashbam on Qoheleth,* 59–68.

28. For a critical edition of his commentary—with English translation, introduction, and notes—see James T. Robinson, "Samuel ibn Tibbon's *Commentary on Ecclesiastes* and the Philosopher's Prooemium," in *Studies in Medieval Jewish History and Literature,* vol. III, edited by I. Twersky and J. M. Harris (Cambridge: Harvard, forthcoming).

29. Mendelssohn's Ecclesiastes commentary and its role in the emergence of modern Jewish thought is discussed by David Sorkin, *Moses Mendelssohn and the Religious Enlightenment* (Berkeley: University of California, 1996), 35–52.

30. Modern Christian commentators often find the value of Koheleth's pessimism and skepticism to be the way that (as they see it) it supposedly clears the ground in preparation for the message of the New Testament. Barton, for example, says, "It is a teaching which is to a Christian chilling and disappointing, but Koheleth's negative work had, no doubt, a function to perform in clearing away outworn conceptions before a new, larger, truer and more inspiring faith could have its birth" (p. 50). However, Barton forgets that he is remarking not on the Book of Ecclesiastes but upon his own reconstruction—the book minus numerous sentences that he considers additions. This reconstruction was not the one that Jews read! Nor does Barton identify the "outworn conceptions" that Koheleth supposedly sweeps away. That toil is profitable? That there is an afterlife? That God's justice is perfect?—these were hardly "swept away." The Jews of the pre-Christian era never discarded the beliefs that Koheleth's observations contradicted. Nor, for that matter, did Christianity.

31. On Ginsberg's theory that Koheleth is a translation from an Aramaic original, see above, n. 13.

32. Hengel, *Judaism and Hellenism,* 1.125.

33. With regard to the anthropomorphism and gender of Israel's deity, see Mark S. Smith, *The Origins of Biblical Monotheism* (New York: Oxford University Press, 2001), 88–93. Israel's deity (*YHWH* or "Yahweh") was consistently viewed as male, though female actions could be ascribed to him, as in Deut. 32:18; Ps. 22:9–19; and Isa. 46:3; 66:9, and 13. Such passages "treat Yahweh as a male deity to whom female imagery was occasionally attributed on a metaphorical level.... Yahweh both encompasses the characteristics and values expressed through gendered metaphors and transcends the categories of sexuality (cf. Job 38:28–29): monotheism is beyond sexuality yet nonetheless expressed through it" (91–92). God continues to be spoken of as a male deity in Ecclesiastes, but specifically masculine imagery (such as his being a "man of war" or "father") has disappeared.

ABBREVIATIONS AND OTHER CONVENTIONS

Abbreviations

AEL	Miriam Lichtheim, *Ancient Egyptian Literature*; 3 vols., Berkeley: Univ. of California, 1973–80.
Avot	Mishnah *Pirke Avot*
B.	Babylonian Talmud
BETL	*Bibliotheca ephemeridum theologicarum lovaniensium*
J.	"Jerusalem" (Land of Israel) Talmud
JBL	*Journal of Biblical Literature*
Koh. R.	Koheleth Rabbah
M.	Mishnah
MT	Masoretic text
NJPS	New Jewish Publication Society translation
Pes. de-R. Kah.	Pesikta de-Rav Kahana
R.	*(preceding a name)* Rabbi
R.	*(following a name of a book)* Rabbah (a midrash compilation)
Song	Song of Songs
Transl.	Translators (of NJPS)

Hebrew Textual Variants (Ketiv and Kerey)

The MT's *ketiv* (written tradition) and *kerey* (recited tradition) differ from each other for occasional words; and when reading the text aloud, the *kerey* is what is traditionally followed. Where differences exist, this edition first prints that word's *ketiv* letters in small type, followed by the vocalized *kerey* letters in normal text type. (This edition's biblical text is excerpted from the *JPS Hebrew-English Tanakh* [1999], as corrected in printings through 2001. For more information on the provenance and preparation of the Hebrew text, see the preface to that volume.)

Transliteration of the Hebrew Consonants

ʾ	alef
ʿ	ayin
b	bet
g	gimel
d	dalet
h	heh
v	vet, vav
z	zayin
ḥ	het
t	tet, tav
y	yod
k	kaf
kh	khaf
l	lamed
m	mem
n	nun
s	samekh, sin
p	peh
f	feh
tz	tzadi
k	kof
r	resh
sh	shin

Pronunciation Guide for Vowels

a	as in *farm*
ai	as in *eye*
e	as in *dent*
ei	as in *hay*
i	as in *hit* or *heat*
o	as in *hope*
u	as in *food*

THE COMMENTARY TO ECCLESIASTES

1 The words of Koheleth son of David, king in Jerusalem.

א דִּבְרֵי֙ קֹהֶ֣לֶת בֶּן־דָּוִ֔ד מֶ֖לֶךְ בִּירוּשָׁלִָֽם׃

2 Utter futility!—said Koheleth—
Utter futility! All is futile!

2 הֲבֵ֤ל הֲבָלִים֙ אָמַ֣ר קֹהֶ֔לֶת
הֲבֵ֥ל הֲבָלִ֖ים הַכֹּ֥ל הָֽבֶל׃

Introduction (1:1–18)

TITLE AND MOTTO (1:1–2)

1:1 The words of Koheleth son of David, king in Jerusalem On the identity of Koheleth, see Title and Author in the introduction. Since the word can appear with the article, *ha-kohelet* ("the Koheleth"; 7:27 [see Comment] and 12:8), it is a title, not a personal name. The word means, approximately, "one who does something in the assembly *(kahal)*." Compare the usages in Ezra 2:55, 57 and Neh. 7:57, 59. Bickermann likens the word to the street-preachers of Ptolemaic times, such as Crates, Menipus, or Bion—philosophers who sought to teach the right way of life to the common man.[1]

A midrash explains that Solomon (who was believed to be the author of Ecclesiastes) was called Koheleth because his words were spoken in assembly, referring to *va-yak-hel,* "and [Solomon] assembled" (NJPS: "convoked") in 1 Kings 8:1 (Koh. R.).

In the light of 12:9, we may surmise that "Koheleth" means something like "teacher to the public." The practice of public teaching is suggested by Prov. 1:20–21 and 8:1–3, in which Wisdom (personified as a woman) goes about the city streets preaching and teaching.

2. Utter futility! [havel havalim]—said Koheleth—Utter futility! All is futile! This sentence (repeated in 12:8) is the narrator's summary of Koheleth's thought. As Rashbam notes, verses 1–2 belong to "the one who arranged [Koheleth's] words as they now are." This same voice will speak again in 12:8 and 12:9–14.

The key term is *hevel* (plural, *havalim;* construct form, *haveil;* and pausal form, *havel*). *Havel havalim* is literally "vapor of vapors," which is to be understood as a superlative: "utter vanity, utter futility" (NJPS), or (as I prefer) "utterly senseless" or "utterly absurd." (See Keywords in the introduction.) Here the superlative is heightened by fluid, alliterative, repetition: *Havel havalim, 'amar ha-kohelet, havel havalim, ha-kol havel.* The reiteration of *hevel* emphasizes the universality of this truth (Rashbam) and also the pervasiveness of this quality.

In the midrashic mode of interpretation, the Targum tells that Koheleth's pronouncement was a response to national tragedies. When Solomon prophetically foresaw the grim future awaiting his kingdom, the Temple, and the Jewish people, he declared that all is *hevel,* understood to mean vain and transitory. These national calamities demonstrated the fragility of human achievements. Another midrash reads this sentence as a statement of human mortality: King David said that a human is like a *hevel*—vapor (Ps. 144:4); however, whereas a vapor, such as from an oven or stove, may have some substance in it, a human is but a *hevel* of *havalim,* a vapor of vapors (Koh. R.).

3 What real value is there for a man
In all the gains he makes beneath the sun?

3 מַה־יִּתְר֖וֹן לָאָדָ֑ם
בְּכָל־עֲמָל֔וֹ שֶֽׁיַּעֲמֹ֖ל תַּ֥חַת הַשָּֽׁמֶשׁ׃

PROLOGUE (1:3–11)

3. ***What real value* [*yitron*] *is there for a man in all the gains* [*'amal*] *he makes beneath the sun?*** Better: "What profit is there for a man in all the toil [*'amal*] he performs beneath the sun?" The context provided by the following poem (1:4–9) has nothing to do with wealth. Rather, by describing the unchangeability of natural phenomena, the poem seeks to demonstrate that human *labors* are futile. (And given that 1:3 asks a question that will be answered in the course of the book, it is likely that *'amal* usually has the same sense elsewhere.)

Koheleth soon answers the question about the profit in toil: There is none; see 2:11. Toil, he believes, does not produce enough of real value to compensate for its misery. Koheleth will bring several arguments for this contention, but first he shows that lack of profit is inherent in the world by using the analogy of natural phenomena. If the unending labors of nature accomplish nothing new and lasting (1:4–11), surely no human exertions, however protracted or intense, can do so (v. 3).

According to R. Benjamin ben Levi in Koheleth Rabbah, the sages worried that this verse could cause an inclination to heresy, for it might be understood to mean that toil in the study of Torah is also without profit. Upon rethinking the issue, they noted that Koheleth did not say "in all toil" but (literally) "in all *his* toil." In contrast, "Torah's toil"—labor in Torah—*is* profitable."

beneath the sun The domain of human life, in short, the world. The term does not include the heavens, which are exclusively God's domain (5:1a), or the underworld (see 9:6). (A synonymous phrase is "beneath [or "under"] the "heavens"; 1:13, 2:3, 3:1.)

Traditional exegesis is unanimous in understanding "beneath the sun" as implying that the converse is true: "above the sun," in the supermundane realm of Torah and the coming eternal life, there *is* profit. The Targum paraphrases, "After one dies, what advantage does he have from all the labor that he performs under the sun in this world, unless he has busied himself with Torah so as to receive a full reward before the Master of the Universe in the hereafter." Ibn Ezra says that "beneath the sun" refers to the mundane world, which is subject to the vicissitudes of time. Hence the soul that strives for illumination in wisdom does indeed have a profit in its toil, because the soul (being immortal) is not of the mundane things "beneath the sun." Rashi offers an additional explanation: What is worthless is any toil one does *instead* of the "sun" (for *taḥat* can mean "instead of" as well as "beneath"). The "sun" was equated with the Torah.

Alternatively, "beneath the sun" may be for emphasis, without implying anything about other realms. Then its purpose would be to emphasize the *universality* of Koheleth's claims within the sphere he examines, namely the world that humans inhabit. It is a way of saying "the entire world." This reading is more likely, because the things Koheleth examines can exist only "beneath the sun," making it pointless to exclude another realm from these judgments. For example, "There is nothing new beneath the sun!" (1:9) is not a way of conceding that there is indeed something new in heaven.

Nature's incessant cyclicity, described in verses 4–7, demonstrates that "there is nothing new beneath the sun," and thus, by analogy and a fortiori, shows that feeble human exertions cannot be expected to affect the course of events.

4 One generation goes, another comes,
But the earth remains the same forever.
5 The sun rises, and the sun sets—
And glides back to where it rises.
6 Southward blowing,
Turning northward,
Ever turning blows the wind;
On its rounds the wind returns.
7 All streams flow into the sea,
Yet the sea is never full;
To the place [from] which they flow
The streams flow back again.

4 דּוֹר הֹלֵךְ וְדוֹר בָּא
וְהָאָרֶץ לְעוֹלָם עֹמָדֶת׃
5 וְזָרַח הַשֶּׁמֶשׁ וּבָא הַשָּׁמֶשׁ
וְאֶל־מְקוֹמוֹ שׁוֹאֵף זוֹרֵחַ הוּא שָׁם׃
6 הוֹלֵךְ אֶל־דָּרוֹם
וְסוֹבֵב אֶל־צָפוֹן
סוֹבֵב ׀ סֹבֵב הוֹלֵךְ הָרוּחַ
וְעַל־סְבִיבֹתָיו שָׁב הָרוּחַ׃
7 כָּל־הַנְּחָלִים הֹלְכִים אֶל־הַיָּם
וְהַיָּם אֵינֶנּוּ מָלֵא
אֶל־מְקוֹם שֶׁהַנְּחָלִים הֹלְכִים
שָׁם הֵם שָׁבִים לָלָכֶת׃

Ibn Ezra sees in the poem the four classical elements of nature: earth, fire (the sun), water, and air. Whether or not this schema (Greek in origin) is present, the phenomena chosen are the mightiest and most invariable of natural elements.

*4. **One generation goes, another comes*** Rashbam reads verse 4 as an elaboration of verse 2, in which "all is *hevel*" is understood to contrast human evanescence with the permanence of the physical earth. There is, however, no allusion to mortality elsewhere in this passage. The word order in verse 4 actually places the emphasis on the replacement of one generation by another (the generation that *goes* is replaced by the one that *comes*), a process like that of the other phenomena described. Compare especially how the rivers flow into the sea without filling it up (v. 7). *'Eretz,* "earth," "world," can mean "the entirety of mankind," like *le monde* in French (e.g., Gen. 11:1, 1 Kings 2:2, and Ps. 33:8). It seems to Koheleth that in spite of the ceaseless movement of generations, mankind is always the same.

Rashi finds a moral lesson here. The wicked will not outlive the wealth they gained by oppression, because their generation will pass away and another will come and take their wealth away from their children. But the humble, who are called "the earth" because they inherit the earth (Ps. 37:11), shall endure.

*5. **The sun rises, and the sun sets*** Its great, laborious trek across the sky merely brings it back to its point of departure.

glides back Hebrew *sho'ef;* better: "pants"—that is, trudges along while panting. This metaphorically evokes the strain of the trek. Contrast the elation of the psalmist (Ps. 19:6) in considering the same phenomenon.

*6. **Southward blowing*** Even the wind, which may seem to wander aimlessly, follows a fixed path. The delay of the subject ("the wind") till late in the sentence is suggestive of an unrelenting pull forward, as does the fourfold repetition of the root *s-b-b* ("go round").

*7. **All streams flow into the sea*** The rivers never fill up the sea once and for all. The sea always takes more water. Koheleth chooses to regard this as an example of frustrated efforts rather than as an accomplishment or a process of renewal.

8 All such things are wearisome:
No man can ever state them;
The eye never has enough of seeing,
Nor the ear enough of hearing.
9 Only that shall happen
Which has happened,

8 כָּל־הַדְּבָרִים יְגֵעִים
לֹא־יוּכַל אִישׁ לְדַבֵּר
לֹא־תִשְׂבַּע עַיִן לִרְאוֹת
וְלֹא־תִמָּלֵא אֹזֶן מִשְּׁמֹעַ׃
9 מַה־שֶּׁהָיָה
הוּא שֶׁיִּהְיֶה

To the place [from] which they flow NJPS implicitly adds a prefixed *mem* ("from"),[2] indicating that the waters flow back to the rivers' sources. Ibn Ezra explains this process precisely: the sea's water evaporates and becomes clouds, whose rain supplies the sweet water to the springs, which feed the rivers. The Targum and Rashi reflect a belief that the waters flow through underground tunnels. Lacking "from," the MT describes the endless flow toward the sea: "To the place to which the streams flow, there they flow back again." Both make sense. The sea can always take more water.

8. All such things are wearisome The MT lacks "such," and the addition of this word unnecessarily restricts the scope of this generalization. Koheleth is speaking about *everything*. Furthermore, the claim is ambiguous, because *devarim* can mean either "things" or "words." In the light of the next sentence, it is better to translate "All words are weary." It is not the natural phenomena but rather human *words* that are "weary," inadequate to communicate the immensity of the repetitions in which the world is locked.

No man can ever state them Better: "Man is unable to speak." (No direct object is stated or implied in *ledabber*.) This is an emotional reaction. Koheleth is not saying that the phenomena are too manifold or complex to describe, but that humans (Koheleth means himself, of course) are fatigued by the attempt to comprehend and express what they see in the world.

The eye never has enough of seeing/Nor the ear enough of hearing Just as the appetite for wealth is never sated by amassing possessions (5:9a and 6:7), so is the human desire for understanding never satisfied by sensory data.

Ben Sira rephrases Koheleth's complaint as an exclamation of awe: "And who can be sated with seeing the appearance (of God's works)?" (Sira 42:25). This is the expected reaction to the stability of God's works. For Koheleth, however, the natural world is so repetitive and tiresome that no one can satisfactorily contemplate it or describe what he sees.

The Targum reads this verse as a warning against inquiry into spheres beyond human grasp: "The ancient prophets wearied themselves [in pondering] all the things that are going to happen in the world in the future, but they could not discover how things would turn out. So too humans have no right to speak of what will come to pass in the future after them, nor is the eye able to see all that happens in the world, nor can the ear be filled by hearing all the words of all inhabitants of the earth." According to this homily, Koheleth advocates a humble acceptance of the limitations of human understanding. In fact, Koheleth does not accept these limitations humbly as a religious duty so much as swallow them as a bitter fact.

9. There is nothing new/Beneath the sun! Koheleth's real concern is not the natural phenomena but rather human efforts. These fail to achieve anything new and can thus attain no true "profit." He is not claiming that specific historical events recur, but

Only that occur
Which has occurred;
There is nothing new
Beneath the sun!
[10] Sometimes there is a phenomenon of which they
say, "Look, this one is new!"—it occurred long since,
in ages that went by before us. [11] The earlier ones are
not remembered; so too those that will occur later
will no more be remembered than those that will
occur at the very end.

וּמַה־שֶּׁנַּעֲשָׂה
ה֖וּא שֶׁיֵּעָשֶׂ֑ה
וְאֵ֥ין כָּל־חָדָ֖שׁ
תַּ֥חַת הַשָּֽׁמֶשׁ׃
10 יֵ֥שׁ דָּבָ֛ר שֶׁיֹּאמַ֥ר רְאֵה־זֶ֖ה חָדָ֣שׁ ה֑וּא
כְּבָר֙ הָיָ֣ה לְעֹֽלָמִ֔ים אֲשֶׁ֥ר הָיָ֖ה מִלְּפָנֵֽנוּ׃
11 אֵ֥ין זִכְר֖וֹן לָרִאשֹׁנִ֑ים וְגַ֨ם לָאַחֲרֹנִ֜ים
שֶׁיִּהְי֗וּ לֹֽא־יִהְיֶ֤ה לָהֶם֙ זִכָּר֔וֹן עִ֥ם שֶׁיִּהְי֖וּ
לָאַחֲרֹנָֽה׃ פ

rather that all *types* of events (wars, say, or national disasters) recur, and therefore nothing that happens can be fundamentally new. We are like the figures in a computer game, whose actions seem to vary with each play but are really just ephemeral variants of possibilities dictated by the software. In life, achievements are an illusion, mere echoes of archetypal events. Compare 1:15 and 3:14.

10. If people suppose that something really new has happened, that is only because the collective memory is faulty.

The Midrash (Koh. R.) views the world as essentially static. God made things just right at Creation, and they need not change. Torah too is unchanging. Torah in its entirety, including Scripture and its later expositions, was given at Sinai. If a scholar thinks he has come up with something new, he should remember that "it has occurred long since" (v. 10b). Another implication is that the scholarship of all generations partakes in the revelation at Sinai: "if you have learned Torah from the mouth of a learned scholar, you should regard it as if your own ears heard it at Mount Sinai." See the homily quoted in the Comment to 12:11.

11. The earlier ones are not remembered; so too those that will occur later will no more be remembered than those that will occur at the very end A NJPS note observes that the literal translation is "will not be remembered like…"; cf. *'im* meaning "like" in 2.16; 7.11; Job 9.26. An alternative translation is, "The earlier [events] are not remembered; so too those that will occur later will not be remembered with those [people] who will be even later." The question here is whether "earlier" and "later" refer to people or events. Rashbam identifies them as past and future people, who will all be forgotten, because he understands the theme of the passage to be human mortality. But since verse 10a describes events, as does as the entire poem about nature, this sentence probably does as well. Earlier events are not remembered by present generations, and our own present will be forgotten by our successors. In any case, "at the very end" does not refer to the end of the world.

KOHELETH INTRODUCES HIMSELF AND HIS UNDERTAKING (1:12–18)

As Koheleth Rabbah observes, from the standpoint of chronology, this verse could start the book. All that precedes is a prologue. This passage is an introduction—presenting the speaker, his station, his qualities, and the task he set himself. Specifically, Koheleth

[12] I, Koheleth, was king in Jerusalem over Israel. [13] I set my mind to study and to probe with wisdom all that happens under the sun.—An unhappy business, that, which God gave men to be concerned with!

12 אֲנִ֣י קֹהֶ֗לֶת הָיִ֥יתִי מֶ֛לֶךְ עַל־יִשְׂרָאֵ֖ל
בִּירוּשָׁלִָֽם׃ 13 וְנָתַ֣תִּי אֶת־לִבִּ֗י לִדְר֤וֹשׁ
וְלָתוּר֙ בַּֽחׇכְמָ֔ה עַ֛ל כׇּל־אֲשֶׁ֥ר נַעֲשָׂ֖ה תַּ֣חַת
הַשָּׁמָ֑יִם ה֣וּא ׀ עִנְיַ֣ן רָ֗ע נָתַ֧ן אֱלֹהִ֛ים לִבְנֵ֥י

introduces himself (1:12) and describes the task he took upon himself: to use wisdom to gain an understanding of the world (v. 13). He states his conclusion again: everything is senseless and distorted (vv. 14–15). He then describes the procedure of his undertaking (vv. 16–17a) and the misery it brings with it (vv. 17b–18).

12. I, Koheleth, was king in Jerusalem over Israel Or: "I am Koheleth. I have been king..." This form resembles the opening of royal inscriptions from neighboring cultures. Examples from Phoenician inscriptions are: "I am Kilamuwa, the son of Hayya"; "I am Azitawadda, blessed by Baal, servant of Baal, whom Awarku, king of the Danunians, made powerful."[3] Such self-identifications (like vv. 12–13) introduce autobiographical accounts of the king's virtues and exploits.

was king The apparent past tense of *hayiti* (usually meaning "was") gave rise to puzzlement and speculation. Was Koheleth *no longer* king? The Midrash draws a story out of this verb. It relates that Solomon became arrogant and disobedient because of his wealth and was deposed by the demon Ashmodai. Wandering about impoverished, Solomon confessed, "I, Koheleth, who was previously named Solomon, *was* king over Israel." Eventually he was restored to rule and realized that "all is vanity."[4] Rashi imagines Koheleth saying, "(I was king) over the whole world, then over Israel, then over Jerusalem alone, then over my stick alone, as it is said, 'I was king in Jerusalem'—but now I am not king." Yet the phrase *hayiti melekh* can mean "I became king" or "I have been king" without implying that he ceased to be so. Nevertheless, the book does have an orientation to the past. Koheleth is looking back on his earlier experiences at some distance, reporting them, and evaluating them. Thus he chooses to say "have been" rather than simply "am" king.

13. I set my mind Literally, "I set my heart." Koheleth thinks of his heart as an entity distinct from his ego, the "I" that speaks. This is most clear in 7:25, where he says (translating literally) "I turned, I and my heart, to know..." His heart is essentially his rational faculty, and it accompanies him in his explorations. The phrase "to speak to one's heart" is found elsewhere in the Bible (e.g., Gen. 8:21; 1 Sam. 27:1), but only Koheleth addresses his heart in the second person. Koheleth speaks "to" and "with" his heart (1:16, 2:14–15, etc.) and directs it to do things (2:1). He also explores "in" his heart (2:3), and the like. His heart, for its part, "sees" wisdom (1:16), conducts itself in wisdom (2:3), and receives pleasure (2:10). Koheleth refers to his heart so frequently—especially in 1:12–2:26 (twelve times)—because he is reflecting on the process of perception and discovery, and the heart (or, as we would say, "mind") has a central role in this process. Koheleth is watching his mind at work.

with wisdom That is, via his own learning and intellect—and nothing else. Wisdom is both the means and the goal of Koheleth's search. He clearly has wisdom already—much of it—but he desires a kind of wisdom he cannot attain; see especially 7:23 and 8:17.

all that happens under the sun Koheleth determines to gain understanding of the world—instead of, say, God's will or plans.

14 I observed all the happenings beneath the sun, and
I found that all is futile and pursuit of wind:
15 A twisted thing that cannot be made straight,
A lack that cannot be made good.

הָאָדָם לַעֲנוֹת בּוֹ׃ 14 רָאִיתִי אֶת־כָּל־
הַמַּעֲשִׂים שֶׁנַּעֲשׂוּ תַּחַת הַשָּׁמֶשׁ וְהִנֵּה
הַכֹּל הֶבֶל וּרְעוּת רוּחַ׃
15 מְעֻוָּת לֹא־יוּכַל לִתְקֹן
וְחֶסְרוֹן לֹא־יוּכַל לְהִמָּנוֹת׃

unhappy business This cannot refer to "all that happens under the sun," for God did not "give" that to mankind, nor can humans be said to "busy" themselves with it. It refers, rather, to the search for understanding. Koheleth sees this search as a hopeless, frustrating task, even when undertaken in wisdom and by the wise (1:12, 16; 8:16–17), of whom the Solomonic Koheleth is the foremost example.

which God gave men God implanted in the human heart a desire for knowledge while preventing them from attaining it. Therefore people cannot find rest and repose or true happiness in wisdom and the examination of created things (Mendelssohn).

The search for understanding may be frustrated, but it is not wrong or in violation of God's will. On the contrary, this is something God *wants* humans do and has, in fact, imposed on them.

business...to be concerned with "Business" (*ʿinyan*) is from the root *ʿ-n-h* meaning "to busy oneself with," and may be understood as "busy-ness." *Lehitʿannot,* "to be concerned with," "to busy oneself with," is from the same root. A homonym of *lehitʿannot* means "to afflict oneself." Some commentators prefer that translation, and both connotations may come into play here.

14. ***all the happenings*** This verse is equivalent to 1:2 and helps define the scope of "all" in that verse. What is *hevel* ("senseless"; NJPS: "futile") is not so much beings or material goods, but rather "happenings," *maʿasim*. A *maʿaseh* (plural *maʿasim*) can mean either a deed or an event. (See Keywords in the introduction.) In Koheleth it is usually the latter, something that "happens" or "comes to pass," though most commentators have understood it to mean (human) "deeds."

The Midrash, and traditional commentators generally, have assumed that this verse does not apply to repentance, good deeds, and study of Torah. This is right, but not because Koheleth is deliberately excluding these matters. They are simply not within the scope of his present concerns.

pursuit of wind Hebrew: *reʿut ruaḥ;* see Keywords in the introduction.

15. As translated, this verse describes "all the happenings beneath the sun" (v. 14). Alternatively, we can read it as two sayings: "A twisted thing cannot be made straight; a lack cannot be made good." The first saying, which seems to be a traditional proverb cited to prove a point, reappears in 7:13. The Egyptian sage Anii uses the twisted stick as a metaphor for a foolish or perverse pupil who, he insists, *can* be educated: "The crooked stick left on the ground . . . if the carpenter takes it, he straightens it, makes of it a noble's staff."[5] In similar fashion, the Targum, Rashi, Rashbam, and others identify the "twisted thing" as a sinful person or a corrupt deed, which *cannot* be corrected. But the quality of events, not human corruption, is Koheleth's subject here.

Not only are all things senseless (v. 14), but also they cannot be improved. These flaws, 7:13 declares, are God's doing. Wrongs cannot be corrected or lacks supplied. Koheleth is

16 I said to myself: "Here I have grown richer and wiser than any that ruled before me over Jerusalem, and my mind has zealously absorbed wisdom and learning." 17 And so I set my mind to appraise wisdom and to appraise madness and folly. And I learned—that this too was pursuit of wind:

16 דִּבַּרְתִּי אֲנִי עִם־לִבִּי לֵאמֹר אֲנִי הִנֵּה
הִגְדַּלְתִּי וְהוֹסַפְתִּי חָכְמָה עַל כָּל־אֲשֶׁר־
הָיָה לְפָנַי עַל־יְרוּשָׁלִָם וְלִבִּי רָאָה הַרְבֵּה
חָכְמָה וָדָעַת׃ 17 וָאֶתְּנָה לִבִּי לָדַעַת
חָכְמָה וְדַעַת הוֹלֵלוֹת וְשִׂכְלוּת יָדַעְתִּי
שֶׁגַּם־זֶה הוּא רַעְיוֹן רוּחַ׃

resigned to the intractability of the world's fundamental wrongs. He does not call for the "fixing" of distortions or the filling out of lacks, but only for resignation to the state of affairs that God has built into the world.

be made good[6]

16. ***I said to myself*** Literally, "I spoke with my heart, saying." Koheleth frequently speaks "to" or "in" his heart; he is reporting his thoughts. See Comment to 1:13.

Here I have grown richer and wiser In preparation for his investigation, Koheleth amassed great learning, well beyond that of his royal predecessors. He succeeded in this venture, but (foreshadowing his later conclusions) he found that this success left him with deep malaise. Wisdom here is knowledge that can be studied, presumably in books. When Koheleth sets about his investigation, he does not explicitly avail himself of this great erudition (except, perhaps, by quoting old proverbs), but he uses only his own powers of reasoning. He does not distinguish his wisdom from that of his predecessors in its nature but only in its quantity. The boast of great wisdom is a cliché in ancient Near Eastern royal inscriptions.

than any that ruled before me over Jerusalem Koheleth seems to be comparing himself to a plurality of predecessors, though the only Israelite king over Jerusalem before Solomon was David. The Hebrew is, literally, "than any before me over Jerusalem." The Targum paraphrases, "all the *sages* who were before me in Jerusalem." But the construction *hayah . . . ʿal* ("were over") implies rulership. Jebusite kings ruled over Jerusalem before David, and there is a tradition of their righteousness. Melchizedek, king of Jerusalem in Abraham's time, paid homage to Abraham's God (Gen. 14:18–20), and see Ps. 10:4. However, no clear traditions exist of Jebusite wisdom. The claim in 1:16 might be a stereotyped claim without the author having actual predecessors in mind.

17. ***to appraise*** More precisely, "to know" or "understand." Koheleth sets out to gain wisdom, which he will immediately evaluate.

wisdom and learning . . . madness and folly The Hebrew is ambiguous. Better: "wisdom-and-knowledge [and] madness-and-folly." Verses 17b–18 show that Koheleth's judgment is really directed at a single thing: "wisdom-and-knowledge" (equivalent to wisdom) alone. (The two concepts are almost identical in Wisdom Literature.) Some commentators consider the phrase "madness-and-folly" as an insertion (based on 2:12b or 7:25) by a later scribe who wished to provide a more acceptable object for the condemnation.[7] More likely, what is assessed in verses 17b–18 is a "knowing" (that is, an understanding) of both wisdom *and* folly. The Book of Proverbs has much to say about both qualities. Koheleth exercised his wisdom, his rational faculty, while evaluating (among other things) the range of human mental capabilities. This is what he judges to be "a pursuit of wind."

18 For as wisdom grows, vexation grows; To increase learning is to increase heartache.	18 כִּ֛י בְּרֹ֥ב חָכְמָ֖ה רָב־כָּ֑עַס וְיוֹסִ֥יף דַּ֖עַת יוֹסִ֥יף מַכְאֽוֹב׃

According to Sforno, Koheleth (Solomon) is alluding to earlier philosophers. "Wisdom," Sforno says, is the truth in speculative thought, while "knowledge of madness" *(daʿat holelot)* refers to the confused erudition of former sages, which lacks an adequate axiomatic basis.

18. For as wisdom grows, vexation grows Koheleth has learned that too much wisdom provokes irritation and frustration. Nonetheless, he will later laud wisdom's benefits. To make sense of this verse, Ibn Ezra explains that one who understands the world will suffer from knowing that his children will eventually die and his wealth will be lost, "and the day of (his) death is placed between his two eyes." This, however, is known to all. More to the point, Mendelssohn identifies the cause of vexation as the inability to attain the desired knowledge of hidden things, especially with regard to divine providence. Still, it is not so much wisdom's failure as its success that arouses Koheleth's chagrin. For, as he will demonstrate by his own experience, wisdom forces its possessor to perceive life's absurdities; thus it is an "unhappy business." But it is not a task that Koheleth avoids.

Reflections and Meditations (2:1–4:16)

AN EXPERIMENT WITH PLEASURE (2:1–26)

Chapter 2 follows a single train of thought but has three major components: pleasure and toil (vv. 1–11); wisdom and folly (vv. 12–17); and toil and pleasure, wisdom and folly (vv. 18–26).

KOHELETH ON PLEASURE

The terms that Koheleth uses in referring to pleasure, namely *simḥah* ("pleasure," "enjoyment") and *tov* ("good," often "pleasure"), are discussed in Keywords in the introduction.

Koheleth has conflicting judgments about pleasure. On the one hand, he affirms its goodness several times (2:24; 3:12, 22; 5:17; 8:15). It is mankind's *ḥeilek,* "portion" (3:22; 5:17; 9:9). On the other hand, as Koheleth's experience shows him, pleasure is inane, ineffectual, and senseless (2:1–2, 11). Thus the toil that produces the means of pleasure proves to be *hevel,* absurd.

All the pleasant things he evaluates and recommends are legitimate. The activities that Koheleth disparages in 2:1–2, describes in 2:4–9, and calls *hevel* in 2:11 are not debased or even especially trivial.[8] Rather, they are the same ones that constitute his own "portion" (2:10), which he gained by wisdom (2:19), and which he praises in the course of the book. Nor are these pleasures in any way improper. They all reasonable and respectable, especially for a king who earned his wealth through work and wisdom. The drinking of wine too is proper, even advisable in moderation (see, for example, Prov. 31:6–7;

2 I said to myself, "Come, I will treat you to merriment. Taste mirth!" That too, I found, was futile.
2 Of revelry I said, "It's mad!"
Of merriment, "What good is that?"

ב אָמַרְתִּי אֲנִי בְּלִבִּי לְכָה־נָּא אֲנַסְּכָה בְשִׂמְחָה וּרְאֵה בְטוֹב וְהִנֵּה גַם־הוּא הָבֶל׃
2 לִשְׂחוֹק אָמַרְתִּי מְהוֹלָל
וּלְשִׂמְחָה מַה־זֹּה עֹשָׂה׃

Ps. 104:15; Eccl. 9:7). Koheleth does censure excess in eating and drinking (10:17, 19), yet nothing suggests that he himself got drunk. Koheleth thus says contradictory things about the same wealth and the same pleasurable activities.

Koheleth's contradictory attitudes about pleasure need not be logically reconciled. People are not always consistent. We can enjoy something that we desire and at the same time find it unsatisfying. We may be "having fun" at a party—eating and drinking and "making merry"—yet underneath it all feel empty and depressed.

Koheleth's attitude toward pleasure seems to have changed over time. When he first immersed himself in pleasure on a grand scale, he discovered its inanity, and it failed to satisfy him. But eventually he came to realize that it is nevertheless *tov* ("good"). It *feels* good, and that may be the best thing available. This is an affirmation of pleasure, albeit a rather downbeat one.

PLEASURE AND TOIL (vv. 1–11)

2:1 treat you Hebrew *'anassekhah,* "give you experience of" or "test you" (from *nissah*).

merriment Hebrew *simḥah.* See Keywords in the introduction.

That too, I found, was futile [hevel] This negative assessment in verses 1b–2 previews Koheleth's findings, which are reiterated in verse 11.

2. revelry Hebrew *seḥoq* (lit. "laughter") stands for merrymaking, not necessarily of a superficial or libertine sort. In Ps. 126:2, for example, *seḥoq* refers to the joy of the returning exiles. See Keywords in the introduction.

What good is that? Literally, "What does this do?" Even if it feels good, it *does* nothing, accomplishes nothing, and Koheleth longs to do something *effective,* to achieve something substantive. He finds, however, that wine, women, song, and even achievements in building and land development (vv. 4–8) fail to provide a sense of achievement and efficacy.

It's mad! Hebrew *meholal,* which sounds like *mahul,* "mixed." This wordplay was the cue for Koheleth Rabbah to explore various historical instances where laughter and joy was "mixed," such as the joy of Elisheba, who married Aaron (Exod. 6:23). Though she was righteous, her joy in her family's exalted priestly station was shattered when her sons entered the Tabernacle to burn incense unlawfully and were killed (Lev. 10). Her joy collapsed in a moment, through no fault of her own. Such tales attempt to give historical specificity to Koheleth's generalities, and in this case they are to the point. Koheleth's happiness is "mixed" because he despairs of the constancy and significance of pleasure, though it is good. Rabbi Pinchas quotes an aphorism, "If the gold is alloyed, what use is pleasure?" and tells a tale of a bridegroom who was killed at his wedding. His father kept it secret until the time came to tell the guests that they should say the benediction of mourners, not the one for a bridegroom. At the funeral, R. Zakkai preached the verse, "Of

[3]I ventured to tempt my flesh with wine, and to grasp folly, while letting my mind direct with wisdom, to the end that I might learn which of the two was better for men to practice in their few days of life under heaven. [4]I multiplied my possessions.
I built myself houses and I planted vineyards. [5]I laid out gardens and groves, in which I planted every kind of fruit tree. [6]I constructed pools of water,

3 תַּרְתִּי בְלִבִּי לִמְשׁוֹךְ בַּיַּיִן אֶת־בְּשָׂרִי וְלִבִּי
נֹהֵג בַּחָכְמָה וְלֶאֱחֹז בְּסִכְלוּת עַד אֲשֶׁר־
אֶרְאֶה אֵי־זֶה טוֹב לִבְנֵי הָאָדָם אֲשֶׁר
יַעֲשׂוּ תַּחַת הַשָּׁמַיִם מִסְפַּר יְמֵי חַיֵּיהֶם׃
4 הִגְדַּלְתִּי מַעֲשָׂי בָּנִיתִי לִי בָּתִּים נָטַעְתִּי
לִי כְּרָמִים׃ 5 עָשִׂיתִי לִי גַּנּוֹת וּפַרְדֵּסִים
וְנָטַעְתִּי בָהֶם עֵץ כָּל־פֶּרִי׃ 6 עָשִׂיתִי לִי

laughter [*seḥoq*] I said, 'It's mad!' Of merriment, 'What good is that?'" The rabbinic commentators shared Koheleth's tragic sense of life's fragility.

3. I ventured to tempt my flesh with wine The Hebrew is difficult. A literal translation would be: "I went about in my heart to draw my flesh with wine." He is figuratively pulling his body with the "cord" of wine. (Compare the metaphor of drawing someone with "cords of love" in Hos. 11:4.)

and to grasp folly This is puzzling, because though Koheleth *examines* folly, he nowhere admits to indulging in it. In 2:9 he states, "In addition, my wisdom remained with me"—through the entire experiment. Possibly this is a pious interpolation condemning the material pleasures to be described. It is also possible that "folly" refers to pleasures (such as Koheleth is about to describe), because they have all been prejudged as foolish (2:2).

while letting my mind direct with wisdom Better: "Leading my heart with wisdom." As in verse 3a, the hidden metaphor is of pulling something with a rope, an action implying both attraction and control.

which of the two was better... to practice Better: "what is good... to do." ("Two" is not implied by biblical Hebrew *'ey-zeh,* which means "what" or "which.") Koheleth is looking for *whatever* behavior might prove good and profitable.

4. I multiplied As Koheleth proceeds to amass wealth and try out the pleasures it brings, he does not just sit about partying, like the foolish nobles he derides in 10:17–19. He energetically develops his resources. Some he produces himself: houses and vineyards, gardens and groves, fruit trees and irrigation pools. These are clearly not frivolous or improper. Others he purchases: slaves, livestock, and treasures. The singers are probably also purchased as slaves. Compare Abraham's holdings in slaves, livestock, and gold, which showed that he was a man of substance, prospering under God's favor (Gen. 12:5; 13:2). Likewise, Solomon's vast projects and possessions were the fruit of his wisdom and God's favor (1 Kings 3:13).

Though not reflected in this translation, almost every verb indicating production and acquisition is accompanied by *li,* "for myself": "I built for myself... planted for myself... made for myself," and so on. This emphasis on "myself" exposes a sort of consumerism, an obsessive striving to fill an undefined but gnawing spiritual need by material goods. This attempt is, of course, hopeless (6:7).

my possessions Or "my deeds." As in royal inscriptions, Koheleth boasts of his material accomplishments. Unlike the usual boasts, Koheleth's description is ironic, meant not to glory in his achievements but to underscore their ultimate inadequacy.[9]

enough to irrigate a forest shooting up with trees.
7 I bought male and female slaves, and I acquired
stewards. I also acquired more cattle, both herds and
flocks, than all who were before me in Jerusalem.
8 I further amassed silver and gold and treasures of
kings and provinces; and I got myself male and
female singers, as well as the luxuries of commoners
—coffers and coffers of them. 9 Thus, I gained more
wealth than anyone before me in Jerusalem. In
addition, my wisdom remained with me: 10 I withheld
from my eyes nothing they asked for, and denied
myself no enjoyment; rather, I got enjoyment out
of all my wealth. And that was all I got out of my
wealth.

בְּרֵכוֹת מָיִם לְהַשְׁקוֹת מֵהֶם יַעַר צוֹמֵחַ
עֵצִים׃ 7 קָנִיתִי עֲבָדִים וּשְׁפָחוֹת וּבְנֵי־
בַיִת הָיָה לִי גַּם מִקְנֶה בָקָר וָצֹאן הַרְבֵּה
הָיָה לִי מִכֹּל שֶׁהָיוּ לְפָנַי בִּירוּשָׁלִָם׃
8 כָּנַסְתִּי לִי גַּם־כֶּסֶף וְזָהָב וּסְגֻלַּת מְלָכִים
וְהַמְּדִינוֹת עָשִׂיתִי לִי שָׁרִים וְשָׁרוֹת
וְתַעֲנוּגֹת בְּנֵי הָאָדָם שִׁדָּה וְשִׁדּוֹת׃
9 וְגָדַלְתִּי וְהוֹסַפְתִּי מִכֹּל שֶׁהָיָה לְפָנַי
בִּירוּשָׁלִָם אַף חָכְמָתִי עָמְדָה לִּי׃ 10 וְכֹל
אֲשֶׁר שָׁאֲלוּ עֵינַי לֹא אָצַלְתִּי מֵהֶם לֹא־
מָנַעְתִּי אֶת־לִבִּי מִכָּל־שִׂמְחָה כִּי־לִבִּי
שָׂמֵחַ מִכָּל־עֲמָלִי וְזֶה־הָיָה חֶלְקִי מִכָּל־
עֲמָלִי׃

7. stewards Literally, "sons of the house," meaning home-born slaves. These are usually called *yelidey bayit,* "those born at home," as opposed to purchased slaves.

8. coffers and coffers Hebrew *shiddah ve-shiddot.* The meaning is uncertain. In the Mishnah, *shiddah* means "coffer. Ibn Ezra explains *shiddah* as "woman"; this makes sense here, since (as he observes), there is otherwise no mention of women as objects of sexual pleasure in a passage that lists a great array of desirable things. We could translate "a good number of concubines." Ibn Ezra derives the word from *shadad,* "plunder," hence "women taken as booty." In biblical times, and even in rabbinic law, purchased concubines were considered a legitimate possession. Even the humane Deuteronomic law code permits the taking of female war-captives as wives, provided that they are treated with a certain decency (Deut. 21:10–14).

9. anyone before me in Jerusalem This phrase could include more than kings. The Targum translates, "all the generations that were before me in Jerusalem." Still, 1:16 alluded to rulers, and Koheleth's boast here too would be most emphatic if it set him in contrast with other royalty.

West Semitic and Mesopotamian royal inscriptions often compare the speaker's accomplishments to his predecessors'. The Phoenician king Kilamuwa boasts "But I, Kilamuwa son of Tamutima (?)—I accomplished what the predecessors [of my family] had not accomplished."[10]

In addition, my wisdom remained with me Or "stood by me." Wisdom served Koheleth as helper and supporter. Its "service" was twofold: it served him well in earning his wealth, and it kept him from abandoning good sense while he was amassing that wealth.

10. And that was all I got out of my wealth Literally, "and this was my portion (*ḥeilek*) from all my toil (*ʿamal*)."[11] Pleasure, Koheleth will say several times, is a man's "portion," his *ḥeilek*. See Keywords in the introduction.

11 Then my thoughts turned to all the fortune my hands had built up, to the wealth I had acquired and won—and oh, it was all futile and pursuit of wind; there was no real value under the sun! 12 For what will the man be like who will succeed the one who is ruling over what was built up long ago?
My thoughts also turned to appraising wisdom and madness and folly. 13 I found that
Wisdom is superior to folly
As light is superior to darkness;
14 A wise man has his eyes in his head,
Whereas a fool walks in darkness.

11 וּפָנִיתִי אֲנִי בְּכָל־מַעֲשַׂי שֶׁעָשׂוּ יָדַי
וּבֶעָמָל שֶׁעָמַלְתִּי לַעֲשׂוֹת וְהִנֵּה הַכֹּל הֶבֶל
וּרְעוּת רוּחַ וְאֵין יִתְרוֹן תַּחַת הַשָּׁמֶשׁ׃
12 וּפָנִיתִי אֲנִי לִרְאוֹת חָכְמָה וְהוֹלֵלוֹת
וְסִכְלוּת
כִּי ׀ מֶה הָאָדָם שֶׁיָּבוֹא אַחֲרֵי הַמֶּלֶךְ אֵת
אֲשֶׁר־כְּבָר עָשׂוּהוּ׃ 13 וְרָאִיתִי אָנִי
שֶׁיֵּשׁ יִתְרוֹן לַחָכְמָה מִן־הַסִּכְלוּת
כִּיתְרוֹן הָאוֹר מִן־הַחֹשֶׁךְ׃
14 הֶחָכָם עֵינָיו בְּרֹאשׁוֹ
וְהַכְּסִיל בַּחֹשֶׁךְ הוֹלֵךְ

11. After observing the pleasure he derived from his wealth, Koheleth turns to assess his toil and the luxuries it produced, and he pronounces them all senseless and devoid of profit. Though pleasure is a man's portion, it is inadequate. By Koheleth's strict reckoning, it is not a *yitron,* a "profit" (NJPS: "of real value"), but it is the best thing available.

WISDOM AND FOLLY (VV. 12–17)

12. NJPS switches the two halves of the verse for clarity. As the Hebrew stands, verse 12b ("For what will the man be like . . .") is parenthetical, explaining what led Koheleth to mull over the consequences of wisdom and folly (v. 12a; "My thoughts . . ."). Then verse 13 states his conclusion.

The Hebrew of verse 12b is almost unintelligible. We should probably change the vocalization from *'aḥarey hammelekh* to *'aḥaray hammolekh* (literally, "after me, who will rule") and translate "who will succeed me and who is to rule over, etc." (Transl.). Koheleth wonders what kind of man will succeed him and have control of his earnings (as "rule" means here). The answer comes in 2:18–19: his successor, who is as likely to be foolish as wise.

wisdom and madness and folly As verse 13 will show, Koheleth is now assessing two things only: wisdom and folly. "Madness and folly" is a single concept, "foolish madness."

13–14a. Koheleth lauds wisdom in superlatives here, but then (in vv. 14b–15) gives vent to his disappointment that the wise and the foolish share one fate. Some scholars suggest that verses 13–14, or verse 14 alone, are quotations of conventional wisdom and that Koheleth is opposing these ideas or restricting their validity. But even if Koheleth is citing someone else's ideas, he does not repudiate them; he states them as facts. Koheleth laments the limits of human wisdom and the fragility of its achievements, but he never doubts its vast superiority to folly.

A wise man has his eyes in his head Koheleth underscores his point by a saying—perhaps his own, perhaps one he has heard—in praise of wisdom: The wise man has sight, which to say, knowledge, and whatever discomfort knowledge may entail, it is the greatest of human powers.

But I also realized that the same fate awaits them
both. 15 So I reflected: "The fate of the fool is also
destined for me; to what advantage, then, have I been
wise?" And I came to the conclusion that that too was
futile, 16 because the wise man, just like the fool, is not
remembered forever; for, as the succeeding days roll
by, both are forgotten. Alas, the wise man dies, just
like the fool!
17 And so I loathed life. For I was distressed by all that
goes on under the sun, because everything is futile
and pursuit of wind.

וְיָדַעְתִּי גַם־אָנִי שֶׁמִּקְרֶה אֶחָד יִקְרֶה
אֶת־כֻּלָּם׃ 15 וְאָמַרְתִּי אֲנִי בְּלִבִּי כְּמִקְרֵה
הַכְּסִיל גַּם־אֲנִי יִקְרֵנִי וְלָמָּה חָכַמְתִּי אֲנִי
אָז יוֹתֵר וְדִבַּרְתִּי בְלִבִּי שֶׁגַּם־זֶה הָבֶל׃
16 כִּי אֵין זִכְרוֹן לֶחָכָם עִם־הַכְּסִיל לְעוֹלָם
בְּשֶׁכְּבָר הַיָּמִים הַבָּאִים הַכֹּל נִשְׁכָּח וְאֵיךְ
יָמוּת הֶחָכָם עִם־הַכְּסִיל׃
17 וְשָׂנֵאתִי אֶת־הַחַיִּים כִּי רַע עָלַי
הַמַּעֲשֶׂה שֶׁנַּעֲשָׂה תַּחַת הַשָּׁמֶשׁ כִּי־הַכֹּל
הֶבֶל וּרְעוּת רוּחַ׃

fate Hebrew *mikreh,* what befalls someone, not something "fated" or preordained in the strict sense. In Ecclesiastes, *mikreh* always refers to the universal fate of death. Since it does not mean "fate" elsewhere in the Bible, its meaning here may have been shaped under the influence of the Greek concept of *tychē,* which means both "fate" and "chance." Even so, *mikreh,* unlike "fate" in the strict sense, does not operate as a mechanism that brings about certain events, but is simply the event itself.[12]

the same fate awaits them both That both the wise and the foolish die is not a failing inherent in wisdom. It is an affront *to* wisdom. The wise deserve better.

15. to what advantage, then, have I been wise? Literally, "why then have I become very wise." The fact that wise and foolish end up the same makes it pointless to grow very wise, but it does not, to Koheleth's mind, cancel wisdom's inherent superiority.

16. not remembered forever Better: "never remembered." Koheleth does not require that the wise man's memory endure for eternity, only that it endure *at all.* But, he observes, in reality, it slips from public consciousness as quickly as the fool's does.

as the succeeding days roll by The Hebrew (literally, "already in the coming days") probably means in the immediate future, soon after death.

both are forgotten The Hebrew for "both" *(ha-kol)* may mean "all," "everyone." Koheleth would not agree with the proverbial assertion that "The name of the righteous is invoked in blessing, but the fame of the wicked rots" (Prov. 10:7).

Alas Hebrew *'eykh;* literally, "how." *'Eykh* (or *'eykhah*) is often an expression of lament, as in 2 Sam. 1:25 and Lam. 1:1.

the wise man dies, just like the fool! What oppresses Koheleth is not so much the inevitability of death as the fact that death deletes distinctions of quality that *should* be respected.

17. And so I loathed life Paradoxically, exasperation at death's unfairness made Koheleth hate life. This statement is a report on past experience, when Koheleth's reflections brought him to the nadir. He will have other moments of despair (compare 4:3), but he will come to realize that the light of life is sweet (11:7).

The Targum has Solomon declaring, "I hated all *evil* life," for he hated the evil deeds that are done in it. According to Rashi, Solomon's despair came from foreseeing that his kingdom would fracture in the days of his son Rehoboam.

18 וְשָׂנֵאתִי אֲנִי אֶת־כָּל־עֲמָלִי שֶׁאֲנִי עָמֵל
תַּחַת הַשָּׁמֶשׁ שֶׁאַנִּיחֶנּוּ לָאָדָם שֶׁיִּהְיֶה
אַחֲרָי׃ 19 וּמִי יוֹדֵעַ הֶחָכָם יִהְיֶה אוֹ סָכָל
וְיִשְׁלַט בְּכָל־עֲמָלִי שֶׁעָמַלְתִּי וְשֶׁחָכַמְתִּי
תַּחַת הַשָּׁמֶשׁ גַּם־זֶה הָבֶל׃ 20 וְסַבּוֹתִי אֲנִי
לְיַאֵשׁ אֶת־לִבִּי עַל כָּל־הֶעָמָל שֶׁעָמַלְתִּי
תַּחַת הַשָּׁמֶשׁ׃ 21 כִּי־יֵשׁ אָדָם שֶׁעֲמָלוֹ
בְּחָכְמָה וּבְדַעַת וּבְכִשְׁרוֹן וּלְאָדָם שֶׁלֹּא
עָמַל־בּוֹ יִתְּנֶנּוּ חֶלְקוֹ גַּם־זֶה הֶבֶל וְרָעָה

18 So, too, I loathed all the wealth that I was gaining
under the sun. For I shall leave it to the man who will
succeed me—19 and who knows whether he will be
wise or foolish?—and he will control all the wealth
that I gained by toil and wisdom under the sun. That
too is futile. 20 And so I came to view with despair all
the gains I had made under the sun. 21 For sometimes
a person whose fortune was made with wisdom,
knowledge, and skill must hand it on to be the
portion of somebody who did not toil for it. That too

For I was distressed by all that goes on under the sun What happens in this world is rendered senseless by death's leveling of distinctions.

all that goes on under the sun Hebrew *ha-ma'aseh she-na'asah taḥat ha-shemesh* (sometimes "under the heavens"); see Keywords in the introduction.

TOIL AND PLEASURE, WISDOM AND FOLLY (vv. 18–26)

Here, Koheleth broods about a single situation: one person toils and another gets the wealth. Whereas in 2:12–17 he reported his experiences and observations and concluded with his reaction to them, Koheleth now begins with his emotional reaction—also a sense of loathing—and proceeds to explain what led up to it.

18. wealth ['amal] that I was gaining ['amel] Better: "toil that I performed." What really distresses Koheleth is not the loss of his wealth but the inconsequentiality of his labors.

19. and who knows whether he will be wise or foolish? It is bad enough that one person will receive what another toiled for. How much the worse if the recipient is a fool!

20. I came Hebrew root: *s-b-b* ("turn"). The Midrash discerns here a change of heart in the speaker. Solomon first loathed the idea of toiling for the benefit of his royal descendants, many of whom would prove unworthy, but then he "turned" and said, "Just as others toiled on my behalf, so I must toil for others," for example by planting trees (Koh. R.). But contrary to the Midrash's portrayal, Koheleth lacks a sense of continuity and responsibility for future generations, which would have given greater meaning to his toil.

despair The verb *yi'esh* occurs only here in the Bible. In rabbinic Hebrew it means "to give up for lost," hence "give up illusions or expectations about something." This sense fits well here, and we could translate: "I turned to rid my heart of illusions." The illusion that Koheleth was earlier subject to, judging from the reasons he gives for disabusing himself of it, was the profitability of toil.

21. For sometimes a person Literally, "For there is a man." Koheleth is the prime example of this type (2:18–19), but it is thus with everyone who earns wealth. Unless he loses it earlier, he one must pass it on to someone else who did not work for it. Koheleth considers this absurd and unfair—"a grave evil"—because he does not seem to feel a connection to future generations.

is futile, and a grave evil. 22 For what does a man get
for all the toiling and worrying he does under the
sun? 23 All his days his thoughts are grief and
heartache, and even at night his mind has no respite.
That too is futile!
24 There is nothing worthwhile for a man but to
eat and drink and afford himself enjoyment with
his means. And even that, I noted, comes from
God. 25 For who eats and who enjoys but myself?

רַבָּה׃ 22 כִּי מֶה־הֹוֶה לָאָדָם בְּכָל־עֲמָלוֹ
וּבְרַעְיוֹן לִבּוֹ שֶׁהוּא עָמֵל תַּחַת הַשָּׁמֶשׁ׃
23 כִּי כָל־יָמָיו מַכְאֹבִים וָכַעַס עִנְיָנוֹ
גַּם־בַּלַּיְלָה לֹא־שָׁכַב לִבּוֹ גַּם־זֶה הֶבֶל
הוּא׃
24 אֵין־טוֹב בָּאָדָם שֶׁיֹּאכַל וְשָׁתָה וְהֶרְאָה
אֶת־נַפְשׁוֹ טוֹב בַּעֲמָלוֹ גַּם־זֹה רָאִיתִי אָנִי
כִּי מִיַּד הָאֱלֹהִים הִיא׃ 25 כִּי מִי יֹאכַל

23. All his days...and even at night The toiler struggles all day, then tosses and turns at night, either obsessed with machinations for amassing wealth or plagued by fears of losing it (cf. 5:11). Alternatively (or additionally), the toiler is hounded by nightmares (cf. 5:2). Koheleth always imagines toil (*'amal*) as mental work. He has the merchant in mind, not the physical laborer.

24. This verse and the others that commend sensual pleasures as the best thing in life (3:12, 22; 5:17; 8:15) underwent radical reinterpretation in rabbinic reading. Sensual pleasure was transformed into the joy of Torah and good deeds. The interpretive principle was as follows:

> Every mention of eating and drinking in the Scroll refers to Torah and good deeds. R. Yonah said that the decisive proof text is "and it will accompany him in his toil *(be-'amalo)* during the days of his life" (8:15). בעמלו *(be-'amalo)* should be understood [by transposition of consonants] as if it read בעולמו *(be-'olamo)* "in his world," meaning *this* life. "The days of his life" refers to the grave. But is there food and drink in the grave that could accompany a person to the grave? [Obviously not, hence] these things refer to Torah and good deeds. (Koh. R., on 2:24)

If *be-'olamo* "in his world" means the present life, then "the days of his life" must refer to something else, for it is axiomatic in midrash that there can be no redundancy in the Bible. "Days of his life" must therefore refer to the grave. But the only good things that one can take to the grave are immaterial values, namely good deeds and the study of Torah.

worthwhile Hebrew *tov;* literally, "good."

afford himself enjoyment with his means [*'amal*] Literally, "show himself good in his toil." The question is not so much what to do with wealth as how to get *something*—a "portion," at least, if not a "profit"—out of one's efforts.

And even that, I noted, comes from God Whether we experience pleasure depends on God, not on human efforts.

25. For who eats and who enjoys but myself? This does not make good sense, because Koheleth believes that *everyone,* and not only he himself, should eat and enjoy. We should follow the Septuagint, the Peshitta, and some Hebrew manuscripts in reading ממנו (*mi-mennu,* "from him") for MT's almost identical-looking ממני (*mi-menni,* "from me") and translate, "for who will eat, or who will fret, apart from Him?" The point is that no one receives life's pleasures or worries apart from *God,* who decides a person's fortune, as the next verse emphasizes and 3:13 and 5:18 restate.

26 To the man, namely, who pleases Him He has given the wisdom and shrewdness to enjoy himself; and to him who displeases, He has given the urge to gather and amass—only for handing on to one who is pleasing to God. That too is futile and pursuit of wind.

וּמִי יָחוּשׁ חוּץ מִמֶּנִּי׃ 26 כִּי לְאָדָם שֶׁטּוֹב
לְפָנָיו נָתַן חָכְמָה וְדַעַת וְשִׂמְחָה וְלַחוֹטֶא
נָתַן עִנְיָן לֶאֱסוֹף וְלִכְנוֹס לָתֵת לְטוֹב לִפְנֵי
הָאֱלֹהִים גַּם־זֶה הֶבֶל וּרְעוּת רוּחַ׃

enjoys Hebrew *yaḥush*. Disparate translations are also possible: "worry" (Targum), and "hurry" (Ibn Ezra). "Worry" fits the context best. As the next verse shows, Koheleth is contrasting a man who frets—thus displeasing God—with a man who "eats," thus pleasing Him.

26. him who displeases Hebrew *ḥote'*, which usually means "sinner." Understood thus, the verse describes an act of divine justice: the sinner loses out to the good person. The traditional commentators all understand the verse this way. The Targum rephrases via expansion: "For to the man (whose works are) proper before the Lord, He gives wisdom and knowledge (in this world), and joy (with the righteous in the hereafter). But to the guilty man He gives a (bad) practice—to gather (wealth) and to store up (much property to be taken from him) and given to a man who is good before God." Rashi points to the way Haman lost his wealth to Mordecai (Esth. 8:2).

However, as many interpreters recognize, the *ḥote'* here is not one who has really sinned, for if he had, then the resulting deprivation would be just, not senseless. The *ḥote'* is rather one who has offended God in some way. Koheleth seems to be using the word facetiously—in quotation marks, as it were. The unfortunate "sinner" has offended God, perhaps for inexplicable reasons (9:1b), or perhaps by pushing too hard for material gain instead of enjoying life, which is what God wants people to do (9:7)

***the wisdom and shrewdness* [*ḥokhmah*] *to enjoy himself* [*simḥah*]** Better read literally: "wisdom and knowledge and enjoyment." The "wisdom" and "knowledge" transferred to the fortunate person can be understood in two ways: the *products* of wisdom (compare 1 Kings 10:4 and Ezek. 28:7), or the *wisdom* to do what is beneficial, namely to take it easy and enjoy what falls to one's lot. Koheleth means this as a paradox: on the one hand, wisdom (which includes savvy and cleverness) is the means of attaining wealth (2:19, 21), and wealth makes pleasure possible (2:10); on the other hand, the person who did not toil had the real wisdom—the good sense to take it easy. Whatever the "logic" of the process, there is still a disjunction between effort and result, and this is senseless.

Koheleth sees himself as an example of a man who toils and strains to accumulate wealth without benefiting from it, and who is a "sinner" and displeases God (see 2:18–23). Koheleth was unable to follow his own advice to avoid immoderate labors and to enjoy what comes to hand. A cloud of an unnamed guilt hangs over him, even if he has not violated God's commandments.

TIME AND ITS CONSTRAINTS (3:1–15)

This passage teaches that everything that happens or is done has its right time, meaning a set of circumstances in which it should happen or be performed, and God determines when this is. In everything we do, we should wait until the time is ripe rather than straining against the natural flow of events. Yet, unfairly, we cannot be certain of discovering when the right time has arrived.

3 A season is set for everything, a time for every experience under heaven:
2 A time for being born and a time for dying,
A time for planting and a time for uprooting the planted;

ג לַכֹּ֖ל זְמָ֑ן וְעֵ֥ת לְכָל־חֵ֖פֶץ תַּ֥חַת הַשָּׁמָֽיִם׃* ס
2 עֵ֥ת לָלֶ֖דֶת וְעֵ֣ת לָמ֑וּת
עֵ֣ת לָטַ֔עַת וְעֵ֖ת לַעֲק֥וֹר נָטֽוּעַ׃

v. 1. בכתב היד שלנו הרשימה בצורת שירה

The Catalogue proper (vv. 1–9) is a memorable poem proceeding in a stately march by a series of pairs, or antinomies, one thing and its opposite. Each pair underscores the point already stated in verse 1; the amassing of pairs drives home that *everything* has its time. Verses 10–15 then draw out the implications of this principle, namely that we do not understand or control the course of events, so the only reasonable approach is to enjoy life as it comes.

The teaching of this unit is reformulated later in 11:1–6 as follows: Things will happen when and where they will. Hence it is only prudent to adapt oneself to the constraints of reality and to avoid excessive effort—*'amal*. Also, since we are ignorant of the future, we should do things at a variety of times and in a variety of ways.

THE CATALOGUE OF TIMES (VV. 1–9)

3:1. ***season . . . time*** Hebrew *zeman . . . 'et*. These words are synonyms, but it is the second that is repeated throughout this poem. "Time" here is not a specific moment in time but rather an occasion or situation that is *right* for something. For example, "a time for war" means whenever the conditions demand and are ripe for entering into war. A "time for laughing" is not a specific date but rather the right circumstances—at a party, say, rather than a funeral. This does not imply that the moments when we fight or laugh are predetermined and independent of human decision, but rather that certain occasions demand a certain type of response.

a season is set Better: "There is a season . . . there is a time." Koheleth does not claim that the time of every action is "set" or predetermined; see previous Comment.

experience Hebrew *ma'aseh,* which includes both deeds that people do and events that happen to them; see Keywords in the introduction.

2. ***being born . . . dying*** This pair epitomizes events that are beyond human control. Their "times" are not the specific dates on which one is born or dies, but rather the right or normal occasions for them to happen. Thus, the "time for being born" means when the embryo is mature and viable, in other words, after nine months of gestation in the case of humans (Koh. R., Rashi). "Time" (*'et*) is used in exactly this way when God reminds Job of his ignorance: "Do you know the season when the mountain goats give birth, can you mark the time when hinds calve? Can you count the months they must complete? Do you know the time they give birth?" (Job 39:1–2).

Similarly, the "time for dying" is the time when a person is ripe for death. The psalmist sets this at 70–80 years (Ps. 90:10). One who expires then is dying "in his time." One who dies prematurely may be said to perish "not in his time" (compare the usage in Eccl. 7:17). Sinners, according to the prevalent belief, are snatched away "before their time" *(we-lo' 'et)* (Job 22:16). Even though this is the *just* time for them to die, it is still not "the time for dying." Koheleth knows that people do not necessarily die when the time is right (8:12–14).

"Being born"[13] and "dying," modern and ancient interpreters often say, indicates that everyone has a predestined life span. Some modern commentators read this as a strong

3 A time for slaying and a time for healing,
A time for tearing down and a time for building up;
4 A time for weeping and a time for laughing,
A time for wailing and a time for dancing;
5 A time for throwing stones and a time for gathering stones,
A time for embracing and a time for shunning embraces;
6 A time for seeking and a time for losing,
A time for keeping and a time for discarding;

3 עֵת לַהֲרוֹג וְעֵת לִרְפּוֹא
עֵת לִפְרוֹץ וְעֵת לִבְנוֹת׃
4 עֵת לִבְכּוֹת וְעֵת לִשְׂחוֹק
עֵת סְפוֹד וְעֵת רְקוֹד׃
5 עֵת לְהַשְׁלִיךְ אֲבָנִים וְעֵת כְּנוֹס אֲבָנִים
עֵת לַחֲבוֹק וְעֵת לִרְחֹק מֵחַבֵּק׃
6 עֵת לְבַקֵּשׁ וְעֵת לְאַבֵּד
עֵת לִשְׁמוֹר וְעֵת לְהַשְׁלִיךְ׃

fatalism: one is born and dies exactly on the dates predetermined for him. But a rigid fatalism is foreign to the Bible or later Jewish thought. On the other hand, the notion of a predetermined but alterable life span is well attested. According to R. Akiva (Koh. R.), a person is allotted a certain life span at birth. If he is righteous, he will fulfill it; if he is not, he will die prematurely. Another opinion offered in Koheleth Rabbah is that righteousness can extend one's life span; cf. 2 Kings 20:6.

planting... uprooting the planted The verb *la'akor,* "uproot," does not refer to harvesting but rather to the deliberate plucking out and destruction of vegetation, as when clearing a field for new cultivation or, possibly, as an act of war (Koh. R.). This is not a seasonal chore, but a sporadic act of destruction. The pair epitomizes beginnings and ends of enterprises, or intermittent changes in one's life-path, as when one abandons an old enterprise and starts a new one. "Tearing down" and "building up" convey the same idea.

4. ***weeping... laughing/wailing... dancing*** "Wailing" *(sefod)* is specifically the bewailing of the dead at a funeral.

The Midrash sees an equivalence between both halves of this verse: weeping and wailing belong to the period of mourning, laughing and dancing, to the time afterwards (Koh. R.).

5. ***throwing stones... gathering stones*** The Midrash identifies the former as the time when a wife is ritually clean and the latter as the time when she is unclean, that is to say, menstruating (Koh. R.). Many commentators similarly see here allusions to having sexual intercourse and abstaining from it. This identification, however, seems arbitrary, and, moreover, "gathering" *(kenos)* does not imply refraining from something.

One might throw stones for a variety of reasons, such as in ruining an enemy's field in war (2 Kings 3:19, 25) or in clearing a field prior to cultivation (Isa. 5:2). One might also gather them for building (thus Targum).

embracing... shunning embraces This pair might indeed allude to sexual intercourse (thus Ibn Ezra) or to embraces of all kinds. The Targum says that there is a time for a husband and wife to embrace and a time for them to refrain, namely during the seven days of mourning. Koheleth Rabbah says that the time to embrace is when you meet righteous people, and the time to shun embraces is when you come upon the wicked.

6. ***seeking... losing*** Is there really an *'et*—an appropriate occasion—to lose something? Some commentators, assuming that there is not, parse the verb *le'abbed* as declarative: to declare something as lost; hence to give up hope of finding it. But this meaning is not attested elsewhere. Koheleth's point may be that there is indeed a time for

7 A time for ripping and a time for sewing,
A time for silence and a time for speaking;
8 A time for loving and a time for hating;
A time for war and a time for peace.
9 What value, then, can the man of affairs get from
what he earns? 10 I have observed the business that

7 עֵ֥ת לִקְר֖וֹעַ וְעֵ֣ת לִתְפּ֑וֹר
עֵ֥ת לַחֲשׁ֖וֹת וְעֵ֥ת לְדַבֵּֽר׃
8 עֵ֤ת לֶֽאֱהֹב֙ וְעֵ֣ת לִשְׂנֹ֔א
עֵ֥ת מִלְחָמָ֖ה וְעֵ֥ת שָׁלֽוֹם׃ ס
9 מַה־יִּתְרוֹן֙ הָֽעוֹשֶׂ֔ה בַּאֲשֶׁ֖ר ה֥וּא עָמֵֽל׃
10 רָאִ֥יתִי אֶת־הָֽעִנְיָ֖ן אֲשֶׁ֨ר נָתַ֧ן אֱלֹהִ֛ים

losing, for the rule that "everything has a time" applies to actions that are seemingly damaging as well as to those that are obviously useful. Moreover, even if one did not intend to lose something, sometimes it may turn out for the best. The disappearance of the asses of Saul's father (1 Sam. 9:3) is an example of a fortuitous loss.

*6–7. **keeping... discarding/ripping... sewing*** These pairs reiterate the basic idea of "seeking... losing."

discarding As an example of how it can be expedient to throw something away, the Targum mentions jettisoning merchandise from a ship in a storm. Koheleth Rabbah tells of a merchant travelling by ship who threw away a chest of coins to frustrate thieves whom he overheard scheming to kill him and his son. He later brought the robbers to court. They pleaded innocence, since the merchant had cast the money away himself. He countered that "there is a time for discarding," meaning that the circumstances demanded this action. These examples are to the point. They do not epitomize predestined times but rather opportune *circumstances* in which it is wise to act in a certain way, even one that involves an apparent loss.

*7. **ripping... sewing*** The Targum plausibly explains the time for ripping as the day of mourning, when one ritually rips one's garments. The right time for sewing follows the mourning period. Koheleth Rabbah understands these acts as symbolic: one "rips" in the time of war and "sews" in the time of peace.

*8. **war... peace*** According to the Midrash, this pair sums up several of the others, namely uprooting/planting, seeking/losing, tearing down/building up, slaying/healing, ripping/sewing, and hating/loving (Koh. R.).

*9. **What value [yitron], then, can the man of affairs get from what he earns ['amel]?*** Better: "What profit [*yitron*] does one who does something [*ha-'oseh*] have in toiling [*'amel*]?" It is not the profitability of earning that is at issue in this unit, but the value of toiling. Koheleth makes a distinction between *'asah* ("doing" what is needed, e.g., to survive) and *'amal* ("toiling," i.e., overdoing). When we struggle and strain in an attempt to grasp something before the occasion presents itself (by scrambling to get rich, for example), our efforts are stymied by the times, for these cannot be forced.

THE FUTILITY OF TOIL (vv. 10–15)

*10. **I have observed the business*** The "business" in question is described in the following verse: trying to understand what God brings to pass, which is undoubtedly a hopeless task. The same statement is made in similar language in 8:17.

to be concerned [la'anot] with Or, "to busy oneself with" (Rashi). *La'anot* might also be read as a homonym meaning "to be afflicted." This would suggest a hostile intent on God's part, which is probably not what Koheleth has uppermost in his mind; he sees

God gave man to be concerned with: 11 He brings
everything to pass precisely at its time; He also puts
eternity in their mind, but without man ever
guessing, from first to last, all the things that God
brings to pass. 12 Thus I realized that the only
worthwhile thing there is for them is to enjoy

לִבְנֵי הָאָדָם לַעֲנוֹת בּוֹ׃ 11 אֶת־הַכֹּל עָשָׂה
יָפֶה בְעִתּוֹ גַּם אֶת־הָעֹלָם נָתַן בְּלִבָּם
מִבְּלִי אֲשֶׁר לֹא־יִמְצָא הָאָדָם אֶת־
הַמַּעֲשֶׂה אֲשֶׁר־עָשָׂה הָאֱלֹהִים מֵרֹאשׁ
וְעַד־סוֹף׃ 12 יָדַעְתִּי כִּי אֵין טוֹב בָּם כִּי

God as more indifferent than antagonistic. However, the ambiguity may be deliberate, connoting affliction.

11a. He brings everything* [*'asah*] *to pass precisely* [*yafeh*] *at its time Better: "He made everything appropriate in its time"; *'asah* means "made" or "caused to happen," while *yafeh* may mean either "beautiful" or "appropriate." (NJPS's "precisely" is doubtful.)

The "everything" here is the "everything" mentioned in verse 1 and exemplified in the pairs of recurrent events in verses 2–8. That is, God made a world in which all things, even death and war, are good and serviceable in their proper time. Koheleth is not focusing on God's initial actions during the seven days of Creation so much as on the quality of the results, the way things are now. As an example, Ibn Ezra mentions death, for which God made a right and proper time, namely old age. Even death is "appropriate" *(yafeh)* if it happens when it should and not prematurely. Probably borrowing from the present verse, Ben Sira uses similar language in speaking of God's providence: "Do not say, 'This is worse than that,' for everything dominates in its own time" (Sira 39:34). ("Dominates" means that it comes to the fore, becomes reality.) In other words, do not say that hail and wild beasts are inherently evil, because God made them for their time, namely the time of punishment (Sira 39:29–30).

11b. He also puts eternity* [*ha-'olam*] *in their mind God made humans *desire* eternity or made us imagine that we will live forever (Ibn Ezra). Nowhere else, however, does *ha-'olam* ("world, aeon, forever") mean "eternity." Others understand *ha-'olam* to mean "the world" and take the sentence to mean that God implanted in humans a desire to possess or understand the world. (In a note, NJPS explains this to mean that God "preoccupies man with the attempt to discover the times of future events"; cf. 8.17.) Rashbam says that what God put in minds is time—that we would know that there are good times and bad times, because if all times were of only one sort, we would not see the need to repent. But these supplements are not supported by the text. In any case, *desire* is irrelevant to this context.

A minor emendation, from העלם *(ha-'olam)* "the world" to העמל *(he-'amal)* "the toil," produces a meaningful text: "but he also placed toil in their hearts" (Ginsberg). The issue of the profitability of *'amal* ("toil") is the theme of verses 9 and 13. Ecclesiastes 8:17 uses similar wording, including the verb *ya'amol* (from *'-m-l*), in speaking of the futile endeavor to understand God's work. This *'amal* is a mental toil, hence it is said to be placed in a man's mind (literally, "heart"). This endeavor is the same as the "business" *(ha-'inyan)* that God "gave" men (1:13). (The same verb, *natan,* "gave, placed," is used in both verses.)

***12. the only worthwhile thing* [*tov*]** Since the quest for knowledge is hopeless, the only "worthwhile" or "good" thing is enjoyment of the pleasures we are granted.

do what is good "Good" by itself can refer to the experience or feeling of pleasure (e.g., 2:1, 3:13, 4:8, 7:14). "What is good" refers to what Koheleth has already concluded is good, in 2:24 (Transl.).

themselves and do what is good in their lifetime;
13 also, that whenever a man does eat and drink and
get enjoyment out of all his wealth, it is a gift of
God.
14 I realized, too, that whatever God has brought to
pass will recur evermore:
Nothing can be added to it
And nothing taken from it—
and God has brought to pass that men revere Him.
15 What is occurring occurred long since,
And what is to occur occurred long since:

אִם־לִשְׂמ֖וֹחַ וְלַעֲשׂ֥וֹת ט֖וֹב בְּחַיָּֽיו׃ 13 וְגַ֤ם
כָּל־הָֽאָדָם֙ שֶׁיֹּאכַ֣ל וְשָׁתָ֔ה וְרָאָ֥ה ט֖וֹב
בְּכָל־עֲמָל֑וֹ מַתַּ֥ת אֱלֹהִ֖ים הִֽיא׃
14 יָדַ֗עְתִּי כִּ֠י כָּל־אֲשֶׁ֨ר יַעֲשֶׂ֤ה הָֽאֱלֹהִים֙
ה֚וּא יִהְיֶ֣ה לְעוֹלָ֔ם
עָלָיו֙ אֵ֣ין לְהוֹסִ֔יף
וּמִמֶּ֖נּוּ אֵ֣ין לִגְרֹ֑עַ
וְהָאֱלֹהִ֣ים עָשָׂ֔ה שֶׁיִּֽרְא֖וּ מִלְּפָנָֽיו׃
15 מַה־שֶּֽׁהָיָה֙ כְּבָ֣ר ה֔וּא
וַאֲשֶׁ֥ר לִהְי֖וֹת כְּבָ֣ר הָיָ֑ה

13. a gift of God It is He who allows or denies people the means and circumstances of pleasure.

14. recur By this translation, the verse means that God has made a world of eternal repetitions, so that man can influence the course of events only to a trivial extent. Though this idea is in accord with 1:1–11, it is probably not the point here. Hebrew *yihyeh* (lit. "will be, will happen") does not denote recurrence, nor is recurrence relevant to the immediate context. See next Comment.

whatever God has brought to pass will recur evermore Translated in accord with 1:1–11. Better: "I know that whatever God makes happen is always what will be." In other words, God is in control, having created a system of times that is opaque to human wisdom (3:11). Whoever has the discernment to recognize this will fear God and share the humility epitomized in the confession of the psalmist: "My times are in your hand" (Ps. 31:16; NJPS: "My fate").

revere Hebrew root *y-r-'*; better, here and throughout Ecclesiastes: "fear." Koheleth's unpredictable and aloof deity provokes real fear and consternation, not only pious reverence.

God has brought to pass that men revere Him What makes people fear God? According to Ibn Ezra, Koheleth is saying that God prevents humans from adding to or subtracting from what He has created, in order to inspire fear. The strict limiting of human effectiveness is what causes them to fear God. According to Rashi, although everything God created was worthy of enduring unchanged forever, sometimes God causes breaches in the natural order, such as the Flood, in order to undermine human overconfidence. In this view, it is the *violation* of the created order—rather than the unchangeable order itself—that causes fear.

15. What is occurring occurred long since Using the words of 1:9a to restate the idea of 3:14. Divine omnipotence overwhelms our puny efforts, and nothing substantially new can interrupt the awesome course of events that God has ordained.

God seeks the pursued Hebrew *ha-'elohim yevakkesh 'et-nirdaf.* We can reflect the verse's intention better by translating: "God seeks what has already been sought," a variant of the first half of this verse, and of 1:9b ("There is nothing new beneath the sun"). The

and God seeks the pursued. 16 And, indeed, I have
observed under the sun:
Alongside justice there is wickedness,
Alongside righteousness there is wickedness.
17 I mused: "God will doom both righteous and
wicked, for there is a time for every experience and
for every happening." 18 So I decided, as regards men,

וְהָאֱלֹהִים יְבַקֵּשׁ אֶת־נִרְדָּף׃ 16 וְעוֹד
רָאִיתִי תַּחַת הַשָּׁמֶשׁ
מְקוֹם הַמִּשְׁפָּט שָׁמָּה הָרֶשַׁע
וּמְקוֹם הַצֶּדֶק שָׁמָּה הָרָשַׁע׃
17 אָמַרְתִּי אֲנִי בְּלִבִּי אֶת־הַצַּדִּיק וְאֶת־
הָרָשָׁע יִשְׁפֹּט הָאֱלֹהִים כִּי־עֵת לְכָל־
חֵפֶץ וְעַל כָּל־הַמַּעֲשֶׂה שָׁם׃ 18 אָמַרְתִּי

roots *b-k-sh* ("seek") and *r-d-f* ("pursue") are near-synonyms; see Ps. 34:15, and compare Zeph. 2:3 with Deut. 16:20.

As the earliest interpreters read this verse, "seeks" means to care for or to be solicitous of, and "pursued" *(nirdaf)* refers to persecuted people. Thus: "God looks after the oppressed." On this basis, Ben Sira shapes Koheleth's saying into a new proverb: "Do not say, 'Who can overcome my power?', for God seeks those who are pursued" (Sira 5:3). According to Koheleth Rabbah, God "always seeks [or: requires] the blood of the pursued from the pursuers," as in choosing the offerings of Abel, who was pursued by Cain (Gen. 4:4), or in saving Noah, who was thought to have been persecuted by his generation (Gen. 7:1). Sforno says this means that God will seek out—and restore—the persecuted of Israel.

INJUSTICE AND JUDGMENT (3:16–22)

Injustice is rife. Koheleth believes, or tries to believe, that God will ultimately execute judgment, yet he realizes that this may come too late, for human beings' ultimate fate wipes out distinctions, including those between the righteous and the wicked, and even between human and beast.

16. Alongside justice there is wickedness Better: "in the place where judgment should be, wickedness is there, and in the place where righteousness should be, wickedness is there." The terms "judgment" and "righteousness" combine to express a single concept: "righteous judgment." The place of righteous judgment is (in principle) the court of law; the wickedness that Koheleth finds there is the judicial acquittal of the guilty in exchange for bribes (Sforno, with reference to Isa. 5:23). Isaiah calls Jerusalem the place "where righteousness dwelt, but now murderers" (1:21).

17. will doom Rather, "will judge" *(yishpot)*. Since "there is a time for every experience and for every happening," judgment too must have its time. The term *shafat* means to give persons their due. Thus, to "judge" the widow and orphan does not mean to render a decision in a case to which they are a party, but rather to give them their *mishpat*, "justice" (that is to say, what is rightly theirs; Deut. 10:18)—and to save them from their oppressors (e.g., Isa. 1:17; Ps. 82:3–4). God will "judge" the righteous and wicked by rewarding the former and punishing the latter.

there Hebrew *sham*, a spatial term that actually comes at the end of the sentence. Perhaps it refers to the place of judgment (v. 16). Many change שם *sham* to שם *sam* ("he placed," "set"), and translate, "For [God] has set a time for every experience and for every happening" (Transl.).

18. The verse's Hebrew is obscure, and this rendering is conjectural. The gist can be discerned: humans are, in the end, no better than animals.

to dissociate them [from] the divine beings and to
face the fact that they are beasts. 19 For in respect of
the fate of man and the fate of beast, they have one
and the same fate: as the one dies so dies the other,
and both have the same lifebreath; man has no
superiority over beast, since both amount to nothing.
20 Both go to the same place; both came from dust
and both return to dust. 21 Who knows if a man's
lifebreath does rise upward and if a beast's breath
does sink down into the earth?
22 I saw that there is nothing better for man than to
enjoy his possessions, since that is his portion. For
who can enable him to see what will happen
afterward?

אֲנִי בְּלִבִּי עַל־דִּבְרַת בְּנֵי הָאָדָם לְבָרָם
הָאֱלֹהִים וְלִרְאוֹת שְׁהֶם־בְּהֵמָה הֵמָּה
לָהֶם׃ 19 כִּי מִקְרֶה בְנֵי־הָאָדָם וּמִקְרֶה
הַבְּהֵמָה וּמִקְרֶה אֶחָד לָהֶם כְּמוֹת זֶה כֵּן
מוֹת זֶה וְרוּחַ אֶחָד לַכֹּל וּמוֹתַר הָאָדָם
מִן־הַבְּהֵמָה אָיִן כִּי הַכֹּל הָבֶל׃ 20 הַכֹּל
הוֹלֵךְ אֶל־מָקוֹם אֶחָד הַכֹּל הָיָה מִן־הֶעָפָר
וְהַכֹּל שָׁב אֶל־הֶעָפָר׃ 21 מִי יוֹדֵעַ רוּחַ בְּנֵי
הָאָדָם הָעֹלָה הִיא לְמָעְלָה וְרוּחַ הַבְּהֵמָה
הַיֹּרֶדֶת הִיא לְמַטָּה לָאָרֶץ׃
22 וְרָאִיתִי כִּי אֵין טוֹב מֵאֲשֶׁר יִשְׂמַח
הָאָדָם בְּמַעֲשָׂיו כִּי־הוּא חֶלְקוֹ כִּי מִי
יְבִיאֶנּוּ לִרְאוֹת בְּמֶה שֶׁיִּהְיֶה אַחֲרָיו׃

and to face the fact The MT vocalizes ולראות as *ve-lir'ot* (lit. "and to see"), while the Septuagint reflects the vocalization *ve-lar'ot* (equivalent to *u-lehar'ot*), "and to show." By the latter reading, God intends to show us that we are no better than the beasts. Contrast Ps. 8:5–6.

19–20. Humans and animals share the same *ruaḥ,* "spirit" or "lifebreath." All living beings have a body (commonly called "flesh") and a *ruaḥ*. This is not an immortal "soul," but the lifebreath (Rashbam defines it as *ḥayyut,* "vitality"), an animating force that gives and preserves life. When God takes this away, the creature dies (Ps. 104:29; Job 34:14–15).

***amount to nothing* [*hevel*]** Or, "are senseless, are meaningless."

In Birkat ha-Shaḥar, the Jewish liturgy before the morning service, part of this verse is combined with reminiscences of other phrases from Ecclesiastes to quite different effect: "For *most* of [human] deeds are nothingness, and the days of their lives are fleeting *(hevel)* before You. And the advantage of human over beast is naught, for all is fleeting." In this prayer, *hevel* does not mean "meaningless," nor are *all* human deeds deemed "nothingness"; in the Jewish view, much of what we do, or can do, has deep significance.

21. Who knows if a man's lifebreath does rise upward Ecclesiastes, alone in the Bible, is aware of the belief that at death the soul goes upward to the heavens, rather than down to Sheol. This idea is not Semitic in origin, but it was found in popular Hellenistic religion, which held that the soul rises to the ether, the heavenly seat of the gods.[14] As the author portrays Koheleth, the sage has heard of this notion, but he does not know if it is true, and he refuses to be comforted by conjecture.

22. his possessions Hebrew *ma'asav* (lit. "his works"), what one has earned and now owns. Rashi emphasizes the suffix "his": a man should take satisfaction in his own earnings and not covet another's. The Targum identifies these "works" as good deeds but also the pleasures of "eating and drinking and making one's heart cheerful."

4 I further observed all the oppression that goes on under the sun: the tears of the oppressed, with none to comfort them; and the power of their oppressors—with none to comfort them. 2 Then I accounted those who died long since more fortunate than those who are still living; 3 and happier than

ד וְשַׁבְתִּי אֲנִי וָאֶרְאֶה אֶת־כָּל־
הָעֲשֻׁקִים אֲשֶׁר נַעֲשִׂים תַּחַת הַשָּׁמֶשׁ
וְהִנֵּה ׀ דִּמְעַת הָעֲשֻׁקִים וְאֵין לָהֶם מְנַחֵם
וּמִיַּד עֹשְׁקֵיהֶם כֹּחַ וְאֵין לָהֶם מְנַחֵם:
2 וְשַׁבֵּחַ אֲנִי אֶת־הַמֵּתִים שֶׁכְּבָר מֵתוּ
מִן־הַחַיִּים אֲשֶׁר הֵמָּה חַיִּים עֲדֶנָה: 3 וְטוֹב

portion Strictly speaking, the benefits one derives from what one earns, not the material possessions themselves.

For who can enable him to see what will happen afterward? "Afterward" can refer either to later in life or after death. Rashbam thinks that the ignorance is specifically with regard to the man's heirs: he should enjoy his possessions now, for he does not know what his heirs may be like; they may be fools and dissipate the inheritance (see 2:18–19). In any case, the only sensible thing to do is to embrace the good experiences life affords us, because all we have—or at least all we know we have—is the present moment.

FELLOWSHIP AND CONFLICT (4:1–16)

This passage is a cluster of five sections sharing the theme of patterns in human relations, both desirable and undesirable. The theme-word here is *shnayim,* "two" or *sheni,* "second," which can also mean "companion" or "fellow," and possibly "successor." This recurrent word is not always reflected in the translation.

NO FELLOWSHIP FOR THE OPPRESSED (vv. 1–3)

4:1. all the oppression that goes on under the sun As Koheleth contemplates social injustice, he realizes that the oppressed weep with none to comfort them. In sharp contrast to the prophets, Koheleth does not demand a cessation to oppression or even condemn the oppressors. The possibility of improvement does not seem to occur to him. In his world, after all, there is nothing new, and "a twisted thing cannot be made straight" (1:15). The oppressed *could,* however, receive comfort from their fellows, and the fact that they do not is what really pains him. Lack of a comforter intensifies the grief of a tragedy. Thus the first chapter of Lamentations several times bewails Jerusalem's isolation by saying, "there is none to comfort her" (1:2, 9, 17, 21; cf. 16). The repetition of "they have none to comfort them" in the present verse is suggestive of Koheleth's hopelessness. Loyal companionship is truly a good thing (4:9–12; 9:9), but the downtrodden are denied even this. This is just the way of the world. Koheleth does not try to provide the missing comfort or even urge his readers to do so.

2. Then I accounted those who died As in 2:17–18, Koheleth declares that he preferred death to life. But—as his narration makes clear—this was his thought earlier, in a moment of despondency. Eventually he will come to affirm the intrinsic value of life (9:7–10; 11:7–12:7).

3. have never witnessed the miseries that go on under the sun Koheleth seems to be most troubled by the effect of the miseries on the *onlookers*—such as himself—who are dismayed at the sight of life's ugliness.

either are those who have not yet come into being
and have never witnessed the miseries that go on
under the sun.

מִשְּׁנֵיהֶם אֵת אֲשֶׁר־עֲדֶן לֹא הָיָה אֲשֶׁר
לֹא־רָאָה אֶת־הַמַּעֲשֶׂה הָרָע אֲשֶׁר נַעֲשָׂה
תַּחַת הַשָּׁמֶשׁ׃

4 I have also noted that all labor and skillful enterprise
come from men's envy of each other—another futility
and pursuit of wind!
5 [True,]
The fool folds his hands together
And has to eat his own flesh.
6 [But no less truly,]
Better is a handful of gratification
Than two fistfuls of labor which is pursuit of wind.

4 וְרָאִיתִי אֲנִי אֶת־כָּל־עָמָל וְאֵת כָּל־
כִּשְׁרוֹן הַמַּעֲשֶׂה כִּי הִיא קִנְאַת־אִישׁ
מֵרֵעֵהוּ גַּם־זֶה הֶבֶל וּרְעוּת רוּחַ׃
5 הַכְּסִיל חֹבֵק אֶת־יָדָיו
וְאֹכֵל אֶת־בְּשָׂרוֹ׃
6 טוֹב מְלֹא כַף נָחַת
מִמְּלֹא חָפְנַיִם עָמָל וּרְעוּת רוּחַ׃

JEALOUSY, THE FUEL OF TOIL (vv. 4–6)

4. all labor ['amal] and skillful enterprise come from men's envy of each other Toil is driven by envy, which, according to Prov. 14:30, is a "rot to the bones."

another futility [hevel] Or: "another absurdity."

5–6. [True,] . . . [But no less truly,] The words in brackets are supplied by NJPS for clarity. Two proverbs, in juxtaposition, teach that moderate labor is better than either idleness (v. 5) or excessive exertions (v. 6b) (Sforno). Both verses have the typical form of proverbs and may be older sayings, or perhaps the author himself composed them (12:9).

5. folds his hands together That is, does not work; cf. Prov. 6.10; 24.33 (Transl.).

eat his own flesh Eating human flesh is a metaphor of destruction in Ps. 27:2, Mic. 3:3, and especially Isa. 49:26. In Aramaic and other Semitic languages, the phrase "eat flesh" is sometimes idiomatic for slandering and cursing (Dan. 3:8; 6:25). That nuance could be a secondary connotation here as well. The underlying picture in this verse, of a foolish man sitting with his hands clasped together and gnawing on his knuckles, is an acrid scene of anxiety and self-destruction.

Ibn Ezra compares the fools in this verse and the preceding. There is a kind of fool who does not envy his fellow, and lacking even that motivation sits idle and consumes what he possesses. When that is gone, rather than working for his food, he starves, and in this way he "eats his flesh." Rashbam similarly explains the "eating" as the fool's body wasting away in hunger, consequent upon his idleness. Koheleth Rabbah, perhaps correctly, identifies "eating his own flesh" as an emotion: One man studies Torah, another neglects it; in the hereafter, the latter sees the former being honored together with the righteous, while he himself stands with the wicked. He "eats his own flesh" in chagrin and envy.

6. gratification Hebrew *naḥat ruaḥ;* literally, "resting of the spirit," hence "inner repose," "calm." This may stand for the earnings of work done in moderation—as opposed to grinding, pointless toil—just as the term *'amal* ("labor") can stand for the *products* of labor.

Better is a handful of gratification than two fistfuls of labor which is pursuit of wind Better to receive modest income from moderate, calm labor than twice as much

7 And I have noted this further futility under the sun:
8 the case of the man who is alone, with no
companion, who has neither son nor brother; yet he
amasses wealth without limit, and his eye is never
sated with riches. For whom, now, is he amassing it
while denying himself enjoyment? That too is a
futility and an unhappy business.

7 וְשַׁבְתִּי אֲנִי וָאֶרְאֶה הֶבֶל תַּחַת הַשָּׁמֶשׁ׃
8 יֵשׁ אֶחָד וְאֵין שֵׁנִי גַּם בֵּן וָאָח אֵין־לוֹ
וְאֵין קֵץ לְכָל־עֲמָלוֹ גַּם־עיניו עֵינוֹ לֹא־
תִשְׂבַּע עֹשֶׁר וּלְמִי ׀ אֲנִי עָמֵל וּמְחַסֵּר
אֶת־נַפְשִׁי מִטּוֹבָה גַּם־זֶה הֶבֶל וְעִנְיַן רָע
הוּא׃

earned by toil and agitation. Proverbs 15:16 expresses essentially the same idea but introduces a religious factor: "Better a little with the fear of the LORD than great wealth with confusion in it."

THE LONE MAN'S LABOR (vv. 7–8)

8. To toil is always pointless, but for a loner to toil thus—compulsively, grimly, without satisfaction—is completely ridiculous, an "unhappy business," because there is no one (at least no one he cares about) to enjoy what he hoards.

The sad state of the loner is not an accidental misfortune, but, as Rashi observes, a chosen condition: He conducts his affairs alone. He does not take a disciple (who is like a son), or a companion in Torah study (who is like a brother), or a business partner, or a wife (who would be a helpmate).

For whom, now, is he amassing it** [*'amel*] **while denying himself enjoyment? The Hebrew is actually in the first person: "For whom, then, am I toiling, while denying myself enjoyment?" Koheleth parenthetically slips into the first person and, as in 2:18–19, shows that when he describes the workaholic loner he really has himself in mind.

COMPANIONSHIP AMONG MEN (vv. 9–12)

This passage responds to the preceding thoughts about the lone man, whom Ibn Ezra calls a "fool" for not taking a companion. The companion that Koheleth has in mind here is clearly another adult male, one who could help fight off an attacker. This suggests the possibility that even an unmarried, childless man, with no one who could share his wealth in the present or inherit it in the future, could alleviate his loneliness through fellowship. The benefits of fellowship that Koheleth lists are rather cheerless ones but still of real value in warding off trouble.

The principle can be extended to other kinds of companionship, as is done in the Midrash. For example, the "two" can be companions in Torah study, with the "third" strand of the cord being their teacher. Or the "two" can be husband and wife, with the "third" strand being God, who grants them children (Koh. R.).

Verses 9a and 12b seem to be based on a graded numerical saying. We might reconstruct the original saying as "Two are better off than one, and a threefold cord is not readily broken." Koheleth splits it and inserts his own commentary. The saying itself is based on an ancient proverb known also from the Babylonian epic "Gilgamesh and Hubaba," which also reflects the two-three gradation. There the hero Gilgamesh wants to persuade his friend Enkidu to go on a dangerous journey with him:

> Stop, Enkidu! The second [i.e., companion] will not die.
> The towed boat will not sink.
> No one can sever the threefold cord.[15]

9 טוֹבִים הַשְּׁנַיִם מִן־הָאֶחָד אֲשֶׁר יֵשׁ־לָהֶם
שָׂכָר טוֹב בַּעֲמָלָם׃ 10 כִּי אִם־יִפֹּלוּ הָאֶחָד
יָקִים אֶת־חֲבֵרוֹ וְאִילוֹ* הָאֶחָד שֶׁיִּפּוֹל
וְאֵין שֵׁנִי לַהֲקִימוֹ׃ 11 גַּם אִם־יִשְׁכְּבוּ שְׁנַיִם
וְחַם לָהֶם וּלְאֶחָד אֵיךְ יֵחָם׃ 12 וְאִם־
יִתְקְפוֹ הָאֶחָד הַשְּׁנַיִם יַעַמְדוּ נֶגְדּוֹ וְהַחוּט
הַמְשֻׁלָּשׁ לֹא בִמְהֵרָה יִנָּתֵק׃

v. 10. שני טעמים

9 Two are better off than one, in that they have greater benefit from their earnings. 10 For should they fall, one can raise the other; but woe betide him who is alone and falls with no companion to raise him! 11 Further, when two lie together they are warm; but how can he who is alone get warm? 12 Also, if one attacks, two can stand up to him. A threefold cord is not readily broken!

9. ***from their earnings*** **[*'amal*]** Better: "in their endeavors." On the frequent ambiguity of the important word *'amal,* see Keywords in the introduction. Here "toil" refers to life's endeavors and tribulations generally, not just to occupational labors or their "earnings." (The benefits these companions get from their *'amal,* described in verse 10, have nothing to do with occupational effort.)

10. ***fall*** Any difficulty or failure; compare Mic. 7:8; Pss. 24:17; 145:14. (After a literal fall, it is not usually difficult to get up.) Ibn Ezra gives sickness as an example.

11. ***Further, when two lie together they are warm*** Rashi says that in addition to its plain meaning (two men lying next to each other to keep warm), the verse can allude to the sexual embrace of husband and wife.

12. ***if one attacks*** That is, if someone else attacks either of them.

A threefold cord is not readily broken! If the companionship of two people is beneficial, how much the more so the fellowship of three!

KINGS AND THEIR SUCCESSORS (vv. 13–16)

An old king is succeeded by another wiser than he, and the young king by others. But soon all are forgotten and their fame has evaporated. The anecdote illustrates the fact that wisdom is effective but fails to secure its gains. Human accomplishments are transient and will be passed on to someone else (cf. 2:18–26). This section has strong affinities to 9:13–15. In both, a poor but wise man uses his skills with short-term success but with no lasting benefit to himself.

The Hebrew text of this passage is very difficult, in ways not reflected in the translation. In the Hebrew, it is often unclear what the pronouns and verbs refer to, and it is not even certain how many "youths" appear in the story, whether two or three. In spite of the uncertainties (which NJPS resolves, in ways open to dispute), the main point of the story is fairly clear: wisdom's practical value is real but ephemeral. The instability of accomplishment, rather than the loss of power as such, is what troubles Koheleth. As he will remind us, favor does not belong to the knowledgeable (9:11).

Many attempts have been made to identify the old king and wise youth with historical characters. The Midrash and traditional commentators suggest pairs such as Nimrod and Abraham, Potiphar and Joseph, Saul and David, Pharaoh and Joseph, Nebuchadnezzar and Daniel. None of these fit the events of Koheleth's anecdote. Modern scholars propose identifications with personages of the Hellenistic period, such as Antiochus III and Ptolemy Philapeter, Antiochus Epiphanes and Alexander Balas, Ptolemy

13 Better a poor but wise youth than an old but
foolish king who no longer has the sense to heed
warnings. 14 For the former can emerge from a
dungeon to become king; while the latter, even if
born to kingship, can become a pauper. 15 [However,]
I reflected about all the living who walk under the
sun with that youthful successor who steps into his
place. 16 Unnumbered are the multitudes of all those
who preceded them; and later generations will not
acclaim him either. For that too is futile and pursuit
of wind.

13 טוֹב יֶלֶד מִסְכֵּן וְחָכָם מִמֶּלֶךְ זָקֵן וּכְסִיל
אֲשֶׁר לֹא־יָדַע לְהִזָּהֵר עוֹד׃ 14 כִּי־מִבֵּית
הָסוּרִים יָצָא לִמְלֹךְ כִּי גַּם בְּמַלְכוּתוֹ נוֹלַד
רָשׁ׃ 15 רָאִיתִי אֶת־כָּל־הַחַיִּים הַמְהַלְּכִים
תַּחַת הַשָּׁמֶשׁ עִם הַיֶּלֶד הַשֵּׁנִי אֲשֶׁר יַעֲמֹד
תַּחְתָּיו׃ 16 אֵין־קֵץ לְכָל־הָעָם לְכֹל אֲשֶׁר־
הָיָה לִפְנֵיהֶם גַּם הָאַחֲרוֹנִים לֹא יִשְׂמְחוּ־
בוֹ כִּי־גַם־זֶה הֶבֶל וְרַעְיוֹן רוּחַ׃

IV and Ptolemy V. But none of them fits the description, and some lived after the book was written.

13. Some hints allow us to fill in the background of events. Since the old king once knew how to be wary, and since the young man was in prison, we may surmise that the latter had been incarcerated for presenting a danger to the king. Then the king dropped his guard.

old but foolish king Some translations incorrectly render "old and foolish king," as if the two traits go together. Rather than being the cause of the king's folly, his old age was an asset that was nullified by it.

14. ***For the former can emerge from a dungeon to become king; while the latter, even if born to kingship, can become a pauper*** This translation phrases the event as a possibility, reasoning that Koheleth is stating a potential, but that does not fit the Hebrew tenses or the context, for Koheleth is presenting the events as an historical incident that proves his point. Better: "For he [the youth] emerged from a dungeon to become king, and in his rule too a poor man was born [*nolad rash*]."

15. ***[However,] I reflected about all the living who walk under the sun with that youthful successor who steps into his place*** Or: "I saw all the living—those who go about under the sun—with the next young man who would arise in his place." The "next young man" is not the youth mentioned in verse 13, but rather whoever comes next in line to displace the once "poor but wise youth."

16. ***Unnumbered are the multitudes of all those who preceded them*** Or: "There was no end to all the people before whom he was"—in other words, all whom he led.

and later generations will not acclaim him either As Koheleth said earlier, "for, as the succeeding days roll by, all are forgotten" (2:16a).

For that too is futile [hevel] and pursuit of wind This comments on the entire situation described, in which one ruler loses his power to the next with little rhyme or reason. Though wisdom can bring a poor man to power, he too is quickly succeeded and forgotten. This is senseless.

17 Be not overeager to go to the House of God: more acceptable is obedience than the offering of fools, for they know nothing [but] to do wrong.

17 שְׁמֹר רגליך רַגְלְךָ כַּאֲשֶׁר תֵּלֵךְ אֶל־בֵּית
הָאֱלֹהִים וְקָרוֹב לִשְׁמֹעַ מִתֵּת הַכְּסִילִים
זָבַח כִּי־אֵינָם יוֹדְעִים לַעֲשׂוֹת רָע׃

Counsels and Teachings (4:17–11:6)

PRUDENCE IN VOWS (4:17–5:6)

Until now, Koheleth has offered mostly reflections and meditations on life and its problems. Now he begins to provide practical advice on getting along in the world, and teachings of this sort will occupy much of the remainder of the book. The main theme of the present unit is caution in making vows. The remarks about going to the Temple, offering sacrifices, avoiding rash speech, and fearing God are all organized around this theme and should be interpreted in this context.

At the Temple, worshipers could vow to pay a voluntary offering to God, sometimes upon fulfillment of a prayer of petition. Failure to pay one's vows would provoke God's wrath. As is usual in Wisdom Literature, the misdeed is condemned as foolish rather than as sinful. Impulsive vows are warned against in Prov. 20:25 and Sira 18:22–23, and payment of vows is demanded in Num. 30:3 and Ps. 50:14b.

In form and content, this passage is prudential wisdom of a conventional cast. Koheleth's observations, in spite of their subversive implications, never lead him to abandon prudence or religious principles. He esteems the Temple rituals, as shown by the fact that in 9:2 he lists people who offer sacrifice among other possessors of virtues.

*17. **Be not overeager to go*** Literally, "Watch your foot when you go." In other words, tread carefully; watch how you behave. This advice pertains to all behavior in the Temple, but the present context applies it particularly to vows.

more acceptable is obedience than the offering of fools As Samuel said, "Surely, obedience is better than sacrifice, compliance than the fat of rams" (1 Sam. 15:22). "Obedience" in both verses is *shamaʿ*; literally, "hear." The word "fools" is, strictly speaking, superfluous, since obedience is better than *anyone's* offerings. Koheleth is focusing on what fools do without intending to restrict the principle to their offerings alone.

for they know nothing [but] to do wrong Literally, "for they do not know how to do wrong," which does not make much sense. NJPS's addition of "but" makes sense but is doubtful grammatically. Rashi paraphrases, "for the fool does not understand that he is doing harm to himself," but this too does not fit the Hebrew. The line has not yet been satisfactorily explained.

5 Keep your mouth from being rash, and let not
your throat be quick to bring forth speech before
God. For God is in heaven and you are on earth; that
is why your words should be few. 2 Just as dreams
come with much brooding, so does foolish utterance
come with much speech. 3 When you make a vow to
God, do not delay to fulfill it. For He has no pleasure
in fools; what you vow, fulfill. 4 It is better not to vow
at all than to vow and not fulfill. 5 Don't let your

ה אַל־תְּבַהֵל עַל־פִּיךָ וְלִבְּךָ אַל־יְמַהֵר
לְהוֹצִיא דָבָר לִפְנֵי הָאֱלֹהִים כִּי הָאֱלֹהִים
בַּשָּׁמַיִם וְאַתָּה עַל־הָאָרֶץ עַל־כֵּן יִהְיוּ
דְבָרֶיךָ מְעַטִּים׃ 2 כִּי בָּא הַחֲלוֹם בְּרֹב
עִנְיָן וְקוֹל כְּסִיל בְּרֹב דְּבָרִים׃ 3 כַּאֲשֶׁר
תִּדֹּר נֶדֶר לֵאלֹהִים אַל־תְּאַחֵר לְשַׁלְּמוֹ
כִּי אֵין חֵפֶץ בַּכְּסִילִים אֵת אֲשֶׁר־תִּדֹּר
שַׁלֵּם׃ 4 טוֹב אֲשֶׁר לֹא־תִדֹּר מִשֶּׁתִּדּוֹר
וְלֹא תְשַׁלֵּם׃ 5 אַל־תִּתֵּן אֶת־פִּיךָ לַחֲטִיא

5:1. Keep your mouth from being rash . . . before God The phrase "before God" or "before the LORD" usually means in the Temple, in God's presence. Thus this admonition refers in particular to pronouncement of vows in the Temple. If you make vows without proper forethought, you may find yourself unable to pay them, that is to say, to bring the promised offerings to the Temple.

This rule can be extended to other types of behavior. Rashi says that one must beware of speaking harsh things toward God. Rashbam says that one should be cautious and sparing of words in prayer, to avoid making a mistake. Ibn Ezra understands this as an admonition to pray only in the words of the fixed liturgy. (In a long digression, he attacks the use of *piyyutim*—elaborate liturgical poems that in his day filled out the liturgy—for being obscure and ungrammatical.)

throat Actually, "heart." Thoughts should be held in the heart until the right time comes for speaking.

God is in heaven and you are on earth From His lofty vantage point, God can see all that happens on earth, whereas humans can barely discern the near future. See "God," in The Teachings of Ecclesiastes in the introduction.

2. brooding **[*'inyan*]** Better: "busyness" (see Comment to 1:13). This verse recalls 2:23, which says that the toiler's thoughts are troubled even at night.

so does foolish utterance come with much speech Literally, "and the voice of the fool comes with many words"—accompanied by blabber. Avot 1:17 phrases the same principle as a matter of morality: "He who multiplies words causes sin."

3–4. A near-quotation of Deuteronomy 23:22–24:

> [22]When you make a vow to the LORD your God, do not put off fulfilling it, for the LORD your God will require it of you, and you will have incurred guilt; [23]whereas you incur no guilt if you refrain from vowing. [24]You must fulfill what has crossed your lips and perform what you have voluntarily vowed to the LORD your God, having made the promise with your own mouth.

Whereas Deuteronomy speaks of guilt, Koheleth warns against folly and the damage that reneging on vows can cause a person.

5. Don't let your mouth bring you into disfavor Literally, "Don't let your mouth make your flesh sin." Others translate, "Don't let your mouth harm your flesh."

mouth bring you into disfavor, and don't plead before the messenger that it was an error, but fear God; else God may be angered by your talk and destroy your possessions. 6 For much dreaming leads to futility and to superfluous talk.

אֶת־בְּשָׂרֶךָ וְאַל־תֹּאמַר לִפְנֵי הַמַּלְאָךְ כִּי
שְׁגָגָה הִיא לָמָּה יִקְצֹף הָאֱלֹהִים עַל־קוֹלֶךָ
וְחִבֵּל אֶת־מַעֲשֵׂה יָדֶיךָ׃ 6 כִּי בְרֹב חֲלֹמוֹת
וַהֲבָלִים וּדְבָרִים הַרְבֵּה כִּי אֶת־הָאֱלֹהִים
יְרָא׃

Rashi glosses "your flesh" as your *sons,* but it probably means "yourself"; rash vows can bring you to sin and harm. Rashi reads this as a warning against public pledges to give charitable donations, which you may later find yourself unable to honor.

and don't plead before the messenger that it was an error Some suggest that this was a messenger sent out by the priests to collect vows. This makes sense, but such a practice is not otherwise attested. The word for "messenger," *mal'akh,* also means "angel." Ibn Ezra thinks of the angel who records everyone's words; others say it is the Angel of Death. The Septuagint and the Peshitta witness to a Hebrew text that had "God" instead of "messenger." The implication is the same, since an angel is God's messenger and an instrument of His will. Deuteronomy 23:22 says that God Himself will seek or demand payment of the vow, meaning that at some time He will call you to account for reneging on vows; this may be the moment Koheleth has in mind.

and destroy your possessions One who reneges on a vow is diminishing what properly belongs to God (which is to say, to the Temple). God will in turn damage that person's property, tit for tat.

6. For much dreaming leads to futility [hevel] and to superfluous talk A difficult sentence. It sounds as if Koheleth were condemning dreams, but that would be pointless. We should probably emend MT; two slight changes in prefix yield: "for many words are like many dreams and absurdities."[16] The subject, in this reading, is words, not dreams. Superfluous talk produces dreams and *hevel*—senseless things, devoid of substance. The Targum and Rashi identify the excessive talk as false prophecy. More plausibly, Ibn Ezra, with attention to the following imperative, says that what is forbidden is only speech that mentions God's name. In context, this statement, which is perhaps a proverb, pertains primarily to impulsive vows.

But fear God For clarity, NJPS moved this clause from the end of verse 6, where it summarizes the unit: Fearing God means watching what you say—the opposite of superfluous talk. "Fear" means true fear, not only reverence, for Koheleth pictures a God who will lash out in anger.

Fear of God is the great virtue advocated by the book of Proverbs (esp. 1:7; 9:10). There, too, the God-fearing man will shun thoughtless vows and vain excuses and will refrain from prattling about things of which he is ignorant.

OPPRESSION AND GREED (5:7–11)

This unit comprises observations loosely connected by the theme of greed: what it does to a society and what it does to an individual.

7 If you see in a province oppression of the poor and
suppression of right and justice, don't wonder at the
fact; for one high official is protected by a higher one,
and both of them by still higher ones. 8 Thus the
greatest advantage in all the land is his: he controls a
field that is cultivated.

7 אִם־עֹ֣שֶׁק רָ֠שׁ וְגֵ֨זֶל מִשְׁפָּ֤ט וָצֶ֙דֶק֙ תִּרְאֶ֣ה
בַמְּדִינָ֔ה אַל־תִּתְמַ֖הּ עַל־הַחֵ֑פֶץ כִּ֣י גָ֠בֹהַּ
מֵעַ֨ל גָּבֹ֙הַּ֙ שֹׁמֵ֔ר וּגְבֹהִ֖ים עֲלֵיהֶֽם׃ 8 וְיִתְר֥וֹן
אֶ֖רֶץ בַּכֹּ֣ל היא הִ֑וא מֶ֥לֶךְ לְשָׂדֶ֖ה נֶעֱבָֽד׃

9 A lover of money never has his fill of money, nor a
lover of wealth his fill of income. That too is futile.
10 As his substance increases, so do those who
consume it; what, then, does the success of its owner

9 אֹהֵ֥ב כֶּ֙סֶף֙ לֹא־יִשְׂבַּ֣ע כֶּ֔סֶף וּמִֽי־אֹהֵ֥ב
בֶּהָמ֖וֹן לֹ֣א תְבוּאָ֑ה גַּם־זֶ֖ה הָֽבֶל׃ 10 בִּרְבוֹת֙
הַטּוֹבָ֔ה רַבּ֖וּ אוֹכְלֶ֑יהָ וּמַה־כִּשְׁרוֹן֙
לִבְעָלֶ֔יהָ כִּ֖י אִם־ראית רְא֥וּת עֵינָֽיו׃

7. in a province Koheleth speaks as a resident of a *medinah,* a province in an empire. This is probably the Hellenistic Ptolemaic empire, ruled from Alexandria. Likewise, the Book of Esther calls the provinces or satrapies of the Persian empire *medinot.* The authors of both books feel the weight of an oppressive and inflexible imperial bureaucracy.

don't wonder at the fact Social and judicial oppression is the way of the world, nothing to be surprised at. Koheleth never expects or demands improvements, even in the distant future. He diagnoses the illness without suggesting a remedy.

for one high official is protected by a higher one, and both of them by still higher ones "Protected" is literally "watches over": one official "watches over" another. Koheleth describes the phenomenon of *protektzia* (as it is known in modern Hebrew), which afflicts all bureaucracies and frustrates attempts to get redress. In Ptolemaic times, the imperial bureaucracy, which was largely an instrument of tax gathering, became very complex and burdensome.

*8. **Thus the greatest advantage*** [*yitron*] ***in all the land is his: he controls a field that is cultivated*** The Hebrew is obscure and no satisfactory solution has been proposed. Literally, "And the advantage of a land in all [regards?] is a king for a cultivated field." Rashbam takes this to mean that everyone must work the land in order to live, and even the ruler "cultivates" the land by requiring subjects to farm it in order to supply his needs. Though obscure, this verse does seem to praise agriculture as advantageous to the country. This natural and productive way of life stands in contrast to the self-serving bureaucracy in verse 7 and the compulsive consumerism of verse 9.

*9. **A lover of money never has his fill of money, nor a lover of wealth his fill of income*** [*tevu'ah*] The appetite for wealth is insatiable; one always craves more. (Instead of loving and desiring riches, a man should be satisfied with the goods *(tovah)* he already owns; 6:3.)

That too is futile [*hevel*] "That" refers either to the love of money or to the *fact* that one who loves money is never satisfied. In the latter case, *hevel* means senseless or absurd.

*10. **As his substance increases, so do those who consume it*** This is one reason that the toiler "never has his fill" of wealth. Compare 2:7–8, which exemplifies this dilemma.

amount to but feasting his eyes? 11 A worker's sleep is
sweet, whether he has much or little to eat; but the
rich man's abundance doesn't let him sleep.
12 Here is a grave evil I have observed under the sun:
riches hoarded by their owner to his misfortune, 13 in
that those riches are lost in some unlucky venture;
and if he begets a son, he has nothing in hand.

11 מְתוּקָה֙ שְׁנַ֣ת הָעֹבֵ֔ד אִם־מְעַ֥ט וְאִם־
הַרְבֵּ֖ה יֹאכֵ֑ל וְהַשָּׂבָע֙ לֶֽעָשִׁ֔יר אֵינֶ֛נּוּ מַנִּ֥יחַֽ
ל֖וֹ לִישֽׁוֹן׃
12 יֵ֚שׁ רָעָ֣ה חוֹלָ֔ה רָאִ֖יתִי תַּ֣חַת הַשָּׁ֑מֶשׁ
עֹ֛שֶׁר שָׁמ֥וּר לִבְעָלָ֖יו לְרָעָתֽוֹ׃ 13 וְאָבַ֛ד
הָעֹ֥שֶׁר הַה֖וּא בְּעִנְיַ֣ן רָ֑ע וְהוֹלִ֣יד בֵּ֔ן וְאֵ֥ין
בְּיָד֖וֹ מְאֽוּמָה׃

what, then, does the success of its owner amount to but feasting his eyes? "Feasting his eyes" is literally "the sight of his eyes." NJPS implies that success *(kishron)* is trivial, amounting to no more than mere vision, not real enjoyment. More likely, the "sight of his eyes" is a *desirable* experience, as the similar expressions in 11:9 and 6:9 indicate. Better: "and the only benefit *(kishron)* for its owner is the sight of his eyes." Wealth is always precarious, because (among other reasons) it excites the envy and greed of others, who will try to take it for themselves. Therefore the only real benefit in wealth is the immediate experience (the "seeing") of pleasure. Koheleth recommends this often (2:24; 3:12, 22; 5:17; 8:15; and more).

11. A worker's Hebrew *ha-ʿoved.* This should probably be vocalized *ha-ʿeved* ("the slave") as the Septuagint understands it, because the contrast between the two halves of this verse hinges on possession of property versus lacking it, not on work versus leisure. (The rich man too works, after all; that is what keeps him awake at night.)

the rich man's abundance doesn't let him sleep The insomnia of the rich is induced by worry about losing wealth to others who are trying to consume it (v. 10; Ibn Ezra and Rashbam, comparing 2:23), and not by overeating. (The slave/worker too may have eaten much; v. 11a.) As Rabban Gamaliel observes, "One who increases property increases worry" (Avot 2:7).

TOIL AND PLEASURE (5:12–6:6)

Koheleth describes three "evils": (1) A man earns wealth but loses it (5:12–14). (2) He leaves this world with nothing, having lived a life of miserable self-deprivation (5:15–16). (3) A man receives wealth from God but is not allowed to enjoy it; rather, a stranger receives its benefit (6:1–6). In 5:17–19, Koheleth describes the desirable situation: A man receives the benefits of his toil and is allowed to enjoy them. The components of this passage, then, are 5:12–14; 5:15–16; 5:17–19; and 6:1–6.

TOIL AND LOSS (vv. 12–14)

Koheleth now depicts a complex scenario to drive home the importance of immediate enjoyment: A man works and hoards his money, then suddenly loses it all. He did not enjoy his wealth while he had it, and now it is gone.

riches hoarded by their owner to his misfortune The "misfortune" or "harm" (*raʿ*, sometimes translated "evil") is the deprivation the stingy man imposed on himself during the hoarding. Rashbam thinks that the misfortune happens afterward: a man may be killed or captured for his money. And if he has begotten a son, he has nothing to give him.

14 כַּאֲשֶׁר יָצָא מִבֶּטֶן אִמּוֹ עָרוֹם יָשׁוּב
לָלֶכֶת כְּשֶׁבָּא וּמְאוּמָה לֹא־יִשָּׂא בַעֲמָלוֹ
שֶׁיֹּלֵךְ בְּיָדוֹ׃ 15 וְגַם־זֹה רָעָה חוֹלָה כָּל־
עֻמַּת שֶׁבָּא כֵּן יֵלֵךְ וּמַה־יִּתְרוֹן לוֹ שֶׁיַּעֲמֹל
לָרוּחַ׃ 16 גַּם כָּל־יָמָיו בַּחֹשֶׁךְ יֹאכֵל וְכָעַס
הַרְבֵּה וְחָלְיוֹ וָקָצֶף׃
17 הִנֵּה אֲשֶׁר־רָאִיתִי אָנִי טוֹב אֲשֶׁר־יָפֶה
לֶאֱכוֹל־וְלִשְׁתּוֹת וְלִרְאוֹת טוֹבָה בְּכָל־
עֲמָלוֹ ׀ שֶׁיַּעֲמֹל תַּחַת־הַשֶּׁמֶשׁ מִסְפַּר
יְמֵי־חַיָּו* אֲשֶׁר־נָתַן־לוֹ הָאֱלֹהִים כִּי־הוּא

v. 17. חסר י'

14 Another grave evil is this: He must depart just as he
came. As he came out of his mother's womb, so must
he depart at last, naked as he came. He can take
nothing of his wealth to carry with him. 15 So what is
the good of his toiling for the wind? 16 Besides, all his
days he eats in darkness, with much vexation and
grief and anger.
17 Only this, I have found, is a real good: that one
should eat and drink and get pleasure with all the
gains he makes under the sun, during the numbered
days of life that God has given him; for that is his

TOIL AND DEATH (vv. 15–16)

A further evil is that this man dies bereft of the wealth he struggled to amass, having lived in grim self-deprivation. Though Koheleth speaks of "a man," this "evil" actually befalls everyone (Ibn Ezra). All humans slave away in grim self-deprivation, but for naught (v. 16). They toil for the wind, and the ledger sheet of their lives ends in a zero balance.

14. ***Another grave evil is this: He must depart just as he came*** NJPS has moved this sentence for clarity from the beginning of verse 15. The move may "improve" the logic, but it is not the way Koheleth segments his description. He first describes the evil of an unexpected loss of wealth (vv. 12–13), observing that this man leaves the world "naked" and impoverished (v. 14). Then he resumes the complaint of verse 14, but now counting it as an *additional* "evil" (v. 15), and adding that the man wasted his life in miserly gloom.

He must depart just as he came "He" is sometimes thought to refer to the son, who has received no inheritance (v. 13b), but it more likely refers to the father, since the next verse speaks of toiling and self-deprivation, which was the father's lot. The problem is not that some people (such as the son) die poor, but that some people (such as the father) waste their lives in dreary labors.

16. ***Besides, all his days he eats in darkness*** He skimps on oil for his lamp. Or perhaps the darkness is the gloom of his spirit.[17]

vexation and grief and anger The opposite of eating and drinking in gladness and joy (9:7). "Grief" is literally "sickness." Sforno says that the typical "sickness" of the wealthy is stinginess: They live poor in order to die rich.

WHAT IS GOOD (vv. 17–19)

17. ***a real good*** Literally, "a good thing that is beautiful" or "...that is appropriate" (*yafeh,* as in 3:11). Here is an area in which humans can imitate God, who makes everything to be *yafeh* in its time.

for that is his portion [ḥeilek] See 3:22. A person's "portion" is not wealth itself, for we are told that a rich man may possess wealth yet neglect to "take his portion" (to use the phrase of v. 18). Rather, the "portion" is the enjoyment of it.

portion. [18] Also, whenever a man is given riches and
property by God, and is also permitted by Him to
enjoy them and to take his portion and get pleasure
for his gains—that is a gift of God. [19] For [such a
man] will not brood much over the days of his life,
because God keeps him busy enjoying himself.

חֶלְקוֹ׃ 18 גַּם כָּל־הָאָדָם אֲשֶׁר נָתַן־לוֹ
הָאֱלֹהִים עֹשֶׁר וּנְכָסִים וְהִשְׁלִיטוֹ לֶאֱכֹל
מִמֶּנּוּ וְלָשֵׂאת אֶת־חֶלְקוֹ וְלִשְׂמֹחַ בַּעֲמָלוֹ
זֹה מַתַּת אֱלֹהִים הִיא׃ 19 כִּי לֹא הַרְבֵּה
יִזְכֹּר אֶת־יְמֵי חַיָּיו כִּי הָאֱלֹהִים מַעֲנֶה
בְּשִׂמְחַת לִבּוֹ׃

6 There is an evil I have observed under the sun, and
a grave one it is for man: [2] that God sometimes grants
a man riches, property, and wealth, so that he does
not want for anything his appetite may crave, but

ו יֵשׁ רָעָה אֲשֶׁר רָאִיתִי תַּחַת הַשָּׁמֶשׁ
וְרַבָּה הִיא עַל־הָאָדָם׃ 2 אִישׁ אֲשֶׁר יִתֶּן־
לוֹ הָאֱלֹהִים עֹשֶׁר וּנְכָסִים וְכָבוֹד וְאֵינֶנּוּ
חָסֵר לְנַפְשׁוֹ ׀ מִכֹּל אֲשֶׁר־יִתְאַוֶּה וְלֹא־

18. gift of God God's gift is to let a man have wealth and keep it. It is his responsibility to "take" his portion by savoring the pleasures available to him.

19. The great benefit in pleasure is that it distracts one from vexatious thoughts. To brood on (lit. "remember") the days of one's life may mean either to be aware of their unhappiness or to recall their brevity. Although the distraction did not work for Koheleth (chapter 2), he can still commend it to others.

In the same vein, the poet of the Egyptian Harper's Song, despairing of the efficacy of mortuary rites to guarantee immortality, urges his listeners to enjoy themselves in the present, to divert their hearts from thoughts of death: "Hence rejoice in your heart! Forgetfulness profits you. Follow your heart as long as you live!"[18]

TOIL WITHOUT PROFIT (6:1–6)

This passage describes an even worse scenario than the two related earlier. There, the toiler lived a dreary existence while hoarding his wealth, then lost it all (5:12–13), or managed to hold on to his wealth but spent a joyless life (5:14–16). Here, God lets a man have everything he wants but prevents him from enjoying it; instead, another man, who did not toil for it, gets the benefit. The irony offends Koheleth's sense of fairness.

Even a man whom God favors with wealth may lose it to another. Then if he has a son, the son inherits nothing. The reason the toiler is prevented from enjoying his wealth is not given. (It is not, in this case, death, since then a son would inherit the property. Perhaps he simply lost his money in an "unlucky venture," as in 5:13.)

As exasperating as the loss of wealth to a stranger may be, it is not what defines the tragedy of this scenario. The real problem is the waste of the opportunity to have the one good thing in life. Even *before* the loss of wealth, and *even if* a man has a son for an heir, and *even if* he lives far beyond the usual life span, his life is wasted unless he has known pleasure (vv. 3–6). The moral: seize the moment, because the next one is beyond your control.

2. wealth Hebrew *kavod; usually* "honor." Sometimes *kavod* is associated with wealth (for example, "wealth, and property, and *kavod*"; 2 Chron. 1:11), but more precisely it is the honor or prestige attendant upon riches. This prestige, Koheleth believes, will be

יַשְׁלִיטֶנּוּ הָאֱלֹהִים לֶאֱכֹל מִמֶּנּוּ כִּי אִישׁ
נָכְרִי יֹאכְלֶנּוּ זֶה הֶבֶל וָחֳלִי רָע הוּא׃
3 אִם־יוֹלִיד אִישׁ מֵאָה וְשָׁנִים רַבּוֹת יִחְיֶה
וְרַב ׀ שֶׁיִּהְיוּ יְמֵי־שָׁנָיו וְנַפְשׁוֹ לֹא־תִשְׂבַּע
מִן־הַטּוֹבָה וְגַם־קְבוּרָה לֹא־הָיְתָה לּוֹ

God does not permit him to enjoy it; instead, a
stranger will enjoy it. That is futility and a grievous ill.
3 Even if a man should beget a hundred children and
live many years—no matter how many the days of his
years may come to, if his gullet is not sated through
his wealth, I say: The stillbirth, though it was not even

transferred along with the wealth to the "stranger." Other intangibles that go along with wealth are "wisdom and knowledge" (2:26).

enjoy it Literally, "eat it," that is, "consume it." Koheleth recommends the timely consumption of wealth.

Rashi reads this verse as referring to a double enjoyment: getting satisfaction from one's own wealth and enjoying the fruits of righteous deeds, and, he adds, the study of Torah. (The latter component he regards as a midrash.) But Koheleth does not give thought to the pleasure of performance of good deeds and study of Torah. In this regard, Rashi and other traditional interpreters have a richer and more subtle sense of the potential meaning of "doing good" and "enjoying the good" (recommended in 3:12 and elsewhere) than the author did.

3. Progeny and long life might be thought sufficient to make life worthwhile but in fact do not. Only actual satisfaction can offset the unhappiness of existence. As a Mesopotamian wisdom book asks rhetorically, "A gloomy life [literally, "a life without light"], what advantage does it have over death?"[19]

no matter how many the days of his years may come to This complaint shows that what troubles Koheleth is not life's brevity so much as the failure to achieve something worthwhile during one's lifetime.

gullet Or: "appetite." *Nefesh,* a rich and complex word, signifies the organ of desire and emotion. Thus via metonymy it can stand for the desires that it houses. The physical location of the *nefesh* was thought to be the throat or neck (as in "for the waters have reached my neck [*nefesh*]," in Ps. 69:2). It means "soul" in the sense of the complex of emotions and thoughts that constitute an individual personality. In the Bible, *nefesh* is not a soul in the theological sense of an immortal spirit.

Verse 3 presents a problem, not visible in NJPS. The clause *ve-gam kevurah lo' hayetah lo* (literally, "moreover, it [or "he"] was not accorded a burial") is actually located in the middle of verse 3, after "if his gullet is not sated through his wealth." In that position, the clause in question can only refer to the man who lacks enjoyment. This is problematic, because it makes it appear as if Koheleth thought that a proper burial would somehow give significance to a cheerless life. NJPS effectively moves the clause to the end of the verse (in the Hebrew), so that it now describes the stillbirth. This change is conjectural and presumes a major copying error.

Alternatively, leaving the clause "moreover, it [or "he"] was not accorded a burial" where it is in the MT, we can grant that Koheleth does take burial seriously, as he shows also in 8:10. Here he lists the lack of a burial as a misfortune that can befall a man even after death, like the quick fading of memory (2:16).

The stillbirth . . . is more fortunate than he The stillbirth too knew no pleasure—no "profit"—but it, at least, was spared the sorrow of seeing life's evils (see 4:3). Likewise,

accorded a burial, is more fortunate than he. 4 Though it comes into futility and departs into darkness, and its very name is covered with darkness, 5 though it has never seen or experienced the sun, it is better off than he—6 yes, even if the other lived a thousand years twice over but never had his fill of enjoyment! For are not both of them bound for the same place? 7 All of man's earning is for the sake of his mouth, yet his

אָמַ֕רְתִּי ט֥וֹב מִמֶּ֖נּוּ הַנָּֽפֶל׃ 4 כִּֽי־בַהֶ֥בֶל בָּ֖א
וּבַחֹ֣שֶׁךְ יֵלֵ֑ךְ וּבַחֹ֖שֶׁךְ שְׁמ֥וֹ יְכֻסֶּֽה׃ 5 גַּם־
שֶׁ֛מֶשׁ לֹא־רָאָ֖ה וְלֹ֣א יָדָ֑ע נַ֥חַת לָזֶ֖ה מִזֶּֽה׃
6 וְאִלּ֣וּ חָיָ֗ה אֶ֤לֶף שָׁנִים֙ פַּעֲמַ֔יִם וְטוֹבָ֖ה לֹ֣א
רָאָ֑ה הֲלֹ֛א אֶל־מָק֥וֹם אֶחָ֖ד הַכֹּ֥ל הוֹלֵֽךְ׃
7 כָּל־עֲמַ֥ל הָאָדָ֖ם לְפִ֑יהוּ וְגַם־הַנֶּ֖פֶשׁ לֹ֥א

both Jeremiah (20:18) and Job (3:10), in misery and frustration, bewail the fact that they were ever born and had to see *'amal* ("toil").

4–5. In the Hebrew, these verses can be read with reference either to the stillbirth or the unfortunate man, an ambiguity that is itself ironic. If the primary referent is the man, we would translate: "[4] For he comes in senselessness [*hevel*] and departs into darkness, and his very name is covered with darkness. [5] Even the one who has never seen or experienced the sun is better off than him." The advantage of the second reading is that verse 4 fits a human life better than a stillbirth, which doesn't even have a name to be forgotten. A human, unlike a stillbirth, comes into life—a senseless one—and passes from there to darkness and oblivion (see 2:16).

5. The subject now switches to the stillbirth.[20] See previous Comment.

better off Only pleasure makes it better to live than never to have been born.

6. Better: "Even if the other lived a thousand years twice over but never had his fill of enjoyment—Oh, are not both of them bound for the same place!" NJPS cannot be right, because an "if" clause cannot be the condition for what precedes, but only for what follows. The textual problem that NJPS is addressing is that the "if" clause is not followed by the expected "then" clause; in other words, the Hebrew syntax is broken. But this broken syntax in fact suggests Koheleth's state of mind. He starts out once again listing conditions for a desirable life, parallel to verse 3, but then suddenly gives up and just exclaims in despair and frustration on the universality of death's power. Koheleth's complaint is illogical, because if life is so bad, why complain that everybody dies? Somehow life is still better than death, for "sweet is the light" (11:7a).

both Hebrew *ha-kol;* better: "all." The stillbirth cannot be said to be "bound" for the underworld whereas it is true that "all"—all the living—are.

THE IMPOSSIBILITY OF SATISFACTION (6:7–9)

Satisfaction in what we currently possess should be distinguished from satisfaction of the desire for what we do not have. The former is "the sight of the eyes"; the latter is the "wandering of the soul"; see Comment to 6:9. The first type of satisfaction is feasible and is what makes life worthwhile (6:2–6). The second is an illusion. Paradoxically, the very attempt to achieve satisfaction places it out of reach. The craving for wealth is insatiable, so it makes no sense to try to amass more.

7. This verse refers to the craving for possessions of all sorts, not food alone (cf. 5:11).

gullet is not sated. 8 What advantage then has the wise
man over the fool, what advantage has the pauper
who knows how to get on in life? 9 Is the feasting of
the eyes more important than the pursuit of desire?
That, too, is futility and pursuit of wind.

תִמָּלֵא׃ 8 כִּי מַה־יּוֹתֵר לֶחָכָם מִן־הַכְּסִיל
מַה־לֶּעָנִי יוֹדֵעַ לַהֲלֹךְ נֶגֶד הַחַיִּים׃ 9 טוֹב
מַרְאֵה עֵינַיִם מֵהֲלָךְ־נָפֶשׁ גַּם־זֶה הֶבֶל
וּרְעוּת רוּחַ׃

***earning* [*ʿamal*]** Or: "toil." See Keywords in the introduction. Proverbs 16:26 makes a similar observation: "The appetite of a laborer labors for him, because his hunger forces him on."

gullet Or: "desire." See Comment to 6:3.

8. This verse interrupts the connection between verses 7 and 9 and may be misplaced. Alternatively, it can be read as parenthetical.[21] In the present context it denies wisdom an advantage (*yoter* = *yitron,* "profit") only when it comes to attaining satisfaction. A *ḥakham* ("wise man") is one who possesses mental powers of any sort, including the acumen one uses in gaining wealth (cf. 2:19, 21), that is, intelligence or ingenuity; see Keywords in the introduction. Since the thirst for wealth is unquenchable, an ingenious man is no better off than an incompetent one.

what advantage has the pauper who knows how to get on in life? A difficult sentence, loosely translated in NJPS. Taken by itself, it seems to mean that if the wise man (who can earn money) has no real advantage over the fool (who cannot), then the (wise) pauper is not aided by his wisdom. In its present context, bracketed by verses 7 and 9, the statement has a more limited focus. It says that a wise (that is, ingenious) man who fails to enjoy wealth has no advantage over the fool.

9. ***Is the feasting of the eyes more important than the pursuit of desire?*** This translation is very paraphrastic. There is no indication that the sentence is a question rather than a statement. We should translate, "Better the sight of the eyes than the wandering [lit. "going"] of desire" (or "soul"; see 6:3 on *nefesh*). This idea is entirely in accord with Koheleth's principles.

This is a typical "better-than" proverb, a form which Koheleth uses often (e.g., 4:6, 9, 13; 5:4). The "sight of the eyes," as in 5:10, is either what one sees or the experience of pleasure. "The wandering of desire" (or "soul") is a yearning for something one does not possess. If we are enjoying a good meal with friends, this is a "sight of the eyes," and it is good. But if we start to think of other things we crave—a better cuisine, perhaps, or prestige, or success, or sex—we lose contact with the actual place and moment, and our soul departs, as it were, and wanders off to another, nonexistent place. Then the moment is depleted of meaning, and we have nothing.

***That, too, is futility* [*hevel*]** The antecedent of "that" is ambiguous. (This occurs frequently in Ecclesiastes and poses a problem in understanding the book. A particularly severe case is 4:13–16, as mentioned there.) Here, "that" could refer to either "the sight of the eyes" or "the wandering of the appetite." Plausibly Koheleth would call either one *hevel*—even "the sight of the eyes," which he praises. (For all his praise of pleasure, he judges it senseless in 2:1 and 11. See "Koheleth on Pleasure" at the start of chapter 2.)

10 Whatever happens, it was designated long ago and
it was known that it would happen; as for man, he
cannot contend with what is stronger than he.
11 Often, much talk means much futility. How does it
benefit a man? 12 Who can possibly know what is best
for a man to do in life—the few days of his fleeting
life? For who can tell him what the future holds for
him under the sun?

10 *מַה־שֶּׁהָיָה כְּבָר נִקְרָא שְׁמוֹ וְנוֹדָע
אֲשֶׁר־הוּא אָדָם וְלֹא־יוּכַל לָדִין עִם
שהתקיף שֶׁתַּקִּיף מִמֶּנּוּ׃ 11 כִּי יֵשׁ־דְּבָרִים
הַרְבֵּה מַרְבִּים הָבֶל מַה־יֹּתֵר לָאָדָם׃ 12 כִּי
מִי־יוֹדֵעַ מַה־טּוֹב לָאָדָם בַּחַיִּים מִסְפַּר
יְמֵי־חַיֵּי הֶבְלוֹ וְיַעֲשֵׂם כַּצֵּל אֲשֶׁר מִי־יַגִּיד
לָאָדָם מַה־יִּהְיֶה אַחֲרָיו תַּחַת הַשָּׁמֶשׁ׃

v. 10. חצי הספר בפסוקים

LIFE IS UNCHANGEABLE AND THE FUTURE IS HIDDEN (6:10–12)

It is futile to argue with God, or even to speak too much. "Whereof one cannot speak, thereof he must keep silent" (Wittgenstein).[22]

10. The Hebrew of this verse is very difficult, but its gist seems to be the same as 1:9 and 3:14–15: God has made a world of eternal repetitions, and humans cannot change the course of events.

It was designated long ago Literally, "and its name was already called"; that is, its nature was already known or was already called into existence.

and it was known that it would happen Whatever happens now was long ago named and known. In other words, "There is nothing new beneath the sun" (1:9).

as for man, he cannot contend with what is stronger than he Better: "and no man can contend with Him who is stronger than he is."[23] (The verb "contend" [*ladin*] is used of strife with persons—including God—but not with things.) We should not struggle with God as, for example, Job did.

Koheleth's outlook contrasts with that of Job, who believes that if he could confront God, there might be a change—and if not a change, at least an explanation; Koheleth expects neither. Silence in the fear of God (6:10b–11; 5:5; 3:14b) is the only prudent behavior in a world in which humans can do little (6:10a; 3:14–15) and understand less (6:12; 3:11).

The two parts of this verse correspond in reverse order to 3:14b–15a; see the commentary there.

12. One should not speak too much (v. 11) because no one knows what is good to do. The prerequisite for discerning what actions are good (in the sense of beneficial) is knowing their consequences. Since the future is hidden, humans are ignorant, and it is best to be silent. This is self-directed irony, because Koheleth himself has been expostulating on what is "good" *(tov)* for human beings to do and will continue in this vein in the next chapter.

Traditional commentators take for granted significant exceptions to Koheleth's skepticism. "For who is he who knows what will benefit man in this life other than to study Torah, for in this is eternal life" (Targum). Furthermore, since we do not know what is good to do (in ordinary matters) and are ignorant of what will happen on earth after our death, we should perform good deeds, through which our children will find blessing (Rashbam).

7 A good name is better than fragrant oil, and the day of death than the day of birth.

ז טוֹב שֵׁם מִשֶּׁמֶן טוֹב וְיוֹם הַמָּוֶת מִיּוֹם הִוָּלְדוֹ׃

the few days of his fleeting* [*hevel*] *life? Following these words, the Hebrew adds "which he passes like a shadow." (This is not shown in NJPS.[24]) The clause is a parenthetical remark about how the days of one's life slip past, leaving behind no trace.

To what kind of shadow can our days be compared? Koheleth Rabbah explains that it is not like the shadow of a date palm or a wall, which has some endurance. As the psalm says, "His days are like a passing shadow" (Ps. 144:4), like a shadow of a bird in flight (Rashi). Similarly, a human breath (also called *hevel*) is not like the more substantial steam of an oven; it is *havel havalim,* literally, "a breath of a breath" (Eccl. 1:1).

what the future holds Within a person's own lifetime ("under the sun"). Rashbam explains it as the future on earth after a person dies. Rashi thinks it means eternity: one should know what good deeds to do in this life for the sake of his existence in the hereafter.

SOME GOOD THINGS (7:1–7)

This passage comprises sayings of the form "Better X than Y." The keyword here is *tov,* "good" (in translation, sometimes "better" or "best"). Koheleth's mistrust of human knowledge does not keep him from offering practical advice and commentary on the human scene. The first line of each couplet has the form and sound of a popular adage. Perhaps the author is quoting a saying and adding a second line of his own, which puts a new twist on the old adage. Possibly, however, he composed them entirely himself (see 12:9).

By means of these sayings, Koheleth calls for a somber awareness of death. Whereas in 5:19 he favored distraction from thoughts of death, here he declares it wise to take death to heart (v. 2b), for that is the reality we face. The purpose of 7:1–4 is not to condemn feasting, but rather to give preference to an open-eyed awareness of mortality. Verses 5–6 reinforce the lesson of sobriety. Verse 7 seems unrelated to the context.

7:1. A proverb can hold multiple meanings; aside from its plain sense, Koheleth's proverb also implies that a reputation is better than elegant funerary preparations, for aromatic oils were used in preparing a corpse for burial. Another implication may be that a (good) reputation is better than being anointed with fragrant unguents, which were distributed as a luxury at banquets.

A good name In the Hebrew, "good" is not stated but implied.

A good name is better than fragrant oil The words themselves glide like oil: *Tov sheim mi-shemen tov*. This is a variant of Prov. 22:1, "A repute [*sheim;* literally, 'a name'] is preferable to great wealth, and grace better than silver and gold." A name *(sheim)* can be a memorial, parallel to *zeikher,* "memory" (Job 18:17; Prov. 10:7; see also Isa. 14:22; 66:22). Rashbam says that "oil" is specifically the oil of the balsam tree, whose fragrance (like a reputation) spreads about. He notes that a name is compared to fine oil in Song 1:3.

the day of death than the day of birth How so? One answer is that our reputation is not secure until we die and can no longer blemish it (Rashbam). As Ben Sira says, "Call no man happy before he dies, for a man is known [only] at his end" (11:28). And Hillel said, "Do not trust yourself till the day of your death" (Avot 2:4).

[2]It is better to go to a house of mourning than to a
house of feasting; for that is the end of every man,
and a living one should take it to heart.
[3]Vexation is better than revelry; for though
the face be sad, the heart may be glad [4]Wise men are
drawn to a house of mourning, and fools to a house
of merrymaking.

2 טוֹב לָלֶכֶת אֶל־בֵּית־אֵבֶל מִלֶּכֶת אֶל־
בֵּית מִשְׁתֶּה בַּאֲשֶׁר הוּא סוֹף כָּל־הָאָדָם
וְהַחַי יִתֵּן אֶל־לִבּוֹ:
3 טוֹב כַּעַס מִשְּׂחֹק כִּי־בְרֹעַ פָּנִים יִיטַב
לֵב: 4 לֵב חֲכָמִים בְּבֵית אֵבֶל וְלֵב כְּסִילִים
בְּבֵית שִׂמְחָה:

Perhaps this verse is a proverb that Koheleth is quoting for the sake of the second sentence, which gives voice to his melancholy outlook (Gordis). Koheleth may be praising death for releasing mortals from the heavy awareness of injustice and from life's toils (4:3; 6:3).

2. This advice seems out of place in a book that emphatically advocates enjoyment of the pleasures of eating and drinking—and recommends merriment for diverting us from sadness (5:19). But Koheleth is not always consistent in what he values, and conflicting counsels may be appropriate in different circumstances. Here he commends sober recognition of the universality of death. Koheleth values knowledge, even though he complains about the discomfort it brings (1:18). If death is our fate, we should face it.

Some see a moral lesson here. Rashbam says that reflecting on death will help us avoid sin. Sforno believes that Koheleth's point is that only at a funeral is it known whether the deceased attained a good reputation, "and one who is living should take it to heart" and try to keep his own name clean (Sforno).

3. ***for though the face be sad, the heart may be glad*** The rhyme attempts to capture the Hebrew's opposition of bad/good idioms. By this translation, the verse means that one's facial expression may belie his true feelings. Thus read, the verse seems to respond to Proverbs 15:13, "A joyful heart makes a cheerful face; a sad heart makes a despondent mood."

The literal translation of verse 3b is, "for in badness of face the heart is made good." This allows for a double entendre. In the light of verse 3a, "badness of face" means a vexed scowl. Rashi explains the "scowl" as a show of anger, which may provide needed chastisement and improve the listener's mind ("heart"). For example, it would have been better for the generation of the Flood if God had earlier shown them an angry face, so as to bring them to the right path (cf. Gen. 6:1–13). It would have been better if David had scolded his sons (cf. 1 Kings 1:6) rather than "laughing" with them. With regard to child rearing, Ben Sira says, "Do not laugh with him [your son], lest you later sorrow with him" (30:10a). ("Laughing" means to behave in a frivolous manner.) Ecclesiastes 7:5 likewise praises chastisement.

4. Literally, "The heart of wise men is in the house of mourning, and the heart of fools is in the house of merrymaking." In other words, the wise are always cognizant of death, while the foolish think only of fun. This verse reiterates verse 2; the "house of merrymaking" *(beyt simḥah)* is the same as the "house of feasting" *(beyt mishteh)* (v. 2).[25] Neither term designates improper behavior, and Koheleth elsewhere recommends both.

It is strange to find a call to contemplate death in an author who (almost alone in the Hebrew Bible) is depressed by human mortality. Nor do we expect to hear disapproval of

5 It is better to listen to a wise man's reproof than to
listen to the praise of fools. 6 For the levity of the fool
is like the crackling of nettles under a kettle. But that
too is illusory; 7 for cheating may rob the wise man of
reason and destroy the prudence of the cautious.

5 טוֹב לִשְׁמֹעַ גַּעֲרַת חָכָם מֵאִישׁ שֹׁמֵעַ
שִׁיר כְּסִילִים׃ 6 כִּי כְקוֹל הַסִּירִים תַּחַת
הַסִּיר כֵּן שְׂחֹק הַכְּסִיל וְגַם־זֶה הָבֶל׃ 7 כִּי
הָעֹשֶׁק יְהוֹלֵל חָכָם וִיאַבֵּד אֶת־לֵב
מַתָּנָה׃

feasting in a work that recommends it warmly (see especially 9:7–10 and 11:9–10). This is an inconsistency less in Koheleth's logic than in his spirit. Just as he knows that enjoyment is good but does not seem disposed to embrace it himself, so too he would rather not brood on death but cannot help doing so.

Possibly this is a proverb that originally meant that one *should* think of death so as to avoid sin (thus Rashbam), but Koheleth would have us understand it cynically: The wise, knowing life's futility, are melancholy (1:18), while fools have a good time.

*5. **praise*** Hebrew *shir,* "song." The fool's merry song is meaningless and grating (see next verse).

6. This saying is onomatopoeic—crackling with repeated *k*-sounds, sibilants, and "*i*" vowels (pronounced "ee"): *Ki ke-khol ha-sirim taḥat ha-sir ken seḥok ha-kesil.* The word *sirim* ("thorns") puns on *sir* ("kettle"). The levity (lit. "laughter") of the fools is as vapid and irritating as nettles crackling in the fire. And thorns, unlike wood, produce no useful heat when burnt; that is, they provide no enlightenment (Rashbam).

illusory [hevel] Better: "senseless"; see Keywords in the introduction. (The levity—literally, "laughter"—of fools is not illusory per se, but an unpleasant reality.)

7. A variant of Deut. 16:19b ("You shall not take bribes, for bribes blind the eyes of the discerning and upset the pleas of the just"); similarly Exod. 23:8. The "wise," that is, the learned, served as judges.

It is hard to connect this verse to either the preceding or following context. Ibn Ezra sees continuity in the way that after mentioning the revelry that might make a wise man foolish, Koheleth adds another thing that can have that effect—cheating. Perhaps a proverb once stood here and provided a better transition. A saying like Prov. 16:8 would fit well: "Better a little with righteousness than a large income with injustice" (suggested by Delitzsch).[26]

cheating Hebrew: *'oshek.* This usually means "oppression," but here its sense is "cheating" or "dishonest money," as in Lev. 5:23 and Ps. 62:11.

may rob Better: "robs." This is a fact, not a possibility.

prudence Hebrew *lev,* literally, "heart, mind."

cautious Hebrew *mattanah;* better: "gift." Though the similar-sounding *matun* means "patient" or "cautious" in postbiblical Hebrew, here as elsewhere *mattanah* means "gift" or "bribe," parallel to *'oshek* ("cheating").

destroy the prudence of the cautious Better: "a gift ruins the mind." See previous two Comments.

8 The end of a matter is better than the beginning
of it.
Better a patient spirit than a haughty spirit.
9 Don't let your spirit be quickly vexed, for vexation
abides in the breasts of fools.
10 Don't say, "How has it happened that former times
were better than these?" For it is not wise of you to
ask that question.

8 טֹ֥וב אַחֲרִ֛ית דָּבָ֖ר מֵֽרֵאשִׁית֑וֹ
טֹ֥וב אֶֽרֶךְ־ר֖וּחַ מִגְּבַהּ־רֽוּחַ׃
9 אַל־תְּבַהֵ֥ל בְּרֽוּחֲךָ֖ לִכְע֑וֹס כִּ֣י כַ֔עַס בְּחֵ֥יק
כְּסִילִ֖ים יָנֽוּחַ׃
10 אַל־תֹּאמַר֙ מֶ֣ה הָיָ֔ה שֶׁהַיָּמִים֙
הָרִ֣אשֹׁנִ֔ים הָי֥וּ טוֹבִ֖ים מֵאֵ֑לֶּה כִּ֛י לֹ֥א
מֵחָכְמָ֖ה שָׁאַ֥לְתָּ עַל־זֶֽה׃

THE SENSIBLE AND PATIENT SPIRIT (7:8–10)

In a world where nothing can be fundamentally changed (1:9; 3:14–15), all that can be controlled is one's own attitudes. One must remain patient for events to run their course.

*8. **The end of a matter is better than the beginning of it*** This recalls 7:1. Only when a series of events reaches its conclusion can we know the outcome; before that we can only guess. Therefore Koheleth advises patience (v. 8b). Rabbi Meir explained the verse by an example: an investment in a stock of goods may lose money at first but finally earn a profit (Koh. R.). This interpretation is in accord with 11:1, "Send your bread forth upon the waters, for after many days you will find it."

matter Hebrew *davar,* which also means "word." Taking it as "word," Rashbam and Rashi understand Koheleth to be advising us to listen patiently to others until they have had their say, for only then can their intentions be known.

patient spirit . . . haughty spirit In a world when one cannot predict or control the outcome of events, the best stance is patience and resignation. The opposite of this is a "haughty" spirit, for only the arrogant would feel confident in their knowledge of what lies ahead. On the face of it, the saying is rather trite, for who would ever favor haughtiness per se? It is the saying's *literal* meaning that gives it interest: "Better a long spirit than a tall spirit." This is a comparison of geometric metaphors about something—the spirit—that actually has neither dimension.[27]

*9. **Don't let your spirit be quickly vexed, for vexation abides in the breasts of fools*** This admonition does not contradict verse 3, for it does not condemn vexation altogether, but only hasty responses. Sometimes anger is justified. Rabbi Eliezer similarly warns, "Be not easily angered" (Avot 2:10).

10. This verse is usually understood as repudiating a sentimental preference for the old days, as if they were better than the present. But Koheleth does not *deny* the proposition that "former times were better than these"; he only admonishes us not to *ask* about this. Perhaps they were better, but it is best not to raise the issue—best not to compare past and present.

Ibn Yaḥyah aptly compares this question to Job's complaints: It expresses grief at a downturn in one's fortunes. The proper attitude toward such a decline is exemplified in Eccl. 7:14, which also teaches the right response to the ups and downs of life: Take things as they come.

11 Wisdom is as good as a patrimony, and even better,
for those who behold the sun. 12 For to be in the
shelter of wisdom is to be also in the shelter of money,
and the advantage of intelligence is that wisdom
preserves the life of him who possesses it.
13 Consider God's doing! Who can straighten what He
has twisted? 14 So in a time of good fortune enjoy the

11 טוֹבָה חָכְמָה עִם־נַחֲלָה וְיֹתֵר לְרֹאֵי
הַשָּׁמֶשׁ׃ 12 כִּי בְּצֵל הַחָכְמָה בְּצֵל הַכָּסֶף
וְיִתְרוֹן דַּעַת הַחָכְמָה תְּחַיֶּה בְעָלֶיהָ׃
13 רְאֵה אֶת־מַעֲשֵׂה הָאֱלֹהִים כִּי מִי יוּכַל
לְתַקֵּן אֵת אֲשֶׁר עִוְּתוֹ׃ 14 בְּיוֹם טוֹבָה הֱיֵה

THE ADVANTAGE OF WISDOM (7:11–12 + 19)

11. Literally, "Wisdom is good with an inheritance." Wisdom is especially effective if one has a material inheritance to back it up. After all, "A poor man's wisdom is scorned, and his words are not heeded" (9:16). Moreover, without wisdom (that is, good sense), the inheritance will not endure (Rashbam).

patrimony Hebrew *naḥalah,* which is almost always a landed inheritance. For Koheleth, this is an especially desirable form of wealth, since it comes without strain and toil.

12. Wisdom brings and secures wealth (Rashi). "Wisdom" in the Bible includes the practical skills needed for financial success; see, for example, Prov. 3:16, 8:18, and 24:3–4.

shelter... shelter Literally, "shade," which implies protection.[28]

the advantage [yitron] of intelligence is that wisdom preserves... life Wealth, though desirable, does not help its owner escape death. This is the message of Prov. 11:4, "Wealth is of no avail on the day of wrath, but righteousness saves from death"; and compare Prov. 11:28. Intelligence (*da'at,* lit. "knowledge") protects its possessors from death (or at least is supposed to do so), not by extending their lives indefinitely, but by preserving them from sudden disaster (Prov. 3:2; 16a, 18; 8:35a; and often).

Verse 19 may originally have stood here; see its Comment, below.

IGNORANCE AND FRAILTY (7:13–14)

Verse 13b echoes 1:15a, but this time Koheleth explicitly imputes the "twisting" to God; thus too in verse 14.

13. ***God's doing*** That is, events such as the misfortunes mentioned in verse 14 and the injustices described in verse 15.

twisted Hebrew *'ivvet.* Job uses the same word in blaming God for perverting justice in his own case (Job 19:6).

14. ***enjoy the good fortune*** Literally, "be in good," that is, enjoy yourself. This is the heart of Koheleth's teaching: We cannot know what will come to pass, so we must grasp whatever blessings the moment offers.

Rashi believes that this good fortune is a reward for righteousness, but Koheleth does not make moral distinctions in this passage. He is referring to the normal ups and downs of life, and he objects to the notion that these necessarily correspond to moral deserts.

good fortune; and in a time of misfortune, reflect:
The one no less than the other was God's doing;
consequently, man may find no fault with Him.
15 In my own brief span of life, I have seen both these
things: sometimes a good man perishes in spite of his
goodness, and sometimes a wicked one endures in
spite of his wickedness. 16 So don't overdo goodness

בְּטוֹב וּבְיוֹם רָעָה רְאֵה גַּם אֶת־זֶה לְעֻמַּת־
זֶה עָשָׂה הָאֱלֹהִים עַל־דִּבְרַת שֶׁלֹּא יִמְצָא
הָאָדָם אַחֲרָיו מְאוּמָה׃
15 אֶת־הַכֹּל רָאִיתִי בִּימֵי הֶבְלִי יֵשׁ צַדִּיק
אֹבֵד בְּצִדְקוֹ וְיֵשׁ רָשָׁע מַאֲרִיךְ בְּרָעָתוֹ׃
16 אַל־תְּהִי צַדִּיק הַרְבֵּה וְאַל־תִּתְחַכַּם

time of misfortune Literally, "day of evil." This is not the time of punishment, as Rashi and Rashbam think, for then the crisis would call for repentance, not a comment like the next sentence. Rather, it is whenever bad things happen, without any visible rationale. Koheleth proceeds to ponder such situations in the next unit.

The one no less than the other was God's doing Literally, "God has made the one to happen next to the other." The issue is the proximity of opposites, not their cause.

God's doing The belief that God is responsible for misfortune may sound radical, but it is found throughout the Bible. Even God is said to assert this powerfully in Isa. 45:7, "I form light and create darkness, I make weal and create woe—I the LORD do all these things."

may find no fault with Him Literally, "can find no fault after him." This rendering is based on a similar Aramaic usage, equating *me'umah* (which usually means "anything") with *mum* or *me'um* "blemish" (Ginsberg). But Koheleth elsewhere uses *'aḥarav* ("after him, afterward") with verbs of knowing to state our ignorance of our own future (3:22, 6:12, 10:14), and we should accordingly translate here: "cannot discover anything about what will be afterward"; God keeps the wheel of fortune turning, so to speak, in order to prevent humans from knowing the future. Similarly, divine jealousy of human knowledge is a motif in the Garden of Eden story (Gen. 3:5, 22).

THE PARADOXES OF JUSTICE (7:15–18, [19], 20–22)

15. In my own brief span [hevel] of life Or, "in my senseless life."

sometimes a good man perishes Literally, "there is a good man who perishes." Koheleth thinks that God's rule is just, but he knows that injustices do occur. Ibn Ezra observed that these violations are anomalies and not the rule. But this does not solve the problem, because God's justice—unlike ours—*could* be perfect.

in spite of... in spite of Hebrew *be-*, a prefixed preposition that usually means "in, by." Better: "in [the condition of]..." The inequitable fates occur in violation of the expected consequences of one's actions.

Sforno reads this as an assertion of the reach of divine justice: God may punish a good person for a long-ago transgression and spare a wicked one for a past good deed. Thus it is wise to fulfill the Commandments precisely.

goodness Hebrew *tzedek;* better: "righteousness."

16–17. don't overdo goodness Literally, "don't be very righteous [*tzaddik*]." We should accept in ourselves a mixture of good and bad. Straining for perfection is

יוֹתֵ֑ר לָ֖מָּה תִּשּׁוֹמֵֽם׃ 17 אַל־תִּרְשַׁ֥ע הַרְבֵּ֖ה
וְאַל־תְּהִ֣י סָכָ֑ל לָ֥מָּה תָמ֖וּת בְּלֹ֥א עִתֶּֽךָ׃
18 ט֚וֹב אֲשֶׁ֣ר תֶּאֱחֹ֣ז בָּזֶ֔ה וְגַם־מִזֶּ֖ה אַל־
תַּנַּ֣ח אֶת־יָדֶ֑ךָ כִּֽי־יְרֵ֥א אֱלֹהִ֖ים יֵצֵ֥א אֶת־
כֻּלָּֽם׃
19 הַֽחָכְמָ֖ה תָּעֹ֣ז לֶחָכָ֑ם מֵֽעֲשָׂרָה֙ שַׁלִּיטִ֔ים
אֲשֶׁ֥ר הָי֖וּ בָּעִֽיר׃

and don't act the wise man to excess, or you may be
dumfounded. 17 Don't overdo wickedness and don't
be a fool, or you may die before your time. 18 It is best
that you grasp the one without letting go of the other,
for one who fears God will do his duty by both.
19 Wisdom is more of a stronghold to a wise man than
ten magnates that a city may contain.

presumptuous, a refusal to accept human limitations. After all, no one can be entirely righteous (v. 20). As examples of excessive "righteousness," Ibn Ezra mentions praying all day and self-affliction, practices he ascribes to the hermits in the lands of Edom and Ishmael. Koheleth Rabbah cites Saul's unwarranted mercy to Agag (1 Sam. 15), which was a false virtue, an attempt to be more righteous than the Creator.

don't act the wise man to excess Better: "Nor be excessively wise." True, the *hitpa'el* stem, to which *tithakkam* belongs, can imply pretense, as in 2 Sam. 13:5, *hithal,* "pretend to be sick." Nevertheless, the parallel admonitions show that Koheleth is warning against *being* certain things, not against feigning. And in Exod. 1:10, Pharaoh uses this same verb to refer to what he believes to be actual wisdom: "Let us deal shrewdly [*nithakkemah*] with them" (NJPS). That is, we should not seek too much wisdom—as Koheleth did—for it may open our eyes to life's absurdities and inequities (see v. 15) and leave us vexed (1:18) and dumbfounded (7:16b).

Don't overdo wickedness Literally, "Don't be very wicked." This sounds as if Koheleth would allow a moderate degree of wickedness. The commentators try to avoid this impression in various ways. Ibn Ezra claims that *rasha'* ("wicked") here refers to worldly matters, in which you should busy yourself only to the degree necessary. However, *rasha'* always refers to real wickedness. Koheleth is not advocating it but rather accepting its inevitability: all humans are inescapably flawed (7:20), but they can at least avoid being *very* wicked.

you may die before your time Koheleth does not abandon the principle that wickedness will, at least usually, result in early death, though he knows that this does not always happen.

18. the one . . . the other Probably referring to the two counsels offered in verses 16–17. Rashi says that the reference is to righteousness and wickedness; grasping wickedness means that if a righteous prophet tells you something that *seems* wicked, you should still take it seriously, as when Samuel commanded Saul to kill Agag (1 Sam. 15:3).

both That is, both counsels, verses 16 and 17. An alternative translation is "will depart from both," that is, from both excessive righteousness and excessive wickedness.

19. This verse disrupts the connection between verses 18 and 20. It makes better sense after verse 12. It perhaps belonged there originally and should be read in that context (Ginsberg).

In the MT, wisdom is more of a protection than ten magnates or "rulers" in the city. The ten magnates are sometimes identified with the "ten notables" who governed some Hellenistic cities, such as Tiberias and, perhaps, Jerusalem (Josephus, *Vita* 13.57). This

20 For there is not one good man on earth who does
what is best and doesn't err.
21 Finally, don't pay attention to everything that is
said, so that you may not hear your slave reviling you;
22 for well you remember the many times that you
yourself have reviled others.
23 All this I tested with wisdom. I thought I could
fathom it, but it eludes me. 24 [The secret of] what
happens is elusive and deep, deep down; who can

20 כִּי אָדָם אֵין צַדִּיק בָּאָרֶץ אֲשֶׁר יַעֲשֶׂה־
טּוֹב וְלֹא יֶחֱטָא׃
21 גַּם לְכָל־הַדְּבָרִים אֲשֶׁר יְדַבֵּרוּ אַל־
תִּתֵּן לִבֶּךָ אֲשֶׁר לֹא־תִשְׁמַע אֶת־עַבְדְּךָ
מְקַלְלֶךָ׃ 22 כִּי גַּם־פְּעָמִים רַבּוֹת יָדַע לִבֶּךָ
אֲשֶׁר גַּם־את אַתָּה קִלַּלְתָּ אֲחֵרִים׃
23 כָּל־זֹה נִסִּיתִי בַחָכְמָה אָמַרְתִּי אֶחְכָּמָה
וְהִיא רְחוֹקָה מִמֶּנִּי׃ 24 רָחוֹק מַה־שֶּׁהָיָה

body, however, was a Roman institution and was not in place before the first century C.E. Nor is it clear how or why "ten magnates" would help the wise man at all. However, by dividing the words differently and repointing them, we can translate "than the *wealth* of magnates" (Transl.).[29] Wisdom is more powerful than great wealth (cf. vv. 11–12).

is more of a stronghold Or: "provides strength to." It is good to have both wisdom and wealth, but of the two, wisdom is the better; see 7:11–12.

20. This gives the reason for the advice of verses 16–18: To be human is to err (compare Ps. 143:2; Prov. 20:9; Job 4:17–19). It is not realistic to expect or demand great righteousness from anyone, including yourself.

21. ***don't pay attention to everything that is said*** Do not listen to gossip, or you'll never be at peace (Ibn Ezra). If you listen to gossip (such as you yourself are guilty of; v. 22), you are just exposing yourself to the sting of insults.

your slave *Even* your slave. If your slave, who is in your power and has the most to fear from you, would revile you, how much the more so would others.

22. ***for well you remember*** Literally, "your heart knows"; the same idiom occurs again in 8:5. You know that people must be gossiping and disparaging you behind your back, because you have done the same to others.

THE INEVITABILITY OF IGNORANCE (7:23–24)

Koheleth summarizes his investigations. He had set out to "study and to probe with wisdom all that happens under the sun" (1:13) but he realizes that he fell short of his goal. He amassed much wisdom—he learned a lot—yet the deeper wisdom eluded him.

23. ***All this*** Apparently, all the things that Koheleth has discussed so far. (Others relate it to 6:12 [Transl.].) Though he was wise in the sense of being learned and intelligent, he could not gain real understanding of what happens in life. Now he looks back on his search and findings and recognizes their inadequacy.

24. ***what happens*** That is, life itself, which is not only mysterious, but also remains elusive and distant—far from even the sage's grasp.

discover it? 25 I put my mind to studying, exploring,
and seeking wisdom and the reason of things, and to

וְעָמֹק ׀ עָמֹק מִי יִמְצָאֶנּוּ׃ 25 סַבּוֹתִי אֲנִי
וְלִבִּי לָדַעַת וְלָתוּר וּבַקֵּשׁ חָכְמָה וְחֶשְׁבּוֹן

WOMAN (7:25–8:1a)

Koheleth did not find wisdom, but he did discover "wickedness, stupidity, madness, and folly." He found these concentrated in womankind.

Koheleth is nothing if not provocative, and this passage in particular has stirred up strong debate. Many attempts have been made to soften the misogynistic tone. Some scholars surmise that Koheleth is quoting an opinion and rebutting it,[30] but there is no indication of either quotation or rebuttal. One common view is that he is condemning only those women who fit the description. By this understanding, we would translate, "I find more bitter than death the woman who is all traps, whose hands are fetters, and whose heart is snares." In Koheleth Rabbah, R. Judah understands the verse this way, as do Rashbam, Sforno, and some modern commentators. But 7:28 shows that Koheleth is denouncing all of womankind, not just the wicked among them, for he cannot find even one (satisfactory) woman in a thousand. Koheleth's castigation of women does resemble what Proverbs says about the "strange" or "forbidden" woman, who entraps a man in adultery. For example, "The mouth of a forbidden woman is a deep pit; he who is doomed by the LORD falls into it" (22:14; cf. 23:27). Koheleth, however, here asserts that *all* women are like that.

Koheleth's remark, unlike anything in Proverbs, condemns woman as such, and not only particular women. It is the only such remark in the Hebrew Bible, and even in Koheleth's own teachings it is not central. In any case, we should not treat Koheleth's grousing about the opposite sex as a philosophical proposition. It is clearly hyperbolic. If Koheleth truly believed that all women were this malign, he could not have urged the enjoyment of life "with a woman you love" (9:9a), for any such enjoyment would be impossible. Perhaps he intends his remark in 7:25–8:1a as a wisecrack rather than a solemn statement. Verse 29 suggests self-directed irony, as if to say: "See what strange things happen when men have engaged in too much reasoning!" Anyway, he doesn't think too highly of men either.

People can be inconsistent in the feelings about the opposite sex. In a Babylonian book of a satirical cast, a slave gives his master reasons for loving a woman, then supplies reasons to avoid it:

> "Servant, listen to me."
> "Yes, master, yes."
> "I will fall in love with a woman."
> "[So], fall in love, master, fall in love. The man who falls in love with a woman forgets sorrow and care."
> "No, servant, I will certainly not fall in love with a woman."
> "[Do not] fall in love, master, do not fall in love. A woman is a pitfall, a pitfall, a hole, a ditch, a woman is a sharp iron dagger that slashes a man's throat."[31]

In 9:9, Koheleth softens his tone and includes women among the agreeable things that a man should enjoy. Koheleth is inconsistent about the other good things in (a man's) life as well. See "Koheleth on Pleasure" at the start of chapter 2.

25. I put my mind to studying Literally, "I turned, I and my heart, to know." See Comment to 1:13.

studying wickedness, stupidity, madness, and folly.
26 Now, I find woman more bitter than death; she is
all traps, her hands are fetters and her heart is snares.
He who is pleasing to God escapes her, and he who
is displeasing is caught by her. 27 See, this is what
I found, said Koheleth, item by item in my search for
the reason of things. 28 As for what I sought further
but did not find, I found only one human being in a
thousand, and the one I found among so many was

וְלָדַעַת רֶשַׁע כֶּסֶל וְהַסִּכְלוּת הוֹלֵלוֹת׃
26 וּמוֹצֶא אֲנִי מַר מִמָּוֶת אֶת־הָאִשָּׁה
אֲשֶׁר־הִיא מְצוֹדִים וַחֲרָמִים לִבָּהּ
אֲסוּרִים יָדֶיהָ טוֹב לִפְנֵי הָאֱלֹהִים יִמָּלֵט
מִמֶּנָּה וְחוֹטֵא יִלָּכֶד בָּהּ׃ 27 רְאֵה זֶה
מָצָאתִי אָמְרָה קֹהֶלֶת אַחַת לְאַחַת
לִמְצֹא חֶשְׁבּוֹן׃ 28 אֲשֶׁר עוֹד־בִּקְשָׁה נַפְשִׁי
וְלֹא מָצָאתִי אָדָם אֶחָד מֵאֶלֶף מָצָאתִי

the reason of things Literally, "calculations" (likewise in vv. 27b and 29b). Koheleth is performing an arithmetical calculation, so to speak, adding one (woman) to another, and coming to an exasperating result: zero (v. 28).

26. ***she is all traps*** What Koheleth fears about women is that they "trap" men by arousing their lust. Sforno explains that "her hands are fetters" means that "once a man begins to be seduced he is like a prisoner and forced to do her will," and "Her heart is snares" refers to her seductive tricks. Alternatively, "her heart" is her own sexual desire, which arouses the man's. Koheleth reveals anxiety about sexual desire in itself, apart from any sins it might entice a man to commit. Contrast his words with the ancient love song motif wherein lovers delight in being "ensnared" by each other's attractions.[32]

He who is pleasing to God . . . he who is displeasing Literally, "good before God . . . a sinner." These are the fortunate and the unfortunate man, respectively—quite apart from his virtue or lack thereof. Since Koheleth does not regard himself as "pleasing to God," he may be implying that he himself was "caught"—unhappily—by a woman's snare. See Comment to 2:26; here too we could translate *ḥote'* as "sinner" in quotation marks, to suggest that the word is used facetiously. Koheleth seems to be targeting Prov. 18:22, "He who finds a wife [*'ishah*] has found happiness [lit. "good"], and has won the favor of the Lord."

27. Koheleth pursues the arithmetical imagery. He implies that he appraised women assiduously, as he did with other pleasant things in 2:1–11. His claim of extensive experience with women alludes to the tradition of Solomon's thousand wives (1 Kings 11:3), who are blamed for leading him into transgression (1 Kings 11:1–8; Neh. 13:25–26).

said Koheleth Read "said the Koheleth"[33]; see Comment on 1:1.

28. ***As for what I sought further*** What Koheleth sought was a woman. A minor emendation from אשר ("as for what") to אשה ("woman") produces a sentence more in line with Hebrew grammar: "I sought a woman continually but did not find one."

human being . . . woman Hebrew *'adam . . . 'ishah*. Of a thousand people, Koheleth found one (good) human being, but none of those thousand was a woman. Alternatively, *'adam,* which usually means "human being," "person," can mean "man" [male] when paired with "woman" [Gen. 2:25].) Then Koheleth is saying that he found one (good) *man* in a thousand but not even one (good) woman. Proverbs 31:10–31 speaks of the rarity of a good woman: "An excellent woman who can find?" (v. 10; NJPS: "What a rare find is a capable wife!"). There the purpose is to extol her preciousness, not to lament her statistical rarity, and the author of that poem believes that such a woman *can* be found. Koheleth does not.

never a woman. 29 But, see, this I did find: God made men plain, but they have engaged in too much reasoning.

וְאִשָּׁה בְכָל־אֵלֶּה לֹא מָצָאתִי׃ 29 לְבַד
רְאֵה־זֶה מָצָאתִי אֲשֶׁר עָשָׂה הָאֱלֹהִים
אֶת־הָאָדָם יָשָׁר וְהֵמָּה בִקְשׁוּ חִשְּׁבֹנוֹת
רַבִּים׃

8 Who is like the wise man, and who knows the meaning of the adage:
"A man's wisdom lights up his face,
So that his deep discontent is dissembled"?

ח מִי כְּהֶחָכָם וּמִי יוֹדֵעַ פֵּשֶׁר דָּבָר
חָכְמַת אָדָם תָּאִיר פָּנָיו
וְעֹז פָּנָיו יְשֻׁנֶּא*׃

v. 1. א׳ במקום ה׳

A third interpretation may be suggested: "man . . . wife."[34] (*'Ishah* can mean "woman" or "wife," and the phrase "find a woman" [*motze' 'ishah*] means to find a wife; e.g., Prov. 18:22, quoted above.[35] Thus "seeking a woman" would mean to look for a wife.) That is, Koheleth constantly sought a woman to marry but never found one—though he did find an occasional man to be a friend—so that married life was another part of happiness that escaped him. (His complaint in 2:18–19, about not knowing who would end up with his wealth, suggests that he at least had no sons.) The misogyny he expressed in 7:26 may be the cause—or result—of this failure.

Most commentators read the words in question as elliptical: "[good] human being" (or man) . . . [good] woman." Rashi paraphrases: "I further sought one among women who was worthy but did not find her, because they are all silly headed." (In commenting on verse 26, however, he allegorizes the woman as heresy.)

29. All of Koheleth's calculations have brought him to just this: the recognition that human cleverness collapses of its own weight. Koheleth seems to be poking fun at himself, for he is the one who undertook such calculations (v. 27). We may not be able to straighten out what God has twisted, but we can surely twist one thing that God made straight: ourselves.

plain Literally, "straight," referring not to the original creation of mankind but to every birth, when one begins life "straight" and direct.

too much reasoning Or "great calculations." Men go astray in seeking "calculations." This is the fault that Koheleth warned against in 7:16b: don't be too clever.

8:1a. Although most commentators understand this as a question that is answered in verse 2 by Koheleth himself, it actually belongs with 7:25–29. (The chapter divisions are very late and unimportant for interpretation.) This sentence and 7:23 bracket that unit by insisting on human ignorance. As Koheleth's own experience showed him, no one can *really* become wise.

Who is like the wise man The MT reads מי כהחכם, which implies that the wise man *does* know the meaning of the adage that follows; but this leaves the next clause with little function, since it is a rhetorical question implying that *no one* knows it. (Also problematic is the uncontracted form of כהחכם, "like the wise man." We would expect כחכם.) However, if these words are divided as מי כה חכם (a reading reflected in the ancient Greek versions), it too is a rhetorical question: "Who is so wise . . . ?" or "Who here is wise?"

2 I do! "Obey the king's orders—and don't rush into

אֲנִי֙ פִּי־מֶ֣לֶךְ שְׁמֹ֔ור וְעַ֕ל דִּבְרַ֖ת שְׁבוּעַ֥ת 2

the adage? Hebrew *davar* (lit. "word, thing"); better: "anything." Thus the rhetorical question continues, ". . . and who understands the meaning of anything?!" The implicit answer is "*no one*"—no one is that wise!

AUTHORITY AND POWER (8:1b–9)

Advice on how to get along in the shadow of the king's arbitrary authority leads to reflections about *shilton,* which can be rendered "rule," "authority," or "control." Earlier wisdom too is aware of the dangers of power. The Book of Proverbs warns about the king's wrath (e.g., "The terror of a king is like the roar of a lion; he who provokes his anger risks his life"; 20:2), but on the whole it is less chary than Koheleth of the king's temper and more confident of his justice. Later, living under the Romans, R. Shemaiah shares Koheleth's suspicions: "Do not become intimate with the authorities" (Avot 1:10). And R. Gamaliel III warns, "Be wary of the authorities, for they bring a man near them only for their own ends. They appear to be friends when it is useful to them, but they do not stand by a man in trouble" (Avot 2:3).

It is virtually impossible that the author or the readers of Ecclesiastes would have access to an actual king. "King" may stand for all authorities within the imperial hierarchy (mentioned in 5:7), whose power was an extension of the king's.

Koheleth Rabbah, Rashi, Rashbam, and other traditional commentators identify the "king" as God, whose command, the Torah, is supreme and must be obeyed. The "oath" (v. 2) is then Israel's pledge of obedience at Mount Horeb. By this reading, the passage is a fervent affirmation of obedience—to God. The Midrash identifies the "wise man" variously as God, Adam, Israel, the Torah scholar, and Moses (Koh. R.).

8:1. Ben Sira rephrases this verse: "The heart of a man changes his face, whether for the better or for the worse" (13:25).

A man's wisdom lights up his face Wisdom gives one a cheerful mien. Perhaps originally meant to praise the effect of wisdom, in this context the saying has a more cynical tenor: It is wise to put on a cheerful face when you are around the ruler (or another powerful man), so as not to arouse his suspicion. A bright face would signify contentment, and a contented underling is less dangerous to his master. As Ben Sira says, "The sign of a good heart is a shining face, while withdrawal [?] and brooding (are signs of) wicked plans" (13:26).

deep discontent Hebrew *'oz panav;* more precisely, "the brazenness of his face."

dissembled Prudence—an aspect of wisdom—will prompt one to disguise feelings such as arrogance and resentment toward the despot.

2. ***I do*** As the text stands, Koheleth is answering his own question via the rest of the verse; but the letters *'ny,* interpreted as "I," are probably accidental and should be deleted.[36]

don't rush NJPS places this phrase before the verse division, whereas MT begins verse 3 with it. By the masoretic division, we would translate, (2) "I counsel thee: keep the king's command, and that in regard of the oath of God. (3a) Be not hasty to go out of his presence" (Old JPS). This agrees with 10:4 but strains the syntax.

uttering an oath by God." 3 Leave his presence; do
not tarry in a dangerous situation, for he can do
anything he pleases; 4 inasmuch as a king's command
is authoritative, and none can say to him, "What are
you doing?" 5 One who obeys orders will not suffer
from the dangerous situation.

אֱלֹהִים׃ 3 אַל־תִּבָּהֵל מִפָּנָיו תֵּלֵךְ אַל־
תַּעֲמֹד בְּדָבָר רָע כִּי כָּל־אֲשֶׁר יַחְפֹּץ
יַעֲשֶׂה׃ 4 בַּאֲשֶׁר דְּבַר־מֶלֶךְ שִׁלְטוֹן וּמִי
יֹאמַר־לוֹ מַה־תַּעֲשֶׂה׃ 5 שׁוֹמֵר מִצְוָה לֹא
יֵדַע דָּבָר רָע

oath by God An oath sworn in God's name. In context, perhaps an avowal of innocence when accused by the king of some wrongdoing.

3. When the king is angry, get out of his way as soon as possible. In 10:4, Koheleth suggests a different way to handle this situation.

4. ***"What are you doing?"*** A challenge to authority; Job uses this very phrase to describe God's despotic authority (9:12b); see also Isa. 45:9.

5. ***One who obeys orders will not suffer from the dangerous situation*** This is not an absolute claim that the obedient never suffer. No one, and certainly not Koheleth, would make that claim. The Hebrew may give that impression, since "the dangerous situation" is, literally, "a bad thing," but in context, the verse teaches that obedience to a ruler will protect a man (a court official is in mind) from the ruler's anger in a particular "dangerous situation."

Since the Hebrew for "orders" is *mitzvah,* "commandment," traditional interpreters could understand the verse to mean that one who obeys God's commands will not suffer evil in the long run.

a time of doom Hebrew *'et u-mishpat,* literally, "a time and judgment." (In hendiadys, a Hebrew usage frequent in Ecclesiastes, "A and B" can mean "A of B"). This phrase occurs in verse 6 as well. *Mishpat* has several meanings, including "law," "judgment," "punishment," and "right condition." Because of this ambiguity, both verses are ambiguous.

"A time of doom" is death itself, seen as a judgment on all humans. This may be synonymous with "a time of misfortune" in 9:12 (Transl.).

"A time of judgment" would be when God punishes the tyrant. The prudent man keeps his head down and remains obedient and pliable, confident that despots will eventually pay for their wickedness. Koheleth affirms divine judgment, though inconsistently (3:17a; 5:5b; 8:12b–13; 11:9b).

Alternatively, *'et u-mishpat* can mean either "the time and right way" or "the right time." This alternative is supported by the next verse and by the tenor of the passage: The wise man knows the right time and way to do things [3:1–8]—such as smiling, or remaining in the ruler's presence, or leaving, or swearing an oath.)

This passage (vv. 1–5) bears a strong resemblance to a passage in the Counsels of Aḥiqar:

> Here is a difficult thing before you:
> Do not stand opposed to the king.
> Quicker than lightning is his anger.
> As for you, take care for yourself.
> May he not ignite (his anger) against your words
> and you consequently depart (life) before your time.

A wise man, however, will bear in mind that there is a
time of doom. 6 For there is a time for every
experience, including the doom; for a man's calamity
overwhelms him. 7 Indeed, he does not know what is
to happen; even when it is on the point of happening,
who can tell him? 8 No man has authority over the
lifebreath—to hold back the lifebreath; there is no

וְעֵת וּמִשְׁפָּט יֵדַע לֵב חָכָם׃ 6 כִּי לְכָל־
חֵפֶץ יֵשׁ עֵת וּמִשְׁפָּט כִּי־רָעַת הָאָדָם רַבָּה
עָלָיו׃ 7 כִּי־אֵינֶנּוּ יֹדֵעַ מַה־שֶּׁיִּהְיֶה כִּי
כַּאֲשֶׁר יִהְיֶה מִי יַגִּיד לוֹ׃ 8 אֵין אָדָם שַׁלִּיט
בָּרוּחַ לִכְלוֹא אֶת־הָרוּחַ וְאֵין שִׁלְטוֹן בְּיוֹם

> If the king's word is commanded you,
> it is a burning fire.
> Quickly do it, lest it ignite against you and burn your hands.
> But rather let the king's words be the delight of your heart. (lines 101–104a).

6. ***For there is a time for every experience*** Literally, "For every matter has time and judgment" (*'et u-mishpat*). On the ambiguity of this phrase, see the Comment on verse 5. Here it can refer to the time of the "judgment" that falls on the ruler, or to the right time and way to do things. The latter is supported by 3:1–9, according to which everything has its right time.

a man's calamity Hebrew *ra'at ha-'adam,* literally, "man's evil" or "...misfortune." This is probably death, which is called an "evil time" in 9:12. A wise man should know the right time and procedure and (as the preceding verses teach) endure unpleasantness patiently, because he knows that the tyrant too will die; see verse 8.

7. ***even when it is on the point of happening, who can tell him?*** Literally, "for *when* it will be, who can tell him?" NJPS understands this to mean that a man does not know when he is close to death. We may take it more broadly: humans do not know *what* lies ahead. As Koheleth says, "And a man cannot even know his time" (9:12a), that is, the time of his death. Human ignorance of the future is a frequent topic in Wisdom Literature; for example, Prov. 27:1; Sira 11:19; and numerous Egyptian parallels. Such statements seek to induce an attitude of humility. Only Koheleth seems truly troubled by this inevitable ignorance.

8. No one, not even the king, is ruler *(shallit)* over one's own lifebreath *(ruaḥ),* able to hold onto it on the day of death. The word for "breath" or "lifebreath," *ruaḥ,* also means "wind." The verse may be deliberately ambiguous so as to imply an analogy: Just as no human controls (*shallit*) the wind *(ruaḥ),* so no one, not even the ruler (called *shallit* in 10:5), can exercise control *(shilton)* on the appointed day of death and keep a grip on his lifebreath *(ruaḥ)*. Rabbi Levi observes that David is called "King David" fifty-two times, but in 1 Kings 2:1, when David's life is drawing to a close, he is called simply "David," for on that day he has no more authority (Koh. R.).

no mustering out from that war Literally, "no release [or "delegation"; *mishlaḥat*] in the war." It is unclear just what the "war" and the *mishlaḥat* (from the root *sh-l-ḥ,* "send") are. Some explain the war as the death-struggle every mortal faces.[37] Thus, according to Rashbam, Koheleth's point is that even if the king sends out his best "commandos" (*mishlaḥat* = a group "sent forth")—even they cannot successfully do battle with the Angel of Death. Or a *mishlaḥat* might be a surrogate sent to battle. Such a thing would be impossible in this "war," since no one can send his son or slave in his place (Koh. R.). Or *mishlaḥat* might mean "release." According to Deut. 20:5–7, certain soldiers

הַמָּ֑וֶת וְאֵ֤ין מִשְׁלַ֙חַת֙ בַּמִּלְחָמָ֔ה וְלֹֽא־
יְמַלֵּ֥ט רֶ֖שַׁע אֶת־בְּעָלָֽיו׃
9 אֶת־כָּל־זֶ֣ה רָאִ֗יתִי וְנָת֤וֹן אֶת־לִבִּי֙ לְכָל־
מַעֲשֶׂ֔ה אֲשֶׁ֥ר נַעֲשָׂ֖ה תַּ֣חַת הַשָּׁ֑מֶשׁ עֵ֗ת

authority over the day of death. There is no mustering out from that war; wickedness is powerless to save its owner.
9 All these things I observed; I noted all that went on under the sun, while men still had authority over men

are to be released from battle, namely those who recently built a house, planted a vineyard, or betrothed a woman, lest they die and another receive their new acquisitions. Koheleth (who is familiar with Deuteronomy; see Comment to 5:3–4) may be denying that such a release is possible in the struggle with death. This means that someone else, a stranger, perhaps, would enjoy the slain soldier's new possessions, an injustice that troubles Koheleth elsewhere (see especially 6:2). In fact, this very calamity is listed among the curses in Deuteronomy (28:30).

wickedness is powerless to save its owner This is self-evident, and no one (including the wicked) would think otherwise. Perhaps we should transpose the letters of רשע ("wickedness") and read עשר ("wealth") (Ginsberg). (Ibn Ezra mentions a similar idea, namely that "wickedness" stands for wealth gained by wickedness.) The fact that *wealth* cannot help one escape death is not a truism, because escape from death does not mean gaining eternal life but rather avoiding disaster and premature death. The rich might think they can prolong their lives by, say, hiring guards or giving bribes, but this would be a delusion. As Prov. 11:4 warns, "Wealth is of no avail on the day of wrath, but righteousness saves from death"; similarly Ezek. 7:19.

9. Koheleth is suspicious of human authority. He sees it as inherently arbitrary and harmful. Yet he is no revolutionary. He does not expect any social change, nor can he even imagine a state where justice is the norm. Human government is just one of many burdensome and injurious realities that people face, and the best one can do is to learn how to maneuver around the dangers and accommodate himself to the constraints. This pessimistic and resigned view of government is common in writings of the postexilic and Hellenistic period.

All these things Namely, the matters described in 8:1b–8 (Rashi).

INJUSTICES (8:10–15)

In 8:10b–15, as in 2:18–26, Koheleth describes a single scenario in several ways, repeatedly calling it *hevel*.

Ibn Ezra connects this unit to the preceding, paraphrasing: "When I set my heart [v. 9a, translated literally], then I saw wicked men, who ruled over people and harmed them [v. 9b], dying without suffering." Koheleth first took some comfort from reminding himself that a time of judgment awaits the tyrant (v. 5), namely his death (v. 8), but then realized that inequitable treatment can continue even beyond death (v. 10), and in any case the wicked may outlive the righteous (vv. 11–12a, 14). Humans are guilty of treating the dead unfairly, but it is God who is responsible for inequitable life spans. At the same time, Koheleth does not shed his assumption that God is fundamentally just. For Koheleth, injustice alongside justice is a paradox, an absurdity.

Koheleth is not making a new discovery. Even the more conventional Wisdom Literature does not claim that people always get what they deserve, whether in length of

to treat them unjustly. 10 And then I saw scoundrels
coming from the Holy Site and being brought to
burial, while such as had acted righteously were
forgotten in the city.
And here is another frustration: 11 the fact that the
sentence imposed for evil deeds is not executed
swiftly, which is why men are emboldened to do
evil—12 the fact that a sinner may do evil a hundred
times and his [punishment] still be delayed. For
although I am aware that "It will be well with those

אֲשֶׁר שָׁלַט הָאָדָם בְּאָדָם לְרַע לוֹ׃ 10 וּבְכֵן
רָאִיתִי רְשָׁעִים קְבֻרִים וָבָאוּ וּמִמְּקוֹם
קָדוֹשׁ יְהַלֵּכוּ וְיִשְׁתַּכְּחוּ בָעִיר אֲשֶׁר כֵּן־
עָשׂוּ
גַּם־זֶה הָבֶל׃ 11 אֲשֶׁר אֵין־נַעֲשָׂה פִתְגָם
מַעֲשֵׂה הָרָעָה מְהֵרָה עַל־כֵּן מָלֵא לֵב
בְּנֵי־הָאָדָם בָּהֶם לַעֲשׂוֹת רָע׃ 12 אֲשֶׁר
חֹטֶא עֹשֶׂה רָע מְאַת וּמַאֲרִיךְ לוֹ כִּי
גַּם־יוֹדֵעַ אָנִי אֲשֶׁר יִהְיֶה־טּוֹב לְיִרְאֵי

life, wealth, health, or other kinds of good fortune. Yet the sages held fast to a belief in God's justice. Other thinkers found consolation in the belief that justice would eventually be realized, either later in this life (Ps. 37) or in life after death (the dominant belief in Judaism after the Bible). Some claimed that the good fortune of the wicked was outweighed by the internal turmoil that supposedly afflicts them (Job 20:14–16; Sira 40:1–11). Others maintained that there was a greater order, opaque to humans, within which apparent injustices make sense (the Book of Job). None of these rationalizations work for Koheleth, who sees the world order as mechanical and indifferent, who fears that justice may come too late to undo the wrong, and who regards death as the end.

10. Holy Site Either the Temple or the synagogue. (In Aramaic synagogue inscriptions of the talmudic period, the synagogue is sometimes called *'atra' kaddisha'*, "the holy site.") Not the cemetery, which is ritually unclean. Koheleth may have seen a funeral cortege proceeding from the synagogue where the dead were eulogized.[38]

forgotten That is, *neglected*.[39] While scoundrels receive elegant obsequies, the bodies of the righteous—presumably the righteous poor, who must rely on public beneficence for proper burial—lie untended.[40] (The verse is usually thought to mean that the memory of the righteous perishes, but Koheleth believes that this happens to everyone [2:16], not just the righteous.)

frustration [hevel] Better: "senseless" or "absurd." What Koheleth describes is not just something that frustrates him, but a reality he considers warped and unreasonable, in other words, absurd. See Comment to verse 14.

11. the sentence imposed for evil deeds is not executed swiftly Koheleth maintains his belief in divine judgment, though well aware that some people die earlier or later than they deserve. This is a deep contradiction that he despairs of solving.

why men are emboldened to do evil When people observe unfair life spans, they assume that "there is no judgment and no Judge" and no cost for evildoing (Rashbam).

12. a hundred times Hebrew *me'at* (מאת) actually means "a hundred of," and it is arbitrary to supply "times." The word is ungrammatical, peculiar in form and meaning. We should read מאז *(me-'az)* "from way back, from of old," with the Septuagint.

his [punishment] still be delayed Koheleth does not deny that humans are called to account for their sins, but he realizes that the value of this judgment is vitiated by the manifest delays in its execution.

who revere God since they revere Him, 13 and it will not be well with the scoundrel, and he will not live long, because he does not revere God"—14 here is a frustration that occurs in the world: sometimes an upright man is requited according to the conduct of the scoundrel; and sometimes the scoundrel is requited according to the conduct of the upright. I say all that is frustration.

הָאֱלֹהִים אֲשֶׁר יִירְאוּ מִלְּפָנָיו׃ 13 וְטוֹב
לֹא־יִהְיֶה לָרָשָׁע וְלֹא־יַאֲרִיךְ יָמִים כַּצֵּל
אֲשֶׁר אֵינֶנּוּ יָרֵא מִלִּפְנֵי אֱלֹהִים׃ 14 יֶשׁ־
הֶבֶל אֲשֶׁר נַעֲשָׂה עַל־הָאָרֶץ אֲשֶׁר ׀ יֵשׁ
צַדִּיקִים אֲשֶׁר מַגִּיעַ אֲלֵהֶם כְּמַעֲשֵׂה
הָרְשָׁעִים וְיֵשׁ רְשָׁעִים שֶׁמַּגִּיעַ אֲלֵהֶם
כְּמַעֲשֵׂה הַצַּדִּיקִים אָמַרְתִּי שֶׁגַּם־זֶה
הָבֶל׃

12b–13. NJPS harmonizes this statement of faith with the pessimistic observations in verses 12a and 14 by inserting quotation marks and adding "although," but nothing in the text justifies this. Mendelssohn does the reverse, ascribing the observation in verse 12a to *other* people while having Koheleth say that he does not think thus, but rather knows that there will come a day of reward and reckoning. (The phrase "I know that" [*yodei'a 'ani;* NJPS: "I am aware that"] always introduces a proposition that is *affirmed,* not an opinion that one has heard and rejects.)

Rashi paraphrases: "Although [God] does not hurry to punish the wicked and to make a distinction between the righteous and the wicked, I know that in the end everyone will receive a fitting reward, and it will be well with those who fear [God]"; and conversely for the wicked. But Koheleth, unlike Rashi, did not believe in a judgment after death and so could not be certain of a reckoning some time in the future.

Whereas earlier commentators found Koheleth's skeptical assertions difficult to accept at face value (and sometimes attributed them to a student or a fool), modern interpreters find it hard to credit him with his expressions of faith. Yet Koheleth's problem is precisely that he holds both to what he observes and to what he believes (in his words, what he says he "knows"). This is a dilemma shared by many believers. They cannot deny the injustice of the Holocaust, to take the extreme case, but they choose not to abandon faith in God's justice. Koheleth "knows" the principle of retribution and nowhere denies it. At the same time, he *also* knows there are cases that violate the rule. It is because Koheleth holds to the axioms of wisdom and religious tradition that he is shocked by their violation.

and he will not live long, because he does not revere God This should be translated "and one who does not fear God, will, like a shadow, not live long."[41] Compare 6:12 and Ps. 144:4, "Man is like a breath; his days are like a passing shadow."

14. Koheleth again observes that sometimes injustices occur. These are phrased as exceptions (literally, "there are upright people who are requited according to the conduct of scoundrels . . ."). Ibn Ezra says that this happens "on rare occasions." This may be so, but their rarity does not right the wrong.

***frustration* [*hevel*]*. . . frustration* [*hevel*]** The usual translations of *hevel,* such as "transient," "vain," or "futile," do not fit this context, because the fact described is none of these. Nor does "frustration" properly characterize the fact of an upright man being treated the same as a scoundrel, and so on. Rashbam is closer to the mark: "something that people are amazed and shocked at," in other words, something that violates reasonable expectations. This too, however, is not quite accurate, because it obscures Koheleth's own anger and frustration by distancing him from these feelings. Koheleth is focusing not on people's reactions but on a quality in the events themselves, their violation of reason, their senselessness.

15 I therefore praised enjoyment. For the only good a man can have under the sun is to eat and drink and enjoy himself. That much can accompany him, in exchange for his wealth, through the days of life that God has granted him under the sun.

16 For I have set my mind to learn wisdom and to observe the business that goes on in the world—even to the extent of going without sleep day and

15 וְשִׁבַּ֤חְתִּֽי אֲנִי֙ אֶת־הַשִּׂמְחָ֔ה אֲשֶׁ֨ר אֵֽין־
ט֤וֹב לָֽאָדָם֙ תַּ֣חַת הַשֶּׁ֔מֶשׁ כִּ֛י אִם־לֶאֱכ֥וֹל
וְלִשְׁתּ֖וֹת וְלִשְׂמ֑וֹחַ וְה֞וּא יִלְוֶ֣נּוּ בַעֲמָל֗וֹ
יְמֵ֥י חַיָּ֛יו אֲשֶׁר־נָֽתַן־ל֥וֹ הָאֱלֹהִ֖ים תַּ֥חַת
הַשָּֽׁמֶשׁ׃

16 כַּאֲשֶׁ֨ר נָתַ֤תִּי אֶת־לִבִּי֙ לָדַ֣עַת חָכְמָ֔ה
וְלִרְאוֹת֙ אֶת־הָ֣עִנְיָ֔ן אֲשֶׁ֥ר נַעֲשָׂ֖ה עַל־
הָאָ֑רֶץ כִּ֣י גַ֤ם בַּיּוֹם֙ וּבַלַּ֔יְלָה שֵׁנָ֕ה בְּעֵינָ֖יו

Psalms 73 considers the prosperity of the wicked and says, "As for me, my feet had almost strayed, my steps were nearly led off course, for I envied the wanton; I saw the wicked at ease.... So I applied myself to understand this, but it seemed a hopeless task [*'amal*]" (vv. 2–3, 16). The psalmist comes to the conclusion that "Those who keep far from You perish; You annihilate all who are untrue to You" (v. 27). Koheleth, however, is keenly aware that *everyone* perishes, and not always at the right time. Further, he realizes that this inequity cannot be accounted for by assertions such as the psalmist's.

***15. I therefore praised enjoyment* [*simḥah*]** Humans cannot undo these injustices; we can only palliate the distress they cause us. A long chain of rabbinical tradition recorded in Koheleth Rabbah says that "every mention of eating and drinking in this scroll refers to Torah and good deeds"; but Koheleth himself does not look to such deeper satisfactions to lighten life's burden.

***That much can accompany him, in exchange for his wealth* [*'amal*]** Better: "This will accompany him in his toil." That is, life itself is toil (see *'amal* in Keywords in the introduction) and the best thing humans can do is grasp random moments of respite.

IGNORANCE, DEATH, AND PLEASURE (8:16–9:10)

In this passage, Koheleth meditates on human ignorance and the universality of death. Once again, he moves from disheartening observations to advice on embracing life's pleasures.

THE FAILURE OF THE SEARCH FOR WISDOM (vv. 16–17)

Koheleth first restates the limits of human wisdom. As he reported in 1:13–18, he began by amassing wisdom, whereby he sought to comprehend life. But this led him only to frustration and chagrin.

16. Referring to Koheleth's undertaking in 1:13–14.

even to the extent of going without sleep day and night Koheleth searched relentlessly and obsessively, "turning" and "going about" the world as he struggled to make sense of what he observed and to reconcile it with what he believed. He constantly ran into dead ends. Consequently, he advises enjoyment of the present moment. But he does not seem to succeed in that either.

night—[17] and I have observed all that God brings to pass. Indeed, man cannot guess the events that occur under the sun. For man tries strenuously, but fails to guess them; and even if a sage should think to discover them he would not be able to guess them.

אֵינֶנּוּ רֹאֶה׃ 17 וְרָאִיתִי אֶת־כָּל־מַעֲשֵׂה
הָאֱלֹהִים כִּי לֹא יוּכַל הָאָדָם לִמְצוֹא
אֶת־הַמַּעֲשֶׂה אֲשֶׁר נַעֲשָׂה תַחַת־הַשֶּׁמֶשׁ
בְּשֶׁל אֲשֶׁר יַעֲמֹל הָאָדָם לְבַקֵּשׁ וְלֹא יִמְצָא
וְגַם אִם־יֹאמַר הֶחָכָם לָדַעַת לֹא יוּכַל
לִמְצֹא׃

9 For all this I noted, and I ascertained all this: that the actions of even the righteous and the wise are determined by God. Even love! Even hate! Man knows none of these in advance—[2] none! For the same fate is in store for all: for the righteous, and for

ט כִּי אֶת־כָּל־זֶה נָתַתִּי אֶל־לִבִּי וְלָבוּר
אֶת־כָּל־זֶה אֲשֶׁר הַצַּדִּיקִים וְהַחֲכָמִים
וַעֲבָדֵיהֶם בְּיַד הָאֱלֹהִים גַּם־אַהֲבָה גַם־
שִׂנְאָה אֵין יוֹדֵעַ הָאָדָם הַכֹּל לִפְנֵיהֶם׃
2 הַכֹּל כַּאֲשֶׁר לַכֹּל מִקְרֶה אֶחָד לַצַּדִּיק

17. guess Hebrew *matza';* better, "find" or "comprehend." Koheleth is proceeding via rational investigation, not guesswork.

even ... a sage This is not a criticism of wisdom but a complaint about its limitations: Even a sage or wise man, who is best equipped to attain understanding (and *deserves* to do so), cannot fathom the nature of events. The quintessential wise man is, of course, Koheleth himself. He is declaring his own inability to understand absurdities such as the injustices described in 8:10–14. The failure of wisdom to penetrate the world's paradoxes is just another of life's inequities.

DEATH AND IGNORANCE (9:1–3)

9:1. determined by God Literally, "in God's hand." This means that God has the overall control of human lives, rather than predetermining every detail.

The righteous and wise might be expected to shape their future by righteous deeds and wise choices. That, after all, is what wisdom is for. But God's enigmatic control of human destiny cripples wisdom's ability to do so.

even love! even hate! These are God's emotions, not humans'. Looking at the unjust allocation of fates, we cannot understand God's favor and disfavor. The divine psychology is opaque, as is shown, for example, by the unfair allocation of life spans, described in 8:14.

2. none! "None" is not in the text. The end of verse 1 and the beginning of verse 2 are difficult and probably textually corrupt. A literal translation of the MT might be "(1b) Man knows neither love nor hate. Everything is before them. (2a) All is as to all [that is, the same thing happens to everyone], inasmuch as all have the same fate." But this is confused and does not say much. By changing הכל *(ha-kol)* "all" to הבל *(hevel)* "senseless" and (like NJPS) treating the first word in verse 2 as part of the sentence ending verse 1, we can translate "Everything before them is *hevel,*" in other words, everything people see is senseless. The next words explain why this is so.

the wicked; for the good and pure, and for the impure; for him who sacrifices, and for him who does not; for him who is pleasing, and for him who is displeasing; and for him who swears, and for him who shuns oaths.
3 That is the sad thing about all that goes on under the sun: that the same fate is in store for all. (Not only that, but men's hearts are full of sadness, and their minds of madness, while they live; and then—to the dead!)
4 For he who is reckoned among the living has something to look forward to—even a live dog is better than a dead lion—
5 since the

וְלָרָשָׁע לַטּוֹב וְלַטָּהוֹר וְלַטָּמֵא וְלַזֹּבֵחַ
וְלַאֲשֶׁר אֵינֶנּוּ זֹבֵחַ כַּטּוֹב כַּחֹטֶא הַנִּשְׁבָּע
כַּאֲשֶׁר שְׁבוּעָה יָרֵא׃ 3 זֶה ׀ רָע בְּכֹל
אֲשֶׁר־נַעֲשָׂה תַּחַת הַשֶּׁמֶשׁ כִּי־מִקְרֶה אֶחָד
לַכֹּל וְגַם לֵב בְּנֵי־הָאָדָם מָלֵא־רָע
וְהוֹלֵלוֹת בִּלְבָבָם בְּחַיֵּיהֶם וְאַחֲרָיו אֶל־
הַמֵּתִים׃ 4 כִּי־מִי אֲשֶׁר יבחר יְחֻבַּר אֶל
כָּל־הַחַיִּים יֵשׁ בִּטָּחוֹן כִּי־לְכֶלֶב חַי הוּא
טוֹב מִן־הָאַרְיֵה הַמֵּת׃ 5 כִּי הַחַיִּים

For the same fate is in store for all In 8:11–14, Koheleth described an injustice that befalls some people. Now he remarks on one that is universal: death itself, because people who deserve different fates share the same one.

the pure That is, those who observe the laws of ritual purity [Transl.].

pleasing, displeasing Literally, "good," "sinner." NJPS understands these terms as in 2:26 and 7:26, but they probably retain their moral sense here. The other terms in the series speak of deeds and moral states.

3. ***the sad thing*** Or: "the worst thing" (Ibn Ezra).[42] The word translated is *ra'*, "bad, evil." It can refer to moral evils, to misfortunes, or to other kinds of badness; see next Comment.

full of sadness Hebrew *malei' ra'*; better: "full of evil." Here *ra'* means moral evil. As Koheleth said in 8:11–12, injustice is demoralizing. If people saw the righteous and the wicked ending up differently, they would not be inclined to do evil. As it stands, they are confused and disheartened during their fleeting lifetime, then they join the dead.

LIFE'S SUPERIORITY TO DEATH (vv. 4–6)

4. Traditional commentators found this verse especially offensive and neutralized it in various ways. Ibn Ezra says that the opinion expressed is that of "other people," not Koheleth. Mendelssohn says that it is the unfortunate notion people arrive at when they doubt the immortality of the soul. In context, however, the thought is clearly Koheleth's and is reminiscent of the "loathing" of life that bursts forth in 2:17 and 4:3.

something to look forward to Hebrew *yesh bittaḥon;* better: "something to trust in," namely the fact that they will die (v. 5a). Rashi, Rashbam, and others see the *bittaḥon* (which they understand to mean "hope") as the possibility that a wicked person will repent before death.

even a live dog is better than a dead lion The dog (an object of contempt in ancient Israel) is at least experiencing life, and this experience is better than nothing. Koheleth's tone is sardonic, but he does believe that knowledge in and of itself gives an advantage to the living; see 9:10.

5. ***since the living know they will die. But the dead know nothing*** Only this, then, is the advantage of the living, the one thing they can "trust in"!

living know they will die. But the dead know
nothing; they have no more recompense, for even
the memory of them has died. 6 Their loves, their
hates, their jealousies have long since perished; and
they have no more share till the end of time in all that
goes on under the sun.

יוֹדְעִים שֶׁיָּמֻתוּ וְהַמֵּתִים אֵינָם יוֹדְעִים
מְאוּמָה וְאֵין־עוֹד לָהֶם שָׂכָר כִּי נִשְׁכַּח
זִכְרָם׃ 6 גַּם אַהֲבָתָם גַּם־שִׂנְאָתָם גַּם־
קִנְאָתָם כְּבָר אָבָדָה וְחֵלֶק אֵין־לָהֶם עוֹד
לְעוֹלָם בְּכֹל אֲשֶׁר־נַעֲשָׂה תַּחַת הַשָּׁמֶשׁ׃

7 Go, eat your bread in gladness, and drink your wine
in joy; for your action was long ago approved by
God. 8 Let your clothes always be freshly washed, and
your head never lack ointment. 9 Enjoy happiness
with a woman you love all the fleeting days of life

7 לֵךְ אֱכֹל בְּשִׂמְחָה לַחְמֶךָ וּשְׁתֵה בְלֶב־
טוֹב יֵינֶךָ כִּי כְבָר רָצָה הָאֱלֹהִים אֶת־
מַעֲשֶׂיךָ׃ 8 בְּכָל־עֵת יִהְיוּ בְגָדֶיךָ לְבָנִים
וְשֶׁמֶן עַל־רֹאשְׁךָ אַל־יֶחְסָר׃ 9 רְאֵה חַיִּים
עִם־אִשָּׁה אֲשֶׁר־אָהַבְתָּ כָּל־יְמֵי חַיֵּי הֶבְלֶךָ

they have no more recompense Koheleth obliquely concedes that the living do have some compensations for life's toil. He will list some of these in 9:7–9.

for even the memory of them has died *If* people were remembered, that might be reckoned an enduring recompense, but they are not (2:16). In this regard, Koheleth unequivocally departs from traditional wisdom, which taught that "The memory of the righteous is for a blessing, but the name of the wicked rots" (Prov. 10:7; different in NJPS). Koheleth sees no such distinctions.

6. ***Their loves, their hates, their jealousies*** These experiences are not necessarily pleasant, but they are *ours,* our "share" or portion (*ḥeilek*) in life. Indeed they are what we most intensely care about, and they all evaporate.

they have no more share [ḥeilek] till the end of time Since Koheleth never suggests that time or the world will end, we should translate, "they nevermore have a portion."

LIFE'S PLEASURES (vv. 7–10)

However inadequate pleasure may be, we should partake of it, simply because that is what we have for the moment, while ahead of us stretches the void without bound.[43]

7. ***approved*** Hebrew *ratzah* ("wanted, willed, approved"); better: "desired." When praising pleasure (2:24, 26; 3:13; 5:18), Koheleth has observed that it is God's gift. Now he goes farther: God not only allows you enjoyment but also *wants* you to have it—if you are one of the fortunate.

8. ***Let your clothes always be freshly washed, and your head never lack ointment*** Rashbam says that these actions represent purity in behavior. Rabbi Judah ha-Nasi taught that the clean clothes and oil represent good deeds and Torah, whereby we keep ourselves morally ready for God's "banquet" on the day of our death (Koh. R.). Ibn Ezra, more plausibly, identifies all these actions as physical luxuries, which he considers inadequate.

9. ***Enjoy happiness*** Literally, "See life," that is, live your life.

with a woman you love In spite of his acrid comments about women in 7:24–29, Koheleth does not think it is good for a man to be alone. A man should share his life with a female companion.

that have been granted to you under the sun—all your fleeting days. For that alone is what you can get out of life and out of the means you acquire under the
sun. [10] Whatever it is in your power to do, do with all your might. For there is no action, no reasoning, no learning, no wisdom in Sheol, where you are going.
[11] I have further observed under the sun that
The race is not won by the swift,

אֲשֶׁר נָתַן־לְךָ תַּחַת הַשֶּׁמֶשׁ כֹּל יְמֵי הֶבְלֶךָ
כִּי הוּא חֶלְקְךָ בַּחַיִּים וּבַעֲמָלְךָ אֲשֶׁר־
אַתָּה עָמֵל תַּחַת הַשָּׁמֶשׁ׃ 10 כֹּל אֲשֶׁר
תִּמְצָא יָדְךָ לַעֲשׂוֹת בְּכֹחֲךָ עֲשֵׂה כִּי אֵין
מַעֲשֶׂה וְחֶשְׁבּוֹן וְדַעַת וְחָכְמָה בִּשְׁאוֹל
אֲשֶׁר אַתָּה הֹלֵךְ שָׁמָּה׃ ס
11 שַׁבְתִּי וְרָאֹה תַחַת־הַשֶּׁמֶשׁ כִּי
לֹא לַקַּלִּים הַמֵּרוֹץ

Some commentators hasten to assure us that "a woman" (rather than "*the* woman") must be one's wife. Others (Barton, for example) are concerned that the text's lack of a definite article might allow for "voluptuousness." Still, the only woman who would be a life-companion is one's wife, and Koheleth does not say "women."

Rashi reads this advice as allegory, "See and understand to learn a trade for supporting yourself with the study of Torah which you possess." The Midrash (which, like Koheleth, had some unpleasant things to say about women in expounding 7:24–29), now quotes an unusually warm commendation of marriage, taken from the Talmud (B. Yevamot 62b): "Whoever is without a wife lives without good, without help, without happiness, without blessing, and without atonement." Rabbi Joshua b. Levi adds: "and without life and without peace."

all your fleeting [hevel] days. For that alone is what you can get out of life and out of the means you acquire under the sun Better: ". . . for this is your portion [*ḥeilek*] in life and in your toil [*ʿamal*] at which you labor under the sun." *ʿAmal* means "toil" in the broad sense of life's exertions; see Keywords in the introduction.

10. with all your might Hebrew *be-koḥakha;* literally, "with your strength," in other words, "in accordance with your abilities." Koheleth does not advocate doing things with one's full power. That would be *ʿamal,* or overdoing, which he often warns against. Rather, he advocates moderate work.

For there is no action, no reasoning, no learning, no wisdom in Sheol, where you are going In the ancient Hebrew view, Sheol, the underworld—like the Greek Hades—was a dreary realm of darkness, inertia, and eternal sleep. (The idea of resurrection is not clearly expressed before Daniel 12, which is later than Ecclesiastes.) We must embrace the pleasures and activities of life, whatever their inadequacies, because they are what we have and all we will have.

TIME AND CONTINGENCY (9:11–12)

Everyone is subject to the vagaries of chance and fortune, which can nullify the advantages of talents and efforts.

11. The race is not won by the swift That is, not *necessarily* won by the swift. They might usually win, but they cannot control the outcome, because unpredictable and uncontrollable factors enter into the results. As Rashbam says, "their running is not always worthwhile, for although they run swiftly, time and chance and accident may happen to them, as to others."

Nor the battle by the valiant;
Nor is bread won by the wise,
Nor wealth by the intelligent,
Nor favor by the learned.
For the time of mischance comes to all. 12 And a man
cannot even know his time. As fishes are enmeshed in
a fatal net, and as birds are trapped in a snare, so men
are caught at the time of calamity, when it comes
upon them without warning.
13 This thing too I observed under the sun about
wisdom, and it affected me profoundly. 14 There was a
little city, with few men in it; and to it came a great
king, who invested it and built mighty siege works

וְלֹא לַגִּבּוֹרִים הַמִּלְחָמָה
וְגַם לֹא לַחֲכָמִים לֶחֶם
וְגַם לֹא לַנְּבֹנִים עֹשֶׁר
וְגַם לֹא לַיֹּדְעִים חֵן
כִּי־עֵת וָפֶגַע יִקְרֶה אֶת־כֻּלָּם: 12 כִּי גַּם
לֹא־יֵדַע הָאָדָם אֶת־עִתּוֹ כַּדָּגִים
שֶׁנֶּאֱחָזִים בִּמְצוֹדָה רָעָה וְכַצִּפֳּרִים
הָאֲחֻזוֹת בַּפָּח כָּהֵם יוּקָשִׁים בְּנֵי הָאָדָם
לְעֵת רָעָה כְּשֶׁתִּפּוֹל עֲלֵיהֶם פִּתְאֹם:
13 גַּם־זֹה רָאִיתִי חָכְמָה תַּחַת הַשָּׁמֶשׁ
וּגְדוֹלָה הִיא אֵלָי: 14 עִיר קְטַנָּה וַאֲנָשִׁים
בָּהּ מְעָט וּבָא־אֵלֶיהָ מֶלֶךְ גָּדוֹל וְסָבַב
אֹתָהּ וּבָנָה עָלֶיהָ מְצוֹדִים גְּדֹלִים:

Nor is bread won by the wise Just as the swiftest runner *should* win a race, the wise *should* have food, if not wealth (Prov. 3:16; 8:18, 21; 22:4; 24:4), and the learned (or "insightful") *should* have favor, that is, the favor "of God and man" (Prov. 3:4, 22; 4:9; 13:15). But this often does not happen.

This verse complains not about ethical injustices, as are the cases of early death for the righteous and long life for sinners, but about a more fundamental inequity, the lack of a dependable connection between efforts and results, or between what one deserves and what one gets. This inequity is what Koheleth throughout calls *hevel.*

time of mischance Hebrew *'et va-fega';* literally, "time and chance." Some explain this as the "time of (mis)chance" par excellence, which is to say, death (Transl.), which is mentioned also in the next verse. Nevertheless, the universality of death does not explain why the swift do not necessarily win the race and so on. Rather, this phrase refers to any unpredictable event that befalls people and confounds their plans and endeavors.

12. And a man cannot even know his time Koheleth turns from ordinary mishaps to the great misfortune, death, which falls upon people suddenly, like a net.

birds The epitome of gullible, ignorant creatures (Prov. 1:17; Hos. 7:11).

WISDOM AND FOLLY (9:13–10:3)

The unit begins with an anecdote demonstrating both the power and the vulnerability of wisdom (9:13–18), then continues this theme with several observations (10:1–3). Some of these have a proverbial cast.

A WISE MAN AND HIS CITY (vv. 13–18)

14. There was a little city No historical event such as described in this anecdote has been identified.

against it. 15 Present in the city was a poor wise man
who might have saved it with his wisdom, but
nobody thought of that poor man. 16 So I observed:
Wisdom is better than valor; but
A poor man's wisdom is scorned,
And his words are not heeded.
17 Words spoken softly by wise men are heeded sooner
than those shouted by a lord in folly.

15 וּמָצָא בָהּ אִישׁ מִסְכֵּן חָכָם וּמִלַּט־הוּא
אֶת־הָעִיר בְּחָכְמָתוֹ וְאָדָם לֹא זָכַר אֶת־
הָאִישׁ הַמִּסְכֵּן הַהוּא׃ 16 וְאָמַרְתִּי אָנִי
טוֹבָה חָכְמָה מִגְּבוּרָה
וְחָכְמַת הַמִּסְכֵּן בְּזוּיָה
וּדְבָרָיו אֵינָם נִשְׁמָעִים׃
17 דִּבְרֵי חֲכָמִים בְּנַחַת נִשְׁמָעִים מִזַּעֲקַת
מוֹשֵׁל בַּכְּסִילִים׃

15. Present in the city was a poor wise man who might have saved it with his wisdom Better: "And he [the king] found in it a man who was poor but wise, and it was he who saved the city by his wisdom." NJPS and many commentators think that the deliverance of the city was only a possibility—the poor man *could* have saved the city but was ignored. Though verse 16b favors this interpretation, verse 15 is not hypothetical. If the wise man had not actually saved the city, how could anyone know that he *could* have done so? Moreover, the first part of Koheleth's conclusion in verse 16 would be unjustified, for it underscores the power that comes with wisdom. The Hebrew has the pronoun "he" in the emphatic position: "and it was he (of all people!) who saved" *(u-millat hu')*.

thought of Hebrew *zakhar;* better: "remembered." (The verb can mean either "gave thought to" or—more usually—"remembered," but it is not used of heeding advice.) The wise man who saved the city was forgotten—his deed was remembered, but his name was lost. We can compare the two women who saved their cities but whose names and identities go unmentioned: the woman of Tebez (Judg. 9:52–55) and the wise woman of Abel Beth Maacah (2 Sam. 20:14–22).

16. So I observed: Wisdom is better than valor This is the conclusion Koheleth draws from the anecdote. If the poor man's wisdom had no effect, this sentence would be untrue.

but/A poor man's wisdom is scorned/And his words are not heeded This saying does not restate the events of the anecdote but rather looks forward to verses 17–18, introducing a further affront to wisdom: In spite of wisdom's inherent efficacy, people tend to disregard it if it is spoken by a poor man.

17. "In folly" is actually "among fools." Ben Sira shares this saying's optimism: "The opinion of the intelligent man is consulted in the assembly, and they pay attention to his words" (21:17). In 9:16b, Koheleth said that wise words are despised if their speaker lacks the power of wealth. Now he states another, contradictory, rule: The words of the wise spoken softly (though vulnerable and often disdained) are heeded more than a ruler's shouts are among fools. This is valid in principle but, to Koheleth's chagrin, is often violated. Ibn Ezra harmonizes verse 17 with the preceding, perhaps correctly, by saying that even though the wisdom of a poor man is commonly ignored, his quiet words are nevertheless paid greater heed than a ruler's are when he is ranting at a bunch of fools. (See next Comment.)

Wisdom Literature, especially in Egypt, emphasized the importance of reserve and quiet in speech as a personal and courtly value. One should wait in silence for the proper

18 Wisdom is more valuable than weapons of war, but
a single error destroys much of value.

18 טוֹבָה חָכְמָה מִכְּלֵי קְרָב וְחוֹטֶא אֶחָד
יְאַבֵּד טוֹבָה הַרְבֵּה׃

10 Dead flies turn the perfumer's ointment fetid
and putrid; so a little folly outweighs massive
wisdom.
2 A wise man's mind tends toward the right hand,
a fool's toward the left. 3 A fool's mind is also wanting
when he travels, and he lets everybody know he is
a fool.

י
זְבוּבֵי מָוֶת יַבְאִישׁ יַבִּיעַ שֶׁמֶן רוֹקֵחַ
יָקָר מֵחָכְמָה מִכָּבוֹד סִכְלוּת מְעָט׃
2 לֵב חָכָם לִימִינוֹ וְלֵב כְּסִיל לִשְׂמֹאלוֹ׃
3 וְגַם־בַּדֶּרֶךְ כשהסכל כְּשֶׁסָּכָל הֹלֵךְ לִבּוֹ
חָסֵר וְאָמַר לַכֹּל סָכָל הוּא׃

moment, then speak carefully and fluently. For example, Ptahhotep teaches: "If you are a man of worth, who sits in his master's council, concentrate on excellence. Your silence is better than chatter. Speak when you know you have a solution."[44] And "Do not boast at your neighbor's side. One has great respect for the silent."[45]

18. ***error*** Hebrew: *ḥote';* actually: "offender" or "sinner," as in 2:26. This verse reiterates the complaint in 9:16b.

WISDOM AND FOLLY (10:1–3)

10:1. This proverb reinforces 9:18: As a fly can spoil the ointment, so can a little folly ruin much wisdom.

2. Whatever wisdom's vulnerabilities, it is much less harmful than folly. Though fools may impede the workings of wisdom, fools harm themselves even more. The thought continues in verse 15.

right... left Connoting efficacy and clumsiness, respectively.

3. ***A fool's mind is also wanting*** His mind (lit. "heart") is absent, meaning that he is foolish.

when he travels Even when merely walking along the road, which requires no special intelligence.

he lets everybody know he is a fool Or: "*it* lets everybody know he is a fool." His heart leaves him and proclaims, "He is a fool!"; as Prov. 12:23b puts it, "The heart of fools cries out, 'Folly!'" The "heart" is an entity in some way distinct from its owner; see 1:13.[46]

GETTING ALONG IN LIFE (10:4–20)

As uncertain, perilous, and frustrating as life can be, it still holds possibilities for prudent and sensible action. In 10:4–20 Koheleth observes some ways of adjusting to the realities one faces.

4 If the wrath of a lord flares up against you, don't
give up your post; for when wrath abates, grave
offenses are pardoned.
5 Here is an evil I have seen under the sun as great
as an error committed by a ruler: 6 Folly was placed
on lofty heights, while rich men sat in low estate.

4 אִם־רוּחַ הַמּוֹשֵׁל תַּעֲלֶה עָלֶיךָ מְקוֹמְךָ
אַל־תַּנַּח כִּי מַרְפֵּא יַנִּיחַ חֲטָאִים גְּדוֹלִים׃
5 יֵשׁ רָעָה רָאִיתִי תַּחַת הַשָּׁמֶשׁ כִּשְׁגָגָה
שֶׁיֹּצָא מִלִּפְנֵי הַשַּׁלִּיט׃ 6 נִתַּן הַסֶּכֶל
בַּמְּרוֹמִים רַבִּים וַעֲשִׁירִים בַּשֵּׁפֶל יֵשֵׁבוּ׃

DEALING WITH THE POWERFUL (vv. 4–7)

Koheleth gives further counsels and comments on the relations between rulers and subjects. (For more on this topic, see 5:7–8, 8:2–9, and 10:16–20.) The ruler and the powerful are seen as irritable, dangerous, and sometimes dissolute. The wise person treads carefully and finds ways to pacify their anger. Proverbs 16:14 and 20:2 teach the same.

4. As Ibn Ezra observes, this verse harks back to 9:17, in which a soft-spoken wise man is contrasted with an enraged, loudmouth ruler. As in 8:1b–4, Koheleth teaches how to behave in the presence of authority.

a lord Hebrew *moshel* ("ruler"), probably a provincial official, beneath the *melekh* "king," who is the subject of 8:3–4.

To Rashi, this refers to the ruler of the universe: If God is angry at you and punishes you for your sins, you should hold fast to your virtues and not think that your righteousness is of no use, for your sufferings will atone for many sins.

don't give up your post Literally, "don't abandon your place," that is to say, don't go away too soon. In 8:3, Koheleth says that one *should* depart. Both counsels are true in different circumstances, and the wise man will recognize which approach the situation calls for.

abates Hebrew *marpei'* means "soothing ability" or "healing ability" in Prov. 12:18b ("The speech of the wise is healing [*marpei'*]"); hence we can translate here "the ability to soothe (anger) can set aside great offenses." Compare: "The king's wrath is a messenger of death, but a wise man can appease it"; Prov. 16:14. The wise man will stay put, bearing the torrent of wrath and pacifying his superior. Ben Sira rephrases: "The man who pleases the great atones for wrongdoing" (Sira 20:28b).

Another interpretation: Literally, "abatement (2 Chron. 36:16) remits grave offenses." For *hinniah,* "to remit," cf. *Abodah Zarah* 13a; cf. *hanaḥah,* "remission of taxes," Esther 2:18 (Transl.).

6–7. Here Koheleth reveals his class bias: In the right and normal order of things, fools are kept in low positions while the rich are appointed to high ones. He is exasperated to see fools and slaves prospering while rich and nobles are humbled. Though he does not assume that the rich are inherently wise (see 10:16–17), he does believe that dislocations in the proper social order are unseemly; compare 10:16. He shares the prejudice of the author of Prov. 30:21–23, who believes that the "earth shudders" when a slave comes to rule or a maid supplants her mistress. Similar attitudes can be found in the Egyptian "prophetic complaints," in which rapid shifts in social status are bewailed as signs of social disorder.[47] The sages of Wisdom Literature, including Koheleth, were socially conservative. They condemned social injustices but did not envision or desire changes in the social structure.

Folly That is, the fool (Ibn Ezra).

7 I have seen slaves on horseback, and nobles walking
on the ground like slaves.
8 He who digs a pit will fall into it; he who breaches a
stone fence will be bitten by a snake. 9 He who
quarries stones will be hurt by them; he who splits
wood will be harmed by it. 10 If the ax has become
dull and he has not whetted the edge, he must exert
more strength. Thus the advantage of a skill [depends

7 רָאִ֥יתִי עֲבָדִ֖ים עַל־סוּסִ֑ים וְשָׂרִ֛ים
הֹלְכִ֥ים כַּעֲבָדִ֖ים עַל־הָאָֽרֶץ׃
8 חֹפֵ֥ר גּוּמָּ֖ץ בּ֣וֹ יִפּ֑וֹל וּפֹרֵ֥ץ גָּדֵ֖ר יִשְּׁכֶ֥נּוּ
נָחָֽשׁ׃ 9 מַסִּ֣יעַ אֲבָנִ֔ים יֵעָצֵ֖ב בָּהֶ֑ם בּוֹקֵ֥עַ
עֵצִ֖ים יִסָּ֥כֶן בָּֽם׃ 10 אִם־קֵהָ֣ה הַבַּרְזֶ֗ל וְהוּא֙
לֹא־פָנִ֣ים קִלְקַ֔ל וַחֲיָלִ֖ים יְגַבֵּ֑ר וְיִתְר֥וֹן

nobles Hebrew *sarim;* not hereditary nobility but men who held high positions in government.

PREPARING FOR THE UNEXPECTED (vv. 8–11)

Though Koheleth is pessimistic about the value of human efforts and sees life as a land full of pitfalls, he does not tell us to give up. We still have to make our way through this murky territory, and Koheleth offers some advice on how to do do so, here speaking in ways typical of the more conventional sages, such as the authors of the Book of Proverbs.

8. This is a variant of a popular saying found in various forms elsewhere (Pss. 7:16; 9:16f.; 35:7f; 57:7; Prov. 26:27, and Sira 27:25–27). Its point is that a person's deeds rebound upon him: "His mischief will recoil upon his own head; his lawlessness will come down upon his skull" (Ps. 7:17). Koheleth employs the proverb differently, not to prove that justice ultimately prevails but to warn against the unanticipated consequences of one's actions. (See next Comment.)

Ibn Ezra connects this observation with the preceding comments on the ruler (vv. 5–7): The ruler's mistakes are a pit he will himself fall into.

will fall . . . will be bitten . . . will be hurt . . . will be harmed Better: "may fall . . . may be bitten," etc. The dangerous actions referred to here are everyday chores, not schemes to harm others. Because these accidents do not happen every time one undertakes the chore, we should translate the verbs as potential. (The Hebrew verb form can represent either a reality or a potentiality.) These mishaps are hazards, not certainties.

bitten by a snake When dismantling a stone wall, a person may get bitten by a poisonous snake that was nesting in it. This is a real danger in the land of Israel, where there are quite a few poisonous serpents (currently some twenty species).

9. ***he who splits wood will be harmed by it*** If the ax slips or a splinter flies into one's eye, for example.

10. ***If the ax has become dull*** This statement shows how the last-mentioned accident might occur. A dull ax, because it must be wielded with greater force, is more likely to slip and cause injury.

Thus the advantage of a skill [depends on the exercise of] prudence The Hebrew is difficult. As translated, it means that it is best to exercise forethought in one's chores, such as by sharpening an ax before use. On *ḥokhmah,* "wisdom," here translated "prudence," see Keywords in the introduction.

on the exercise of] prudence. [11] If the snake bites
because no spell was uttered, no advantage is gained
by the trained charmer.
[12] A wise man's talk brings him favor, but a fool's
lips are his undoing. [13] His talk begins as silliness and
ends as disastrous madness. [14] Yet the fool talks and
talks!
A man cannot know what will happen; who can tell
him what the future holds?
[15] A fool's exertions tire him out, for he doesn't know
how to get to a town.
[16] Alas for you, O land whose king is a lackey and

הכשיר הַכְשֵׁר חָכְמָה׃ 11 אִם־יִשֹּׁךְ הַנָּחָשׁ
בְּלוֹא־לָחַשׁ וְאֵין יִתְרוֹן לְבַעַל הַלָּשׁוֹן׃
12 דִּבְרֵי פִי־חָכָם חֵן וְשִׂפְתוֹת כְּסִיל
תְּבַלְּעֶנּוּ׃ 13 תְּחִלַּת דִּבְרֵי־פִיהוּ סִכְלוּת
וְאַחֲרִית פִּיהוּ הוֹלֵלוּת רָעָה׃ 14 וְהַסָּכָל
יַרְבֶּה דְבָרִים
לֹא־יֵדַע הָאָדָם מַה־שֶּׁיִּהְיֶה וַאֲשֶׁר יִהְיֶה
מֵאַחֲרָיו מִי יַגִּיד לוֹ׃
15 עֲמַל הַכְּסִילִים תְּיַגְּעֶנּוּ אֲשֶׁר לֹא־יָדַע
לָלֶכֶת אֶל־עִיר׃
16 אִי־לָךְ אֶרֶץ שֶׁמַּלְכֵּךְ נָעַר וְשָׂרַיִךְ בַּבֹּקֶר

11. If the snake bites because no spell was uttered, no advantage is gained by the trained charmer Since snake charming was a form of "wisdom" (see Isa. 3:3; Ps. 58:6), this verse too counsels the timely application of wisdom. If a snake charmer does not mesmerize the snake quickly enough and thus gets bitten, such skill is of no avail.

SPEECH, WISE AND FOOLISH (vv. 12–15)

Perhaps prompted by mention of the spell of the snake charmer (who is, literally, "the possessor of a tongue"), Koheleth now turns to proverbs on the consequences of speech, good and bad. The speech of the wise man benefits him, the speech of the fool harms him—yet it is the latter who talks the most. Compare 5:5–6; 6:11.

12. A wise man's talk brings him favor Compare Prov. 3:4.

a fool's lips are his undoing Literally, "the fool's lips devour him." For this image, compare 4:5. Cannibalism is also a harsh metaphor for destruction in Ps. 27:2, Mic. 3:3, and especially Isa. 49:26.

13. begins as silliness and ends as disastrous madness Fools' chatter gets worse and worse until it devastates them. They do not know the "time for silence" (3:7).

14. A man cannot know what will happen Given human ignorance of the future, it is only reasonable to be reticent in speech; thus too 6:11–12.

15. A fool's exertions tire him out This is an afterthought to the comments on folly. It is more relevant to 10:3 and perhaps originally followed it.

he doesn't know how to get to a town The fool reveals his folly and exhausts himself because he cannot even figure out how to get to town, the best-known place in the region.

THE RULING CLASS (vv. 16–20)

16. lackey Hebrew *na'ar,* "youth, lackey, slave." The latter sense is supported by the antithesis to the "master" in verse 17 (see Comment there). (On the possibility that a king can rise from low estate, see 4:13). Koheleth (like the author of Prov. 30:22) believes that a slave or lowly person who has come to power, having risen so far above his station,

whose ministers dine in the morning! 17 Happy are
you, O land whose king is a master and whose
ministers dine at the proper time—with restraint, not
with guzzling!
18 Through slothfulness the ceiling sags,
Through lazy hands the house caves in.
19 They make a banquet for revelry; wine makes life
merry, and money answers every need.
20 Don't revile a king even among your intimates.

יֹאכֵלוּ׃ 17 אַשְׁרֵיךְ אֶרֶץ שֶׁמַּלְכֵּךְ בֶּן־חוֹרִים
וְשָׂרַיִךְ בָּעֵת יֹאכֵלוּ בִּגְבוּרָה וְלֹא בַשְּׁתִי׃
18 בַּעֲצַלְתַּיִם יִמַּךְ הַמְּקָרֶה
וּבְשִׁפְלוּת יָדַיִם יִדְלֹף הַבָּיִת׃
19 לִשְׂחוֹק עֹשִׂים לֶחֶם וְיַיִן יְשַׂמַּח חַיִּים
וְהַכֶּסֶף יַעֲנֶה אֶת־הַכֹּל׃
20 גַּם בְּמַדָּעֲךָ מֶלֶךְ אַל־תְּקַלֵּל

will be unworthy and degenerate. As Prov. 19:10 opines: "Luxury is not fitting for a dullard, much less that a servant rule over princes." One wonders whether the author here has specific aristocrats in mind.

whose ministers dine in the morning That is, they start feasting in the morning—and continue all day. They are like "a scoundrel sated with food" (Prov. 30:22).

17. master Hebrew *ben ḥorim;* better: "freeman" or "noble," a member by birth of the well-to-do classes.

whose ministers dine at the proper time—with restraint, not with guzzling Everything has its proper time and manner, and moderation is always in order.

18. Through slothfulness A proverb entirely in the mode of the Book of Proverbs, cited as a parenthetical reinforcement of verses 16–17.

caves in Or "leaks." Flat roofs in Israel were covered with lime, which, if not maintained by fresh plastering, would crack and allow seepage.

19. banquet Hebrew *leḥem,* literally, "bread," which refers to all kinds of solid food.

They make a banquet for revelry This describes the lifestyle of the wealthy, continuing verse 17. Banqueting is in principle a legitimate activity, enjoyed by both types of rich people, the dissolute and the temperate.

wine makes life merry An old saying, appearing in Ps. 104:15 and Judg. 9:13. "Makes merry" is *yesammaḥ,* in other words, "gives *simḥah.*" *Simḥah* designates the experience of pleasure that Koheleth praises; see Keywords in the introduction. Neither he nor the other sages objected to the pleasures of of food and wine. As Ben Sira says, "Joy of heart and happiness of soul: wine drunk at the proper time and temperately" (31:27, Greek). The wealthy are not condemned for enjoying these pleasures, but rather for failing to do so in the proper time and measure.

money answers every need Alternatively: "money keeps them all busy!" The verb *ya'aneh* (from the root *'-n-h*) usually means "answer," though not in the sense of "provide"). Here, however, it is used in the same way as *ma'aneh* in 5:19, where NJPS translates "keeps him busy."[48] The fact that money keeps them occupied is evidence of their good fortune. What is unfair is that the dissolute rich have these resources.

20. even among your intimates Or: "even in your thoughts" (*madda'* = "mind"; thus Ibn Ezra, NJPS note). This is hyperbole: Don't even *think* about it! You might let your thoughts slip out in an unguarded moment (Gordis). This remark is a wry

Don't revile a rich man even in your bedchamber;
For a bird of the air may carry the utterance,
And a winged creature may report the word.

וּבְחַדְרֵי מִשְׁכָּבְךָ אַל־תְּקַלֵּל עָשִׁיר
כִּי עוֹף הַשָּׁמַיִם יוֹלִיךְ אֶת־הַקּוֹל
וּבַעַל הכנפים כְּנָפַיִם יַגֵּיד דָּבָר׃

11 Send your bread forth upon the waters; for after
many days you will find it. 2 Distribute portions to

יא שַׁלַּח לַחְמְךָ עַל־פְּנֵי הַמָּיִם כִּי־
בְרֹב הַיָּמִים תִּמְצָאֶנּוּ׃ 2 תֶּן־חֵלֶק לְשִׁבְעָה

afterthought, as if Koheleth realizes that he himself has just insulted the king and the wealthy.

For a bird...may carry the utterance A proverbial warning against reckless speech.

LIVING WITH UNCERTAINTY (11:1–6)

Prepare for all eventualities, says Koheleth, because you cannot know what lies ahead and you cannot change the course of events. Instead of pondering life's mysteries and the hidden future, adapt yourself to various possible outcomes. This is also the practical message of 3:1–15.

11:1. Send your bread forth upon the waters To send forth one's bread "upon the waters" means giving it up, surrendering expectation of personal benefit from it. Yet, paradoxically, if you do this you *can* expect to benefit.

Perform deeds of charity, Koheleth advises, giving alms and assistance to a number of people in need ("seven or... eight"). Though you do not know how your reward will come, it will. The "giving" may include more than charitable donations. Rashbam paraphrases, "Do a favor for a man from whom you never expect to benefit, because in the far future he will do a favor for you" (Rashbam).

The Midrash tells an anecdote of a man who was shipwrecked and washed ashore naked. Rabbi Bar Kappara took him home, fed him, and clothed him. He turned out to be a Roman proconsul, who at a later time acceded to the rabbi's request to show mercy to some Jews who had been arrested.

Ancient Wisdom Literature includes a number of parallels. The Egyptian instruction of Anchsheshonq, a near contemporary of Ecclesiastes, says, "Do a good deed and throw it in the water; when it dries up you will find it."[49] This is close enough to Koheleth's saying to indicate that he was using (and reshaping) a popular proverb. Ben Sira similarly advises: "Lose your money for the sake of a brother or friend, and don't let it rust under a stone" (29:10). The righteousness you store up instead of wealth will save you from all evil (Sira 29:11–13; see also Sira 3:31 and Ps. 112:9).

Others understand this figure as advice on investments: Send your merchandise over the seas, but divide it among several boats for safety's sake. Or, more broadly, take chances, such as in commercial investments, but don't put all your eggs in one basket. That way, you will not lose all your wealth in "some unlucky venture" (5:13). The sayings in Anchsheshonq and Ben Sira, however, support the first interpretation.

2. Distribute portions to seven or even to eight Assist several needy people (Rashi). The next line shows that this is advised not so much for the sake of the virtue

וְגַם לִשְׁמוֹנָה כִּי לֹא תֵדַע מַה־יִּהְיֶה רָעָה
עַל־הָאָרֶץ׃
3 אִם־יִמָּלְאוּ הֶעָבִים גֶּשֶׁם עַל־הָאָרֶץ
יָרִיקוּ וְאִם־יִפּוֹל עֵץ בַּדָּרוֹם וְאִם בַּצָּפוֹן
מְקוֹם שֶׁיִּפּוֹל הָעֵץ שָׁם יְהוּא׃ 4 שֹׁמֵר רוּחַ
לֹא יִזְרָע וְרֹאֶה בֶעָבִים לֹא יִקְצוֹר׃
5 כַּאֲשֶׁר אֵינְךָ יוֹדֵעַ מַה־דֶּרֶךְ הָרוּחַ

seven or even to eight, for you cannot know what
misfortune may occur on earth.
3 If the clouds are filled, they will pour down rain on
the earth; and if a tree falls to the south or to the
north, the tree will stay where it falls. 4 If one watches
the wind, he will never sow; and if one observes the
clouds, he will never reap. 5 Just as you do not know
how the lifebreath passes into the limbs within the

of benevolence as for the practical value of the good you will gain thereby, in case you too face adversity.

for you cannot know what misfortune may occur on earth You yourself may need assistance. Egyptian Wisdom Literature also advises helping others in expectation of reciprocation if need arise, for no one knows what the future will bring. Ptahhotep says:

> Satisfy your acquaintances with what has accrued to you,
> as is possible for the one whom god favors.
> As for him who neglects to satisfy his acquaintances,
> it will be said, "This is a selfish soul!"
> One does not know what will happen, such that he might understand the morrow.[50]

3. Not only misfortunes are beyond human control, but also all events—for which natural phenomena such as clouds, trees falling, and winds blowing are analogies. They will happen when (v. 3a) and how (v. 3b) they will.

South . . . north Together signifying "anywhere."[51]

4. ***If one watches the wind [ruaḥ] . . . observes the clouds*** There is a time to plant and a time to harvest, but this does not mean waiting idly for exactly the best moment. A farmer who constantly frets about the weather, waiting for a windless day before sowing (lest the seeds be blown away) or for a cloudless day before reaping (so that the grain will be dry), will never do what needs to be done. This principle applies to all tasks, not only the two mentioned. Forethought and timely action are important, but planning too meticulously for the incalculable can paralyze initiative. On these same grounds, Koheleth elsewhere urges the reader to enjoy the moment as soon as the opportunity presents itself (7:14), because the future is unknown (6:12; 7:14), and death or "some unlucky venture" (5:13) may intervene.

5. A great mystery is how the lifebreath animates the fetus within the womb. A midrash recognizes this as one of seven great mysteries hidden from humans, the others being the day of one's death; the timing of the (messianic) consolation; the profundity of (divine) judgment; the source from which one will profit; what is in a friend's heart; what is in a woman's pregnancy (that is, what kind of child she will have); and when the kingdom of Edom (= Rome) will fall (Koh. R.). These are valid examples of Koheleth's principle of uncertainty and show that rather than being cynical or even unorthodox, it arises from deep humility. Koheleth has come a great distance from the man who set out "to study and to probe with wisdom all that happens under the sun" (1:13). He is settling for a wisdom that can operate within the narrow confines of human comprehension.

lifebreath [ruaḥ] See Keywords in the introduction.

womb of the pregnant woman, so you cannot foresee
the actions of God, who causes all things to happen.
6 Sow your seed in the morning, and don't hold back
your hand in the evening, since you don't know
which is going to succeed, the one or the other, or if
both are equally good.

7 How sweet is the light, what a delight for the eyes to
behold the sun! 8 Even if a man lives many years, let

כַּעֲצָמִים* בְּבֶטֶן הַמְּלֵאָה כָּכָה לֹא תֵדַע
אֶת־מַעֲשֵׂה הָאֱלֹהִים אֲשֶׁר יַעֲשֶׂה אֶת־
הַכֹּל׃ 6 בַּבֹּקֶר זְרַע אֶת־זַרְעֶךָ וְלָעֶרֶב אַל־
תַּנַּח יָדֶךָ כִּי אֵינְךָ יוֹדֵעַ אֵי זֶה יִכְשַׁר הֲזֶה
אוֹ־זֶה וְאִם־שְׁנֵיהֶם כְּאֶחָד טוֹבִים׃

7 וּמָתוֹק הָאוֹר וְטוֹב לַעֵינַיִם לִרְאוֹת אֶת־
הַשָּׁמֶשׁ׃ 8 כִּי אִם־שָׁנִים הַרְבֵּה יִחְיֶה

v. 5. בנוסח אחר "בעצמים"

pregnant woman Literally, "the full one," a usage found in rabbinic Hebrew.

foresee Hebrew *teda'* (from the root *y-d-'*); better: "know" or "understand." (The analogy in this verse shows that its concern is with understanding how things work rather than knowing what will happen in the future.)

6. ***Sow your seed in the morning, and don't hold back your hand in the evening*** This does not mean that we should labor without pause (that would be *'amal,* "toil"!) but rather that we should undertake our tasks whenever the opportunity arises, because we cannot determine the best time for every action. This recapitulates the advice of verses 1–5 and rounds out the unit, which teaches that we should compensate for ignorance by preparing for multiple possibilities.

"Sowing" can represent all gainful investments of work or wealth. "Morning" and "evening" also calls to mind youth and old age. The Midrash applies Koheleth's advice to the study of Torah in both youth and old age as well as to marrying and begetting children when young and also (if a man's wife dies) when old (Koh. R.). In other words, live life fully to the end. This exhortation leads into the next unit.

since you don't know which is going to succeed, the one or the other, or if both are equally good We should respond to ignorance not by inaction or passivity but by being flexible and diversifying our efforts and investments.

Conclusion (11:7–12:8)

This long unit comprises two sections urging enjoyment of life while it is still possible.

THE LIGHT OF LIFE (11:7–10)

7. Just to be alive is good, even though life's taste is often bitter.

8. ***even if a man lives many years, let him enjoy himself in all of them*** We should not take time for granted, Koheleth teaches, however much of it we seem to have. Since we do not know in advance how long we will live, we must begin enjoying ourselves while young and continue throughout life. To be sure, in 11:9–12:1 Koheleth speaks as if we

הָאָדָם בְּכֻלָּם יִשְׂמָח וְיִזְכֹּר אֶת־יְמֵי
הַחֹשֶׁךְ כִּי־הַרְבֵּה יִהְיוּ כָּל־שֶׁבָּא הָבֶל׃

him enjoy himself in all of them, remembering how many the days of darkness are going to be. The only future is nothingness!

9 שְׂמַח בָּחוּר בְּיַלְדוּתֶיךָ וִיטִיבְךָ לִבְּךָ
בִּימֵי בְחוּרוֹתֶךָ וְהַלֵּךְ בְּדַרְכֵי לִבְּךָ
וּבְמַרְאֵי* עֵינֶיךָ וְדָע כִּי עַל־כָּל־אֵלֶּה

9 O youth, enjoy yourself while you are young! Let your heart lead you to enjoyment in the days of your youth. Follow the desires of your heart and the glances of your eyes—but know well that God will

v. 9. י׳ במקום ה׳

can fully enjoy ourselves only during our youth, for "days of sorrow" may arrive to prevent further joys. But the advice in 11:8 is still valid, and some good things may remain available even in old age (cf. 9:7–9).

remembering how many the days of darkness are going to be We should remember death so as to appreciate life. Paradoxically, this thought can remind us to seize the very pleasures that (according to 5:19) will divert our thoughts from our demise.

The only future is nothingness [***hevel***] Hebrew *kol she-ba' havel;* alternatively: "Everything that comes is senseless," devoid of meaning. Life is this way, and so is what follows.

9. The present verse cautions that while enjoying life, one must keep within the bounds of morality. The pleasures that Koheleth recommends are always moderate and legitimate. He advocates only temperate pleasures and disdains excess, as shown by his contempt for the dissolute nobility in 10:17–19.

Some early readers worried that the advice here to follow one's desires might be conducive to hedonism or heresy (see Koh. R. 1:3). As a precaution, some manuscripts of the Septuagint add "innocently" after "your heart" in verse 9, and the Septuagint renders the end of verse 10: "for the youth and ignorance is vanity." In the same vein Ben Sira nearly reverses Koheleth's advice: "Do *not* follow your heart and your eyes, to go in evil delights" (5:2). For subsequent commentators, too, the first part of this verse was unsettling. Ibn Ezra and Rashi hear the imperative as facetious: Go ahead and sin, and see what happens to you!

Follow the desires of your heart and the glances of your eyes Do what you wish to do and pursue the pleasures you see before you. "Glances of your eyes" is literally "sights of your eyes," as in 6:9, meaning satisfaction as opposed to vain yearning. Other sages offered similar advice, such as the Egyptian Ptahhotep:

> Follow your heart as long as you live,
> Do no more than is required,
> Do not shorten the time of following the heart. (lines 186–88)

will call you to account Literally, "bring you to judgment." The Rabbis were uneasy about Koheleth's advice in this verse, for did not Moses say, "and you shall not go astray after your heart and after your eyes" (Num. 15:39)? But when they heard the caveat that followed, "but know well that God will call you to account for all such things" (11:9b), they exclaimed, "Well has Solomon spoken!" (Koh. R.).

Many modern commentators (e.g., Ginsberg and Crenshaw) believe that 11:9b is a later precautionary addition. In addition to expressing a traditional sentiment, the caveat interrupts a series of imperatives. It is not, however, out of line with Koheleth's thought.

call you to account for all such things—10 and banish
care from your mind, and pluck sorrow out of your
flesh! For youth and black hair are fleeting.

יְבִיאֲךָ הָאֱלֹהִים בַּמִּשְׁפָּט׃ 10 וְהָסֵר כַּעַס
מִלִּבֶּךָ וְהַעֲבֵר רָעָה מִבְּשָׂרֶךָ כִּי־הַיַּלְדוּת
וְהַשַּׁחֲרוּת הָבֶל׃

He basically believes in divine justice (see 3:17 and 8:6a) and assumes that people will be held accountable for their deeds (5:3–5), though he disputes the predictability and timeliness of judgment.

10. banish care In addition to immersing ourselves in pleasures, we should rid ourselves of malaise and irritation. As Prov. 14:13 observes and as Koheleth experienced (2:10–11), it is possible for our heart to be sad even while we indulge in diversions and pleasures.

black hair Hebrew *shaḥarut,* literally "blackness," from *shaḥor,* "black"; it signifies youth, just as "grey hair" commonly means old age in the Bible. Others derive *shaḥarut* from *shaḥar,* "dawn," which would also be a metaphor for youth.

fleeting **[*havel*]** In this context, *hevel* does seem to mean "fleeting." See Keywords in the introduction.

THE DARKNESS OF DEATH (12:1–8)

A poem and its introduction now reinforce the advice of 11:9–10. This is the most difficult section of the book. Its Hebrew is difficult, sometimes obscure, and its imagery is enigmatic. Interpreters have read it through three primary lenses: allegorical, literal, and eschatological.

1. *Allegorical.* Since ancient times, most commentators have seen the poem as an allegory, an encoded narrative of the degeneration of the aging body. Each image is identified with some part of the body and its deterioration. Some statements are taken literally, some as metaphors. The problem with this approach is its arbitrariness. An interpreter identifies an image with one or several parts of the body or a process of bodily deterioration without providing a way to control the decoding. Nor do all the images seem good symbols of bodily deterioration.

2. *Literal.* In a literal reading, the items of the description are just what they are said to be. One such interpretation has verses 2–6 describing an estate falling into disrepair. The event as a whole, rather than the individual elements, represents human deterioration and death.[52] Another literal reading, proposed in the present commentary, construes verse 2b as a reference to old age and verses 3–5a as a description of the funeral of the lord of an estate. In favor of this is the syntax of verses 3–5 (not reflected in NJPS), according to which the events described all happen on the day in which "the man is going to his eternal home, and the mourners walk about in the streets" (v. 5b). This is the time of the funeral procession. Even within this literal reading, some symbolism is recognized. For example, the luminaries' growing dark (v. 2a) represents the coming of death, and the breaking of the vessels (v. 6) represents death and burial.

3. *Eschatological.* This type of reading can be combined with either of the first two. The imagery that pictures the death and funeral of an individual is also suggestive of a day of vast calamity or even the destruction of the world. Koheleth is not describing the actual day of judgment or the world's end; he is depicting the death of an individual human with overtones of cosmic disaster. It is as if Koheleth is saying, when you die, a world *is* ending—*yours*.

12 So appreciate your vigor in the days of your youth, before those days of sorrow come and

יב וּזְכֹר֙ אֶת־בּ֣וֹרְאֶ֔יךָ בִּימֵ֖י בְּחוּרֹתֶ֑יךָ
עַ֣ד אֲשֶׁ֤ר לֹא־יָבֹ֙אוּ֙ יְמֵ֣י הָֽרָעָ֔ה וְהִגִּ֣יעוּ

Some motifs in the poem resemble the disastrous day of judgment described in the Prophets and called "the day of the LORD" and equivalent terms (Amos 5:18, 20; 8:3, 9; Hos. 1:4–5; 5:9; Isa. 3:18–4:1, and often). The prophets often used language suggestive of the destruction of the world, though they had in mind widespread disaster rather than a true end. They described a time when God will come to punish both Israel and the nations. It is dark and overhung with clouds (Ezek. 30:3), which connote misery and fright. Further, it is

> A day of darkness and gloom,
> A day of densest cloud. . . .
> Peoples tremble before them,
> All faces turn ashen. . . .
> Sun and moon are darkened,
> And stars withdraw their brightness. (Joel 2:2a, 6, 10b; compare Zeph. 1:15)

On the cruel and violent day of retribution, God will come

> To make the earth a desolation,
> To wipe out the sinners upon it.
> The stars and constellations of heaven
> Shall not give off their light;
> The sun shall go dark when it arises,
> And the moon shall diffuse no glow. (Isa. 13:9b–10)

The prophetic descriptions of "the day of the LORD" themselves draw upon funeral imagery and laments.

In Koheleth's telling, the two events—the end of a world and the end of a person—resonate in each other. The poem is intended to be mysterious and ambiguous, and the process of interpreting it may be as important as the particular solution one arrives at. Koheleth sets us in a dark and broken landscape through which we must find our way with few guideposts. In a fundamental sense, however, the obscurity of the details does not prevent us from understanding the poem; in fact, it is hard to fail. The gist of the poem is clear: Enjoy life before you grow old and die.

Clear too is the poetic power of the passage. The scene is weird and unsettling, evocative of diminution, quaking, darkening, silence, and fear. The poem depicts the inevitable aging and death of the youth who is addressed in 11:9 and who merges with the "you" of the reader in 12:1–7. We can never fully penetrate the fog of the scene, but when we peer through the murk of the images, metaphors, and symbols, we realize with a shudder that we are descrying our own obliteration.

The following exposition cites interpretations explicitly according to all three lines of interpretation described above.[53] Within the allegorical approach, a number of proposed decodings are mentioned. The allegorical decodings cited below are gathered from the Midrash (Koh. R.), the Targum, the Talmud (B. Shabbat 152a), and traditional commentators (especially Ibn Ezra, Rashi, and Rashbam). Some of these are widely accepted by modern commentators too.

12:1. appreciate your vigor Hebrew *zekhor 'et bor'eykha*; its plain sense is "remember your Creator." NJPS instead identifies *bor'eykha* with a rabbinic word *bori,*

those years arrive of which you will say, "I have no
pleasure in them"; 2 before sun and light and moon
and stars grow dark, and the clouds come back again
after the rain:

שָׁנִ֔ים אֲשֶׁ֣ר תֹּאמַ֔ר אֵֽין־לִ֥י בָהֶ֖ם חֵֽפֶץ׃
2 עַ֣ד אֲשֶׁ֤ר לֹֽא־תֶחְשַׁךְ֙ הַשֶּׁ֙מֶשׁ֙ וְהָא֔וֹר
וְהַיָּרֵ֖חַ וְהַכּוֹכָבִ֑ים וְשָׁ֥בוּ הֶעָבִ֖ים אַחַ֥ר
הַגָּֽשֶׁם׃

meaning "health" or "vigor." Many other commentators have likewise felt that "remember your Creator" is too pietistic to suit Koheleth, and they also wonder how remembering God would be relevant to the exhortation to enjoy life. Nevertheless, the advice "remember your Creator" fits well in the passage, echoing and reinforcing the cautionary note in 11:9b ("but know well that God will call you to account for all such things"). Both sentences counterbalance the advice to enjoy life with an admonition to remember that God is watching over your acts.

Rabbi Akiva saw a triple meaning in the word *bor'eykha,* reading it as *be'erka,* "your well" (semen); *boreka,* "your pit" (the grave); and *bor'eykha,* "your Creator" (God) (Lev. R. 18.1).

those years arrive of which you will say, "I have no pleasure in them" When one is old, weak, and ill, many of life's pleasures become impossible.

2. ***before sun and light and moon and stars grow dark*** *Allegorical:* The light of the face or nose or forehead dims. Or, the eyes cannot see the sun. Or, the light stands for the eyes or nose, which lose their keenness, and the moon is the cheeks or the soul, which grows pale. Or, the stars are the eyeballs or the cheeks, which grow dim or dull. *Literal*: A metaphor of the moment of death. The light that goes out is the light of life; see 11:7. *Eschatological*: On the day of the Lord, "Sun and moon are darkened, and stars withdraw their brightness" (Joel 2:10b). Thus God said to Egypt:

> When you are snuffed out,
> I will cover the sky
> And darken its stars;
> I will cover the sun with clouds
> and the moon shall not give its light.
> All the lights that shine in the sky
> I will darken above you;
> And I will bring darkness upon your land
> —declares the Lord God. (Ezek. 32:7–8)

the clouds come back again after the rain *Allegorical*: As one ages, vision grows blurry from tears. *Literal*: The survivors' weeping and gloom are constant. *Eschatological*: The day of the Lord is "a day of cloud" (Ezek 30:3b) and "a day of densest cloud" (Joel 2:2a).

Rashbam recognized eschatological overtones in this image but interpreted them as descriptive of aging rather than death. With regard to the clouds' returning, he says, "Before there comes to you darkness after darkness, you should be quick to repent. This verse is like 'I clothe the skies in blackness, and make their raiment sackcloth' (Isa. 50:3). It is a metaphor for the world becoming dark to [people] in their great sorrow."

3 When the guards of the house become shaky,
And the men of valor are bent,
And the maids that grind, grown few, are idle,
And the ladies that peer through the windows grow dim,
4 And the doors to the street are shut—
With the noise of the hand mill growing fainter,

3 בַּיּוֹם שֶׁיָּזֻעוּ שֹׁמְרֵי הַבַּיִת
וְהִתְעַוְּתוּ אַנְשֵׁי הֶחָיִל
וּבָטְלוּ הַטֹּחֲנוֹת כִּי מִעֵטוּ
וְחָשְׁכוּ הָרֹאוֹת בָּאֲרֻבּוֹת׃
4 וְסֻגְּרוּ דְלָתַיִם בַּשּׁוּק
בִּשְׁפַל קוֹל הַטַּחֲנָה

*3. **When the guards of the house become shaky*** *Allegorical*: The knees—or flanks, or ribs, or legs, or arms, or hands—tremble. *Literal*: The "keepers" (not necessarily "guards") of the house are the menservants, who shudder in mourning and dismay. *Eschatological*: On the day of judgment, fear and trembling are everywhere. (The word for "shake," *yazu'u,* is a strong one, meaning to quake in terror.) As Isaiah describes it:

> Therefore all hands shall grow limp,
> And all men's hearts shall sink;
> And, overcome by terror,
> They shall be seized by pangs and throes,
> Writhe like a woman in travail. (Isa. 13:7–8a)

And the men of valor are bent *Allegorical*: The arms, or legs, or spine, weaken or bend. *Literal*: The valorous (possibly "rich"; cf. Ruth 2:1) men are bent in fear and mourning. *Eschatological*: Universal terror. In similar terms, Isaiah describes his reaction to the grim day of judgment: "I am too bent [NJPS: "anguished"] to hear, too frightened to see" (Isa. 21:3b).

And the maids that grind, grown few, are idle *Allegorical*: The teeth fall out. *Literal*: The mill-maids cease their work for the funeral. *Eschatological*: Depopulation puts an end to normal activities. Compare Isa. 13:12: "I will make people scarcer than fine gold, and men than gold of Ophir."

And the ladies that peer through the windows grow dim *Allegorical:* The eyes grow weak or blind. *Literal*: The women of the house go dark, that is, grow melancholy in grief. (The figure of eyes going dark indicates deep grief; see Lam. 5:17b.) Or, their appearance becomes sickly and grim. The growing dark of the "appearance" (*ha-ro'ot,* or "visage") indicates wasting away with hunger and disease; see Lam. 4:8. *Eschatological*: Fear and gloom are everywhere; compare Joel 2:6.

*4. **And the doors to the street are shut*** More precisely, "double doors." *Allegorical*: The bodily apertures, or ears, or lips, suffer or close. Or, the anus and bladder suffer retention. *Literal*: During the funeral, doors—possibly to the town bazaar—are closed. (The street or bazaar [*shuk*] is mentioned at the end of 12:5 as the place where the lamenters go. Participation in a cortege was a communal duty and could bring the activities in a village or estate to a halt.[54]) *Eschatological*: People hide in terror from the cataclysm.

With the noise of the mill growing fainter *Allegorical*: The stomach fails to "grind" the food. *Literal*: The grinding of grain, one of the background sounds of ordinary domestic life, ceases. Or, the voice diminishes. *Eschatological*: Normal sounds cease. Compare the disaster when Babylon is judged: "And I will banish from them the

And the song of the bird growing feebler,
And all the strains of music dying down;
5 When one is afraid of heights
And there is terror on the road.—
For the almond tree may blossom,
The grasshopper be burdened,

וְיָקוּם֙ לְק֣וֹל הַצִּפּ֔וֹר
וְיִשַּׁ֖חוּ כָּל־בְּנ֥וֹת הַשִּֽׁיר׃
5 גַּ֣ם מִגָּבֹ֤הַּ יִרָ֙אוּ֙
וְחַתְחַתִּ֣ים בַּדֶּ֔רֶךְ
וְיָנֵ֤אץ הַשָּׁקֵד֙
וְיִסְתַּבֵּ֣ל הֶֽחָגָ֔ב

sound of mirth and gladness, the voice of bridegroom and bride, the sound of the grinder and the light of the lamp. This whole land shall be a desolate ruin" (Jer. 25:10–11a).

And the song of the bird growing feebler The Hebrew is obscure, literally, "and one rises to the voice of a bird" or "the bird rises to song" (in other words, begins to sing). The NJPS paraphrase, made according to the context, matches a proposed emendation that is doubtful.[55] *Allegorical*: If translated "and one rises to the voice of a bird," the line means that an old person sleeps lightly and wakes up at dawn. *Literal*: If translated "and the bird begins to sing," the line might allude to the mourning sound of birds of ill omen; see Mic. 1:8b: "I will lament as sadly as the jackals, as mournfully as the ostriches"; see also Job 30:28–31. The funerary wailing recalls such sounds. *Eschatological*: The eerie hoots of birds of ill omen are heard in a depopulated world, when owls and kites roost in desolate cities (see, for example, Isa. 13:21; 34:13; Jer. 50:39).[56]

And all the strains of music dying down Literally, "the daughters of song bow low." *Allegorical*: The aging voice rasps or loses pitch or becomes weak. Or, deafness sets in and the old person can barely hear the sound of singing. *Literal*: The "daughters of song" are singing women, probably professional mourners who chant their laments while bowing to the ground. In 2 Chron. 35:25, lamentations are sung by trained lamenters, male and female, called "singers." *Eschatological*: This represents communal lamentation after the cataclysm.

5. When one is afraid of heights Or: "and they fear also what is on high." *Allegorical*: Even the allegorizers must construe this literally: The aged are afraid of walking up hills. *Literal*: This may mean that the mourners fear Him who is on high, namely, God (thus Ibn Yaḥyah).

And there is terror on the road *Allegorical*: Old people are timid when walking along the road, or they are uncertain how to get from one place to another. *Literal*: Scenes of dismay mark the processional. This may refer to the formalized expression of grief in the mourning rites. *Eschatological*: There are terrors everywhere, on high and on the road. The eschatological allusions end here, with the possible exception of the end of verse 5.

For the almond tree may blossom *Allegorical*: The hair grows white. Or, the hipbone ("almond") protrudes because of leanness. *Literal*: The next three images show a *contrast* to human fate. Nature, but not man, is reborn in the spring.[57] Compare Job 14:7–10, "There is hope for a tree; if it is cut down, it will renew itself…"

The grasshopper be burdened *Allegorical*: The old man is bent over. Or, the buttocks droop. Or, sex becomes onerous. Or, the penis fails to become erect. Or, an actual grasshopper feels heavy to the weakened oldster. *Literal*: The "grasshopper" may be the carob tree, whose pods resemble the locust. (In English this same tree is called the "locust.") This tree becomes "burdened" or (better) "laden" with fruit. In a footnote,

And the caper bush may bud again;
But man sets out for his eternal abode,
With mourners all around in the street.—
6 Before the silver cord snaps
And the golden bowl crashes,
The jar is shattered at the spring,
And the jug is smashed at the cistern.

וְתָפֵר הָאֲבִיּוֹנָה
כִּי־הֹלֵךְ הָאָדָם֙ אֶל־בֵּית עוֹלָמוֹ
וְסָבְבוּ בַשּׁוּק הַסֹּפְדִים׃
6 עַד אֲשֶׁר לֹא־ירחק יֵרָתֵק֙ חֶבֶל הַכֶּסֶף
וְתָרֻץ גֻּלַּת הַזָּהָב
וְתִשָּׁבֶר כַּד֙ עַל־הַמַּבּוּעַ
וְנָרֹץ הַגַּלְגַּל אֶל־הַבּוֹר׃

NJPS translators suggest an emendation, חצב (*ḥatzav*) for MT's חגב (*ḥagav*), which yields: "The squill resumes its burden." The squill is a bulbous plant and its "burden" would be its blossom-stalk and leaves—a sign of renewal.

And the caper bush may bud again The MT has *ve-tafer;* lit. "is annulled," which is obscure. NJPS associates this with *ve-tifraḥ,* "and buds." We should probably emend to the latter reading. These plants, after seeming dead for part of the year, revive—unlike humans (cf. Job 14:7–10) (Transl.). *Allegorical* (reading "annulled"): Sexual desire is dulled, or aphrodisiacs fail. ("Caper bush" is *'aviyyonah,* which appears in the Bible only here and which sounds like *'avah* "to desire.") *Literal*: The caper regains its vitality and blossoms again.

eternal abode The grave.

With mourners all around in the street Better: "and the mourners walk about in the street." *Allegorical*: Maggots crawl over the corpse. *Literal*: This is the funeral procession. (The "mourners"—*sofedim*—are the trained chanters of laments, not the bereaved family.) *Eschatological*: Communal lament is heard on the day of judgment. Amos says,

In every square there shall be lamenting,
In every street cries of "Ah, woe!"
And the farmhand shall be
Called to mourn,
And those skilled in wailing *(mispeid)*
To lament. (5:16b)

6. The images in this verse are symbols of death. There are probably four different images with essentially the same intent: Humans die and descend to the grave. Some read the images as a single complex picture of breakage, to the same effect.[58]

Before the silver cord snaps First, the cord holding the bowl snaps, meaning that one's hold on life is sundered.

And the golden bowl crashes The bowl, apparently representing life or perhaps the physical body that is its vessel, falls and disintegrates.

The jar is shattered at the spring The jar, also representing human life, falls and breaks. Humans are often compared to pots (Isa. 29:16; 64:7; Jer. 18:6). Deliberately broken vessels are often found in Jewish tombs of the Second Temple period. They were perhaps smashed as part of a funeral rite symbolizing the shattering of life.[59]

And the jug is smashed at the cistern Since *bor,* "cistern," is also used of the grave (e.g., Prov. 28:17; Isa. 14:15; 38:18), this image suggests a body lying useless in the grave.

7 And the dust returns to the ground
As it was,
And the lifebreath returns to God
Who bestowed it.
8 Utter futility—said Koheleth—
All is futile!

7 וְיָשֹׁ֧ב הֶעָפָ֛ר עַל־הָאָ֖רֶץ
כְּשֶׁהָיָ֑ה
וְהָר֣וּחַ תָּשׁ֔וּב אֶל־הָאֱלֹהִ֖ים
אֲשֶׁ֥ר נְתָנָֽהּ׃
8 הֲבֵ֧ל הֲבָלִ֛ים אָמַ֥ר הַקּוֹהֶ֖לֶת
הַכֹּ֥ל הָֽבֶל׃

*7. **And the dust returns to the ground as it was*** The human body—"dust" in origin (3:20; see Gen. 2:7, 3:19), like vessels of clay—lies worthless and disintegrated, like the shards of a smashed jug.

And the lifebreath returns to God who bestowed it The lifebreath (*ruaḥ*) is given to all creatures at birth and leaves them at death. This clause does not imply an afterlife but simply the decomposition of the living being. The *ruaḥ* is not the immortal soul but the force that animates all creatures: "take away their breath [*ruaḥ*], they perish and turn again into dust; send back Your breath, they are created, and You renew the face of the earth" (Ps. 104:29b–30). When God takes back the *ruaḥ,* they die.

*8. **Utter futility** [**havel havalim**]**—said Koheleth—All is futile!*** This verse is the pivot between the poem on dying and the epilogue; it belongs to both units. The pronouncements in 1:2 and 12:8 summarize Koheleth's teachings and bracket the book between them. Human life ends in *hevel,* the ultimate void or absurdity. The teaching of Koheleth thus ends where it began. Though he complains that he did not find the wisdom he sought (7:23–24) and that the world remained opaque (8:16–17), he has in fact discovered a wisdom, a more modest, pragmatic one—different from philosophical understanding of life he set out to seek. His honesty and his simple counsels have provided a way to face life frankly and to experience whatever pleasures we are granted. We must accept both our limitations and life's inequities not by avoiding them but by living in the present, which is all we can have. See Keywords in the introduction and Comment to 1:2.

Epilogue (12:9–14)

In the epilogue, a different voice speaks, and it is of an anonymous teacher. This voice addresses the reader as "my son," in typical Wisdom fashion, and speaks about Koheleth in the third person. Koheleth is treated as a personage of the past, whose teachings are admired but viewed with a certain hesitation. This same voice speaks about Koheleth in 1:2, 7:27, and 12:8.

Traditional commentators assumed that because the epilogue is part of the Book of Koheleth, it was composed by Koheleth, which is to say, Solomon. Since the nineteenth century, commentators have assumed that because the epilogue speaks *about* Koheleth, it was added to the book by a later editor. This editor supposedly considered Koheleth's words too unorthodox and sought to counteract them with pious assurances and precepts.

Some recent studies have argued that the epilogue is really spoken by the narrator of the book, who presents the wisdom of Koheleth, supposedly an ancient sage, by quoting it

9 A further word: Because Koheleth was a sage, he
continued to instruct the people. He listened to and
tested the soundness of many maxims. 10 Koheleth
sought to discover useful sayings and recorded
genuinely truthful sayings. 11 The sayings of the wise

9 וְיֹתֵ֕ר שֶׁהָיָ֥ה קֹהֶ֖לֶת חָכָ֑ם ע֗וֹד לִמַּד־
דַּ֙עַת֙ אֶת־הָעָ֔ם וְאִזֵּ֣ן וְחִקֵּ֔ר תִּקֵּ֖ן מְשָׁלִ֥ים
הַרְבֵּֽה׃ 10 בִּקֵּ֣שׁ קֹהֶ֔לֶת לִמְצֹ֖א דִּבְרֵי־חֵ֑פֶץ
וְכָת֥וּב יֹ֖שֶׁר דִּבְרֵ֥י אֱמֶֽת׃ 11 דִּבְרֵ֤י חֲכָמִים֙

extensively.[60] The author of the epilogue (whose viewpoint is final and decisive and therefore probably that of the author of the entire book), looks back at Koheleth and summarizes his work.

While showing respect for Koheleth, the epilogist keeps a certain distance from his teaching—and from other recorded Wisdom as well: the words of the wise are fine and good, but they also must be handled gingerly (12:11–12). The epilogist by no means repudiates Koheleth, yet he cautions that wisdom holds certain dangers. The postscript in 12:13–14 reminds us that wisdom, originating in human intellect and tradition, takes second rank to piety and obedience to God's law.

The words of the wise are not always comfortable, pious, and traditional, as the books of Ecclesiastes and Job prove. They can sting, and they must be approached with care. As R. Eliezer b. Hyrcanus was later to admonish,

> Warm yourself before the fire of the wise, but be wary of their words lest you get burnt. For their bite is the bite of a jackal, and their sting is the sting of a scorpion, and their hiss is the hiss of a serpent, and all their words are like fiery coals (Avot 2:10).

The epilogue uses terms related to scribal practices in the ancient Near East. Scribes often appended colophons—concluding notes describing who copied the text and related information. The epilogue formulates some of these concepts in narrative form. Notably the equivalent of the Hebrew phrase *'asot sefarim* (v. 12; NJPS: "the making of many books") is found in Akkadian and Aramaic in the sense of "compose" or "compile" books. It has been suggested that as a technical scribal term, *tikken* (v. 9; NJPS: "tested the soundness," literally "corrected") meant "edit" or "arrange,"[61] but "compose" is also possible.

9. he continued to instruct the people This implies that the words quoted in this book are a selection of Koheleth's teachings and—very importantly—that they were not intended as esoteric teachings, too dangerous for the public's ears.

He listened to and tested the soundness Hebrew *ve-'izzen ve-ḥikker tikken;* better: "Having listened and investigated, he composed…" The word *tikken* is a verb that implies authorship.

10. Koheleth sought to discover useful sayings and recorded genuinely truthful sayings Koheleth both sought out useful proverbs and composed some of his own. (The verb translated "recorded" is *katuv,* "wrote," which can indicate authorship as well as recording the sayings of others.[62])

11. like goads, like nails fixed The sayings prod people to better behavior. At the same time, again like ox goads, they sting and provoke.

in prodding sticks Hebrew *ba'aley 'asuppot;* better: "[by] masters of collections." These are the experts in proverb collections, parallel to "the wise." Rabbinic Hebrew uses *be'alim* of men expert in different kinds of literature. For example, *ba'aley miqra'* are "experts in Scripture," and *ba'aley 'aggadah* are "experts in Aggadah" (see Gen. Rab. 41.1,

כַּדָּרְבֹנוֹת וּכְמַשְׂמְרוֹת נְטוּעִים בַּעֲלֵי
אֲסֻפּוֹת נִתְּנוּ מֵרֹעֶה אֶחָד׃
12 וְיֹתֵר מֵהֵמָּה בְּנִי הִזָּהֵר

are like goads, like nails fixed in prodding sticks. They were given by one Shepherd.
12 A further word: Against them, my son, be warned!

Lev. Rab. 36:2, and the Alpha Beta d'Ben Sira 24). These *be'alim* are not the texts' authors but rather learned specialists in them. (The idea that one should study the collections of proverbs for the sake of higher learning as well as basic education is found in Prov. 1:5–6.) But the words of these "masters of collections" are themselves Wisdom Literature. The epilogist places Koheleth in this category.

They were given by one Shepherd The "one shepherd" is almost always assumed to be God. By this reading, words of wisdom—even unconventional ones like Koheleth's—ultimately derive from God. The traditional understanding has been a rich source of rabbinic exposition. A homily in B. Hagigah 3b uses this verse to advocate an extraordinary openness to different opinions in the study of Torah, with which wisdom is midrashically identified. (*'Asuppot,* translated above as "collections," can also mean "assemblies.")

> *Ba'aley 'asuppot*: These are the students of the wise, who sit in many assemblies and occupy themselves with the Torah—some pronouncing ritually unclean and others pronouncing [similar persons or objects] clean, some prohibiting and others permitting [identical things], some disqualifying [a person from being a witness or a priest], and others declaring (him) fit.
>
> A man might say, "If this is so, how can I learn Torah?" Therefore Scripture says, "*They were given by one Shepherd.*" One God gave them [that is, the different interpretations of Torah]; one leader spoke them from the mouth of the Lord of all creation (blessed be He), for it is written, "*God spoke all these words*" (Exod. 20:1). You, too, make your ear like a hopper and get a perceptive heart to hear the words of those who pronounce unclean and the words of those who pronounce clean, the words of those who prohibit and the words of those who permit, the words of those who disqualify and the words of those who declare fit.

The key is "all these words" in Exod 20:1, just before the words of the Covenant. All scholars of Torah are speaking God's words, as it were, even when arriving at diverse and contradictory opinions. Some of these scholars must be wrong, yet God is speaking through them too, for not only the substance of the words but the very activity of studying Torah and judging thereby *is* Torah and proceeds from the ultimate source of wisdom, the "one Shepherd."

The difficulty with the traditional understanding of "by one Shepherd" is that the metaphor of shepherd for God refers to his role protecting and providing for people—a role that is not relevant here. A shepherd does not "give" words or commands. Nor, unlike law and prophecy, are the words of the wise ever considered to be given by God. An alternative translation is, "given by a shepherd." This simply continues the metaphor of goads and nails, which are "given" in the sense of being "set" or poked in an animal. (Compare *natan,* meaning "stick into," in Deut. 15:17.) Thus this verse should be translated, "The words of the sages are like goads/And [those of] the masters of collections are like implanted nails, stuck in by a shepherd."[63] The sages prod their flocks along, at once stinging and guiding them for their own benefit. Hence the warning in the next verse.

12. A further word: Against them, my son, be warned! Be wary when reading the words of the wise. This refers not only to unorthodox writings like Ecclesiastes, which is not specifically mentioned in the preceding verse, but to wisdom books generally.

The making of many books is without limit
And much study is a wearying of the flesh.
13 The sum of the matter, when all is said and done:
Revere God and observe His commandments! For
this applies to all mankind: 14 that God will call every
creature to account for everything unknown, be it
good or bad.

The sum of the matter, when all is said and done: Revere God and observe His commandments! For this applies to all mankind.

עֲשׂוֹת סְפָרִים הַרְבֵּה אֵין קֵץ
וְלַהַג הַרְבֵּה יְגִעַת בָּשָׂר:
13 סוֹף דָּבָר הַכֹּל נִשְׁמָע אֶת־הָאֱלֹהִים יְרָא
וְאֶת־מִצְוֺתָיו שְׁמוֹר כִּי־זֶה כָּל־הָאָדָם:
14 כִּי אֶת־כָּל־מַעֲשֶׂה הָאֱלֹהִים יָבִא
בְמִשְׁפָּט עַל כָּל־נֶעְלָם אִם־טוֹב וְאִם־
רָע:*

[סוֹף דָּבָר הַכֹּל נִשְׁמָע אֶת־הָאֱלֹהִים יְרָא
וְאֶת־מִצְוֺתָיו שְׁמוֹר כִּי־זֶה כָּל־הָאָדָם:*]

v. 14. סכום הפסוקים של הספר 222 וחציו 6.10
end. במסורת הקריאה נשנה הפסוק לפני האחרון

תם ונשלם תהילה לאל בורא עולם

The making of many books is without limit Writing books of wisdom continues without end, and one can become overwhelmed with all their ideas.

And much study is a wearying of the flesh Study is praiseworthy but should not be overdone.

13. ***The sum of the matter*** Hebrew *sof davar,* literally, "the end of the matter." The use of this and similar phrases elsewhere (see especially Dan. 7:28), shows that it marks the end of the book or other major textual unit. We should probably translate, "The end of the matter. Everything has been heard." Its purpose is to indicate that the words of the book proper are finished and what follows is a postscript.

Revere God and observe His commandments! Koheleth would not disagree. Whatever his doubts and worries, he advocates fear of God (5:5; 7:18) and insists on divine judgment (3:17; 11:9). The epilogue, however, states the principle firmly and definitively.

For this applies to all mankind This principle pertains to everyone and not only to the wise and learned.

14. ***God will call every creature to account*** God will judge every deed, even hidden ones. Just as Koheleth allowed indulgence in material pleasures in moderation—provided that we remember that we will have to answer for our behavior (11:9), so the epilogue allows us to study and explore wisdom in moderation—so long as we fear God, obey His commandments, and remain conscious of His watchful eye.

Whether the last two verses of the book are by the same author as the rest of Ecclesiastes or by a later scribe, they belong indelibly to the canonical Book of Ecclesiastes and are definitive for the book's meaning as it stands. The book allows readers to probe the ways of God and man, wherever this may lead, so long as we make the fear of God and obedience to the Commandments the final standard of behavior.

The sum of the matter In some Masoretic editions, and in public readings, verse 13 is repeated, so that the book not end with a threat.

NOTES TO THE COMMENTARY

1. E. Bickermann, *Four Strange Books,* 143.

2. Reading הלכים משם for MT's הלכים שם, "go, there," a correction which assumes the early loss during copying of one of two similar adjacent letters (haplography).

3. John L. Gibson, *Textbook of Syrian Semitic Inscriptions* (1971–82), 3.34, 47.

4. Variants of this story appear in Koh. R.; Targum; Pes. de-R. Kah. 26b; and J. Sanhedrin 20c.

5. *AEL* 2.145.

6. The MT reads להמנות *(lehimmanot),* "be counted," which does not make good sense here. NJPS paraphrases this as "be made good," but it is doubtful that this is the same as "be counted." By a minor emendation to להמלות *(lehimmalot,* from the root *m-l-'*) the word means "be filled."

7. Thus Fox, *A Time to Tear Down,* 173–74.

8. In contrast, Alsheikh believes that all the sensual pleasures Koheleth describes are folly. Some commentators make a qualitative distinction between different kinds of pleasure. For example, C. D. Ginsburg, p. 276, says that Koheleth is denouncing "pleasure and mirth" while allowing "innocent cheerfulness and pleasure." But nothing indicates this distinction. Equally artificial is a distinction between pleasures passively received (which Koheleth supposedly affirms) versus actively pursued ones (which he supposedly condemns); thus H.-W. Hertzberg (*Der Prediger* [*Kommentar zum Alten Testament, neue Folge* XVII, 4. Gütersloh, 1963] 86).

9. Discussed by Seow, 150–151. See further Seow, "Qohelet's Autobiography," in *Fortunate the Eyes that See: Essays in Honor of David Noel Freedman,* ed. A. B. Beck et al. (Grand Rapids, MI: Eerdmans), 275–87.

10. Gibson, *Textbook,* 3.34.

11. Septuagint and a few Heb. manuscripts have "(in exchange) for"; cf. 2.24; 3.13, 22; 5.17 (Transl.).

12. For an analysis of Koheleth's use of *mikreh,* see Peter Machinist, "Fate, *Miqreh,* and Reason: Some Reflections on Qohelet and Biblical Thought," in *Solving Riddles and Untying Knots,* ed. Z. Zevit et al. (Winona Lake, IN: Eisenbrauns), 159-75.

13. As an NJPS note says, the literal meaning of *laledit* is "giving birth." But while the *qal* of the verb *yalad* elsewhere does have this meaning, the infinitive of a transitive verb can have an intransitive sense (e.g. *litboaḥ,* "to be killed" in Jer. 25:34), and this is required by the parallelism.

14. Hengel, *Judaism and Hellenism,* 1.124; references 2.84.

15. Version A, ll. 103–4. Translated from the Hebrew of A. Shaffer, *Eretz Israel* 8 (1967), 246–50 and 9 (1969), 159–60.

16. MT reads כי ברב חלמות והבלים ודברים הרבה, but כי כרב חלמות והבלים דברים הרבה would make more sense.

17. The Septuagint reads ואבל (*va-'evel*) "and in mourning" for MT's יאכל (*yo'khel*), "eats," hence "all his days are [spent] in darkness and mourning" (Transl.).

18. *AEL* 1.196–97.

19. A. Gianto, "Human Destiny in Emar and Qohelet," in *Qohelet in the Context of Wisdom* (*BETL*; Leuven, 1998), 473–79, at 475.

20. See Fox, *A Time to Tear Down,* 243–44.

21. Emendation (from *gam,* "also," to *'im*) yields: "(7b) And if the gullet is not sated, (8) what advantage has the wise man over the fool, he who knows how to get on in life over the pauper?" (Transl.; Ginsberg). Or, to the same effect, the "if" can be understood as implicit, without emendation.

22. Tractatus Logico-Philosophicus § 7.

23. This sentence requires a minor emendation, from אדם ולא יוכל לדין, "man, and he cannot contend" to ואדם לא יוכל לדין, "and man cannot contend."

24. MT *ve-ya'asem ka-tzel 'asher.* The meaning of the Hebrew is obscured in NJPS, which (as a footnote explains) treats the second two words as a mistranslation of an underlying Aramaic *beṭul d-* or *meṭul d-,* "because." The hypothesized translator thought that *ṭl* in *mṭwl d-* was the homograph that meant "shadow." It is, however, unlikely that the translator would confuse the extremely common conjunction *meṭul* with a noun that would have the form *ṭll'* or *ṭwl'.* On the theory of Aramaic origin, see note 11 in the introduction.

25. The near-synonymity is shown by the fact that an ancient fragment from Qumran substitutes [*s*]*imḥah,* "pleasure," for *mishteh,* "feasting" in v. 2.

26. The Koheleth fragment from Qumran (4QQoh[a]) originally had some words before 7:7. They are now lost. Perhaps there was once a sentence supplying a transition to v. 7.

27. David E. S. Stein, personal communication.

28. Emendation (from *btzl . . . btzl* ["in the shade" . . . "in the shade"] to *b'l . . . b'l* ["the possessor of" . . . "the possessor of"]) yields: "For the possessor of wisdom becomes a possessor of money" (Transl.). To be sure, צ and ע are similar in some scripts. Nevertheless, "shade" makes good sense as a metaphor, and emendation is not necessary.

29. MT has מעשׂרה שליטים *(me-'asarah shallitim)*; the proposed emendation is to מעשר השליטים *(me-'osher ha-shallitim).*

30. Thus N. Lohfink, "War Koheleth ein Frauenfeind?" *BETL* 51, 259–87.

31. "The Dialogue of Pessimism," in B. Foster, *Before the Muses,* 816.

32. Discussed in M. V. Fox, *The Song of Songs and the Ancient Egyptian Love Songs* (Madison, WI: Univ. of Wisconsin, 1985), 289–90. This motif appears in Song 7:6, "The locks of your head are like purple:/A king is held captive in the tresses." The "king" is the young man who is speaking. Similarly Song 4:9, "You have captured my heart,/My own, my bride,/You have captured my heart/With one glance of your eyes,/With one coil of your necklace."

33. The Hebrew has אמרה קהלת, using a feminine verb. Elsewhere "Koheleth" is treated as masculine, though its grammatical form is feminine. We should redivide the words as אמר הקהלת, "the Koheleth says," as in 12:8.

34. The "man . . . woman" explanation is followed in Fox, *A Time,* 270–72. The "man . . . wife" explanation, however, requires fewer assumptions.

35. A. Ehrlich, *Randglossen zur hebräischen Bibel* (Leipzig, 1908–1914, repr. Hildesheim, 1968), vol. 7.

36. An original ישנאנו "changes it," at the end of the preceding sentence, could have been miscopied as ישנא אני ("changed" + "I"), as the MT has it.

37. Ehrlich, *Randglossen,* 7.89.

38. See B. Megillah 28b; Rosh ha-Shanah 25a; Mo'ed Katan 21b. However, the practice is not established for Second Temple times.

39. For *shakhaḥ* denoting neglect rather than a lapse of memory, see Pss. 9:19; 102:5; Isa. 49:15; Deut. 24:19.

40. A variant in the Septuagint and some Hebrew manuscripts reads וישתבחו, "were praised" for MT's וישתכחו, "were forgotten." The word *ken,* here translated "righteously," can also

mean "thus." Hence the sentence can be translated, "and those who did thus [that is, wickedly] were praised in the city." Both variants make sense.

41. "Shadow" is not represented in NJPS, because it understands Hebrew *ka-tzel 'asher* as equivalent to Aramaic *me-tul d-*; see note 24.

42. Though Ibn Ezra does not emend, we should probably assume the loss during copying of one of two adjacent letters (haplography) and reading זה הרע "this is the worst thing" for MT's זה רע, which might be translated "this is a bad thing."

43. Compare the Egyptian "Harper Song" (mid–fourteenth century B.C.E.): "Follow your heart as long as you live!/Put myrrh on your head,/Dress in fine linen,/Anoint yourself with oils fit for a god./Heap up your joys,/Let your heart not sink!/ Follow your heart and your happiness./Do your things on earth as your heart commands!/When there comes to you that day of mourning,/The Weary-Hearted [Osiris, the god of the netherworld] hears not their mourning,/Wailing saves no man from the pit! [*Refrain*:] Make holiday,/Do not weary of it!/Lo, none is allowed to take his goods with him,/Lo, none who departs comes back again!" (*AEL* 1.196–97).

44. *AEL* 1.70.

45. *AEL* 1.66.

46. Koheleth speaks of his heart in a way reminiscent of the Egyptian conception. In the Egyptian idiom, when your heart "leaves" you, you are deprived of resources. A girl in an Egyptian love song scolds her heart for deserting her and making her foolish (see Fox, *Song of Songs,* 53, 59). The notion of the fool's heart betraying its owner also recalls the Book of the Dead, in which the heart is perceived as a potential accuser of the deceased. In Spell 28, the deceased declares: "I have my heart and control it. It shall not tell what I have done.... Obey me, my heart, (for) I am your lord while you are in my body."

47. For example, from the Complaints of Ipuwer: "Lo, citizens are put to the grindstones,/Wearers of fine linen are beaten with [sticks]./Those who never saw daylight go out unhindered,/Those who were on their husbands' beds, 'Let them lie on boards,' [one repeats]." (Ipuwer, *AEL* 1.153).

48. This explanation parses *ma'aneh* in 5:19 and *ya'aneh* in 10:19 as *hiphil* causitive forms of *'-n-h,* which in the intransitive means "be busy" (1:13, 3:10, and elsewhere).

49. *AEL* 3.174.

50. Ptahhotep 339–43, my translation; cf. *AEL* 1.69. The last quoted line is a frequently cited Egyptian proverb, which appears also in Prov. 27:1. See also the Wisdom of Anii, 21.4–10 (*AEL* 2.141–142).

51. Emendation (of *'eitz,* "tree" to *heitz,* "arrow") yields: "if a thunderbolt (lit. arrow; cf., e.g., 2 Sam. 22.15) falls... where the thunderbolt falls, only there will it strike" (Transl.).

52. Thus H. Witzenrath, *Süss ist das Licht* (St. Ottilien: EOS, 1979), 46–50. John Sawyer ("The Ruined House in Ecclesiastes 12," *JBL* 94 [1976], 519–31) tries to trace an extended description of a ruined estate, which represents the failure of human efforts.

53. In *A Time to Tear Down and a Time to Build Up* (1999), I argue in favor of reading the poem as a mostly literal description of a death and funeral, with strong eschatological resonances. Seow develops the eschatological reading in "Kohelet's Eschatological Poem" (*JBL* 118 [1999], 209–34). Some observations herein are taken from his article as well as his commentary.

54. Sira 7:34 and 38:16–17 indicate that participation in funerals was an important communal obligation. Both B. Mo'ed Katan 27b and J. Bikkurim 65c (cf. Shulḥan Arukh, Yoreh De'ah § 361.4) say that everyone is obliged to rise and accompany a cortege for at least a symbolic four paces.

55. The NJPS relates ויקם לקול *(ve-yakum le-kol)* to ויקמל קול *(ve-yikmal kol),* which is proposed as an emendation by Ginsberg. But *ve-yikmal* (from the root *k-m-l*) means "wither" or "decay," not "grow feebler."

56. The apocalypse of Revelation in Christian Scripture speaks of "Babylon" becoming a "haunt for every unclean and despicable bird" (18:2).

57. H.-W. Hertzberg, *Der Prediger*; O. Loretz, *Qohelet und der alte Orient* (Freiburg: Herder, 1964), 191–92). Seow, however, translates "The almond becomes revolting, the locust droops, and the caper comes to naught." He associates the imagery with decay and death (*Ecclesiastes,* 347).

58. Seow (*JBL* 118 [1999], 228–30) argues for a single image: the shattering of an elaborate and durable lamp on a silver lampstand. He notes that lamps are very commonly found in tombs, where they symbolized hope in the netherworld. Koheleth is implying that "all hope of life will be snuffed out forever" (230).

59. Ibid., 231.

60. Thus Fox, *A Time to Tear Down* (Excursus III) and in earlier studies. Several ancient Near Eastern Wisdom texts use a brief narrative to frame the words of the sage who speaks in the book.

Longman (37–39) goes so far as to argue that the real purpose of the book is revealed in the epilogue, in which the author warns against speculative and skeptical wisdom like Koheleth's. This probably makes too deep a divide between Koheleth's and the epilogist's thinking.

Christianson (*A Time to Tell,* chap. I) analyzes in depth the literary mechanism of the frame-narrative (given in the voice of the epilogist speaking about Koheleth) to show how the framing affects our perception of Koheleth as a person.

61. Michael Fishbane, *Biblical Interpretation in Ancient Israel* (Oxford: Clarendon Press, 1985), 30–32.

62. According to an NJPS footnote, *we-khatuv* is equivalent to *we-khatov,* an infinitive employed as a narrative tense, as in Esth. 9:16 and elsewhere. Alternatively, we can vocalize *we-khatov*.

63. In Hebrew, *'ehad* usually means "one," but it can also mean "a" or an indefinite "some"; e.g., 1 Sam. 24:15; 26:20; 1 Kings 19:4, 5. In Aramaic, the cognate *hdh/hd'* is an indefinite article in Ezra 4:8; Dan. 2:31, 6:18; and often in Syriac.